Mary, Bearer of Life

Mary, Bearer of Life

Christopher Cocksworth

scm press

© Christopher Cocksworth 2023

Published in 2023 by SCM Press
Editorial office
3rd Floor, Invicta House,
108–114 Golden Lane,
London EC1Y 0TG, UK

www.scmpress.co.uk

SCM Press is an imprint of Hymns Ancient & Modern Ltd
(a registered charity)

Hymns Ancient & Modern® is a registered trademark of
Hymns Ancient & Modern Ltd
13A Hellesdon Park Road, Norwich,
Norfolk NR6 5DR, UK

British Library Cataloguing in Publication data
A catalogue record for this book is available
from the British Library

ISBN 978-0-334-06200-4

Typeset by Regent Typesetting
Printed and bound in Great Britain by
CPI Group (UK) Ltd

For my mother
with thanks

Contents

Preface

'Where is she?' I thought, as I marvelled at the restored Frauenkirche in Dresden. The eleventh-century Romanesque church first built on the site and dedicated to 'Our Lady', pulled down in the seventeenth century, rebuilt in a Protestant Baroque style, destroyed through allied bombing in 1945 and rebuilt again after the fall of the Berlin Wall, showed no sign of Mary herself or any other women in its architecture. Mary's absence in the Frauenkirche symbolized a sense that had been growing in me about my own life and heart, and about the theological and spiritual tradition that had shaped and mothered me, and to which I owed so much. The idea for this book grew steadily from about that point and merged with other theological interests that focused on perhaps the most basic of Christian convictions – that life is a gift of the God of life. I am grateful for a period of sabbatical leave which allowed time for reading, writing and some travelling. Although Covid restrictions in 2021 only allowed for a short time in Germany and a slightly longer time in the South Caucasus, they were profound times in all sorts of ways, not least for the help they gave to my thinking about Mary. I draw upon those experiences in the pages that follow and some of the theological and spiritual characters to whom they introduced me.

My time in Germany was split between Erfurt and Wittenberg, cities that played such a formative part in the Reformation. Intrigued by his views on Mary, I was on the trail of Martin Luther. Part of me felt like part of him: drawn to Mary in affection on the one hand, yet conscious of how misplaced attention to Mary can disrupt the clarity of the gospel on the other. I visited the Mariendom in Erfurt, the cathedral dedicated to Mary that Luther would have known well in his university days and that had a particular association with a charming but exotic medieval mythology about Mary meeting a unicorn. I walked through the streets of the city where Luther made sense of his terrifying thunderstorm experience in nearby Stotternheim when he had called out to St Anne, Mary's mother, to save him. I prayed in the monastery where he later implored Mary to turn away Christ's wrath. And so I came to taste something of the spiritual air that Luther breathed and found so stale. All that was reinforced in Wittenberg where Luther was sent to oversee a group of Augustinian monasteries and to teach in the newly founded university. I was fascinated by the position of the bronze relief of Mary being crowned Queen of Heaven right next to the door of the Elector of Saxony's Schlosskirche where Luther is said to have nailed his 95 Theses. I was intrigued that the church where Luther had served as a parish priest before the Reformation, and as parish pastor during it, was called the Marienkirche. I could see that the stone relief of the crowned Mary in heaven holding the infant Christ above the west door of the Marienkirche belonged to a religious culture that seemed to place Mary somewhere between the worshippers and her son, and risked – entirely against Mary's own desires – deflecting them from him.

There is certainly no such risk in the Marienkirche now, dominated as it is by the magnificent Cranach altar piece. Lucas Cranach, a Reformation artist, paints a stark and contemporary crucifixion. Luther is preaching from a short biblical text and pointing to the cross while on the other side of the picture the people of Wittenberg look on and listen. Its simplicity is stark and its combination of cross, Bible, preached word and activated faith is a brilliant précis of Reformation theology. Mary, so familiar in traditional depictions of the crucifixion before the Reformation, is nowhere to be seen. Above the crucifixion we see the three sacraments that Luther recognized: Lord's Supper, Baptism and Reconciliation. Luther sits at the

table of the Lord with the other disciples and, fittingly, is given
the chalice that he had demanded be restored to the people.
Cranach's altar piece in Weimar, where the political centre of
the Reformation was forced to retreat after the Schmalkaldic
war in the mid-sixteenth century, has an even more dramatic
version of the crucifixion. As Jesus dies on the cross for the sins
of the world, we see him also to the side of the cross battling
with the devil and turning the spear which had stricken him
into a weapon that defeats evil once and for all. On the other
side of the cross stands John the Baptist gesturing to Cranach
and Luther, pointing them to the cross. Blood spurts from the
pierced side of Jesus not, as in previous images, into a cup held
safely in the hands of Mary, but on to Cranach's head. Behind
the cross, Adam dances free from the tomb. Jesus dies for all
and for me. On the wings of the altar piece the deposed Elector of Saxony, John Frederik, who had staked his kingdom on
the Reformation, prays with his wife. Their godly children do
the same on the other side of the cross. Mary's absence from
the altar piece struck a particular note of irony in me because
many years before, when John Frederik was a young man and
the reform of the Church was in its early days, Luther had
written his sermon on Mary's Magnificat for him, commending Mary not only as mother of the Lord but as a paradigm of
evangelical faith: a model for reformed Christians who placed
their faith solely in the grace of God in Christ. It was as if one
of the costs of the theological, spiritual, social and political
convulsions of the Reformation was paid by Mary. Despite the
intentions of the mainline reformers, Mary had been ejected
from the life of the Church.

Wittenberg's Marienkirche is known as the Mother Church
of the Reformation. The only appearance Mary makes in the
building is the one I mentioned earlier on the outside of the
west wall above a door which is no longer used. Luther may
have said that Mary is mother to us all but there seemed to be
no positive part she could play in the reform of the Church of
her son, except to remain out of sight and not to get in the way.
But Mary will not go away, not even in historic Wittenberg,

carefully preserved to tell the Reformation's story. I saw her making a tentative, temporary but determined reappearance in three places. The castle of the Thuringian rulers who had supported Luther now housed an exhibition of modern Christian art. From Marc Chagall's *Mother and Child* crucifixion, to Käthe Kollwitz's *Mary and Elizabeth*, to the more contemporary Katerina Belinka's striking depiction of a pregnant woman, Mary was very present. Farther down the main street, between the great Schlosskirche and Marienkirche, three well-produced posters brightened some hoardings which covered up some building work. *Glauben, Hoffnung, Liebe* – Faith, Hope and Love – they proclaimed, each with a biblical text to define them. Mary's Magnificat had been chosen for love. More off the beaten track but still in the historic part of the city, a huge mural adorned a bare wall. Mary, bearing her sacred heart, was texting on an iPhone. Wittenberg, the heart of the rediscovery of the overwhelming goodness and unfathomable grace of God, to which the whole Church – and I, like Cranach, standing at the foot of the cross – owed so much, told its own history of Mary: medieval devotion with more than a touch of excess, Reformation, then absence, followed eventually by contemporary return, subtly but firmly saying, 'Can woman forget her nursing child, or show no compassion for the child of her womb?' (Isa. 49.15. Unless otherwise noted, all Bible references are taken from the NRSVA).

Any discussion of Mary's place in the Church takes one deeply into the sixteenth-century debates which convulsed the Western Church, with Catholic and Reformed emphases vying with each other. So, it was refreshing to be able to spend time with the Orthodox traditions of the Eastern Church. Oriental Orthodox Churches – who had made their own protest against majority views in the Church in the fifth century – have always struck me as gentler on the evangelical eye than at least some forms of Greek Orthodoxy. Perhaps it is the absence of an iconostasis in the churches, the familiarity with extempore prayer and the enjoyment of Bible study and the love of hymnody. Or perhaps it is something less tangible that gives one the sense that these ancient Coptic, Ethiopian, Syrian, Iraqi, Armenian and other traditions have preserved a close connection with the early centuries of the Church that is deeply enriching. One of the many gifts of my time with the Armenian Church was the discovery of the revered Gregory of Narek and his intensely spiritual poetry of the tenth century. Narek became a good friend during the writing of this book and his love of Christ, of the Church, and of Mary, nicely complemented the fourth-century poetry of Ephrem the Syrian that I already knew, with its similarly profound poetry that plays with biblical imagery in all sorts of imaginative ways. I draw on both writers in the pages that follow.

Conscious of the way Mary has evoked such strong theological emotions, I knew that writing about her would not be straightforward. However, the greatest challenge to my confidence proved not to be that any consideration of Mary so soon touches upon profound issues that have caused Christians to argue vehemently with each other in the Western Church since well before the Reformation, or even the further level of complexity and contention that feminist critiques of Marian tradition have permanently and rightly introduced. What made me wonder whether I should dare to write a book on Mary was the recognition that two dimensions of my person and background made me, in a very real sense, alien to insights that would come instinctively to others. I was writing about Mary – a woman and a mother – as a man. Moreover, I was writing about Mary as someone formed in the Anglican Evangelical tradition which, though generally respectful to Mary, saw no dynamic place for her in the life of faith. On the first, I came to accept that being neither a woman nor a mother would bring limitations to my understanding of Mary that, even though they could be reduced by listening better to women and mothers, could not be fully overcome. At the same time, I decided that I needed to claim my own voice as a man whose life has been richly blessed by my own mother, by the other mothers I have known and loved and by the mothering I received from women, men and, moreover, from the Church herself. I say a little more about my experience of mothers and mothering in Chapter 1.

On the second – my distance from an inhabited, deeply formed Marian piety – I came to the view that, although there would be insights I would miss without the deep spiritual dynamic present among Christians more devoted to Mary than I, there was at the same time some value in writing positively about Mary from a position of genuine theological enquiry rather than as someone propounding or defending one's own spirituality. Having said that, I should add also that while my formative theological, spiritual and ecclesial experiences have not offered a ready place for Mary, I have found myself increasingly drawn towards her over the years. Some of the reasons for that journey are also given in Chapter 1. As the book has progressed, that journey has continued in various ways aided by study of the Bible, prayer, reading, observing, conversing, contemplating and more. There was one occasion in the early hours of a night, when, kneeling before an icon of the cross with Mary and the beloved disciple at either side of Jesus, I was so moved by the agony of a mother witnessing the death of her son that I felt more affectively connected with the presence and pain of God the Father in the dying of Jesus than I ever had before; and Mary too became more present to me than she had been previously. The Roman Catholic Church's Congregation for the Doctrine of the Church offers wise advice to anyone who claims to have had some sort of encounter with Mary when it says,

> Private revelation ... can be a genuine help in understanding the Gospel and living it better at a particular moment in time; therefore it should not be disregarded ... The criterion for the truth and value of a private revelation is therefore its orientation to Christ himself.[1]

My own experience of being drawn closer to Mary is of being brought closer to her son. She is my companion with whom I travel as I follow Jesus. She is my sister from whom I learn as I seek to be faithful to him. She is my mother whom I have taken into my home because, as the mother of my Lord, she belongs to him and so belongs to me, for I belong to Christ.

I am grateful to other companions, sisters, brothers, mothers and fathers who have encouraged me to write this book and sustained me through it, including those who have suggested over the years that I write about Mary, Christine Smith the first among them; and I am especially thankful to David Shervington and the team at SCM Press for helping that idea come to fruition, as well as to Sebastian, artist, son and sommelier, for creating such a dynamic image of Mary for the front cover. David has been a positive and reassuring publisher throughout the writing of the book and I have enjoyed working with him and his colleagues. Additional help at a late stage to prepare the manuscript for the publisher was provided by Declan Kelly, and I am grateful to him. A succession of interns and research assistants have been an encouragement over the years as I – and they with me – have lived with and tested out the ideas that have grown into this book. Helen Walker and Matthew Murphy, with their characteristic commitment, have stimulated my thinking and helped to sharpen the text, especially in the ethical sections, and I should say how greatly I have been helped by conversations with Matthew about matters of peace and international security, as will be evident from the ethical section at the end of Chapter 4 on nuclear weapons. Helen's mother, Christine Walker, kindly provided two translations of texts. I am indebted to them both for that assistance. From his first days as Bishop's Intern, through his training for ordained ministry to his first profession as a monk, Charlie Annis has been a regular source of theological wisdom and spiritual nourishment from whom I have learned a great deal, including about Mary. I am deeply grateful to him and for his permission to publish one of his poems in Chapter 5. Christine Camfield has given unfailing support not only for my writing projects but also my several other endeavours as well as the general demands of office. Christine's commitment to this book included a readiness to proofread the text with her usual sharpness of eye and astuteness of mind, and I am very thankful.

Members of The Faith and Order Commission of the Church of England, whose breadth and depth of theological understanding I relied upon in very many ways during the ten years I chaired the Commission, gave patient support to my developing thought and offered new perspectives to take me on to the next stage. There are many others across the Churches – Lutheran, Roman Catholic, Orthodox, Reformed, Methodist, Pentecostal and Independent, many of them in different parts of the world – whose influence abounds in the pages that follow. I am deeply grateful to them, even though, for reasons I know they will understand, I cannot mention them all by name. I would like to have done more justice to them and to all of those who have contributed to my thinking and praying over the years, but while the faults of what follows are mine, the better fruit owes much to them. Among the several Anglicans who have supported and strengthened me is Ashley Cocksworth, whose theological agility and breadth of learning go on deepening my own theological journey in a way that brings joy to a father. Ashley's wife, Hannah, together with Rochelle and Friederike, the wives of two other sons, have given me the privilege of seeing and admiring another generation of mothers. Charlotte, my wife, has been a mother of unending goodness to our five children and, for over four decades, has proved to me the power and cost of enduring love. My own mother, Auriol Cocksworth – 93 as I write – has known and loved me through all the days of my life. I have been greatly blessed by her irrepressible love of life, and it is a delight to dedicate this book to her.

Notes

1 Congregation for the Doctrine of the Faith, *Theological Commentary on the Message of Fatima*, 26 June 2000, quoted in The Anglican–Roman Catholic International Commission, *Mary: Grace and Hope in Christ* (London: Morehouse, 2005), paragraph 73.

I

Introducing Mary: Bearer of Life

> And in his divine, provident mercy
> he made you the restored lot of fragrant flowers,
> replacing the divinely planted Garden of Eden,
> by setting in you the Tree of Life and of immortality,
> to bring forth through you the Fruit of Life
> by whom the whole universe is restored.
> ('Litany for the Assumption of the Blessed
> Bearer of God', Gregory of Narek)[1]

Life is universal. Everything that lives is bound together in the common reality of life.[2] For those of us who believe in God, life is a gift given by the source of life. The Jewish scribe Ezra put it this way when he prayed:

> You are the Lord, you alone;
> you have made heaven, the heaven of heavens,
> with all their host, the earth and all that is on it,
> the seas and all that is in them.
> To all of them you give life,
> and the host of heaven worships you.
> (Neh. 9.6)

For those of us who are Christians, we believe that God, the source of life, not only created life but took the form of that created life in Jesus Christ. We believe, in the language of St John's Gospel, that the Word who is God and is with God, through whom 'all things came into being', was born as a human life so that we 'may have life in his name' (John 1.3, 20.31). We believe that this Word who 'became flesh and lived among us' was *necessarily*, as St Paul put it, 'born of a woman' (Gal. 4.4) and, therefore, that God incarnate (God made flesh, John 1.14) has a mother from whom, in the words of an early Christian liturgy, 'God took flesh'. Her name is Mary. Since at least the fourth century, Christians have also called this Jewish woman *Theotokos* – God-bearer: the one who bears God as the Mother of God.[3]

The title of this book – *Mary, Bearer of Life* – is inspired by that ancient title. I could have called the book 'Mary, Mother of Life', taking a cue from some Orthodox liturgies that speak of Mary in this way,[4] or from the fourth-century bishop of Salamis, Epiphanius, who described Mary as 'Mother of the living', or from the sermons of Pope Francis who preaches tenderly about Mary as the mother who gives life.[5] But I felt there was wisdom in following the pattern of the original definition's wording of Mary as God-bearer, the one who bears the God of life into human life. I was also conscious of the theological instincts of – among others – the sixteenth-century reformer, Philip Melanchthon, when he asked of Mary, 'does she give life?'[6] and of the care Epiphanius himself centuries before him took to show that though he called Mary 'Mother of the living', he was clear that it is her son, Jesus Christ, who gives us – Mary included – life itself.[7]

Already, though, we can see the inseparability of Jesus and his mother. God is the source of life *and* God comes to us to be born into our life through Mary to renew life within us. Jesus has come to bring us into fullness of life, and although, in a graphic image from the earliest known Christian sermon, we 'killed' the 'Author of life', God nevertheless raised him to life (Acts 3.15). God's own 'eternal Spirit' (Heb. 9.14) – the 'Spirit of life' (Rom. 8.2), as Paul says, and 'the Lord and Giver of life', in the words of the Nicene Creed – is given to make this life of the new creation that has been accomplished in Christ a lived reality for all people, so that we 'may take hold of the life that really is life' (1 Tim. 6.19).[8] This gift of life renewed is God's gift for the salvation of the whole world, for the renewal of life throughout the whole fabric of creation. As God's Word spoke created life into being, God calls new life to rise from the old in the resurrection of Christ, the Word made flesh. This life of God, Creator and Redeemer, came to us in human form in and through Mary. In that sense, without Mary, there is no life of the kingdom of God, no coming of the new creation, no (in Irenaeus' words) 'Gospel of life'.[9] 'No Mary, no Jesus', we might say; or, more fully, 'no *believing* and *obeying* Mary, no saving and redeeming Christ'. That is why I have found myself over the years coming to the view that to be truer to Jesus, some of us – myself included – need to be fairer to Mary. So, in writing about life and what it means to live well, I have been drawn to Mary, Jesus' mother, from whom he learned so much about life and how to live it well. My aim, then, in this book is to reflect on the life of Mary in order to understand more fully the life that she bore into the world and the life that her son invites us to live in his Spirit. At the end of this chapter, I will lay out the journey through Mary's life that I would like us to take together. Before doing so there are some further words of explanation about my interest in Mary, Jesus' mother, that may be helpful for readers.

There is no doubt that Mary has divided Christians in the past. Different assessments of her significance in the story of salvation have caused us to say hard things about and to each other and our church communities.[10] Today, even where Christians try to be respectful to each other and are more understanding of different perspectives, there remains a degree of incomprehension between those who feel that some pay too much attention to Mary and those who feel that some neglect her. Points of disagreement between Christians have always been of interest to me. Why do those who confess a common faith in Christ and share the same holy scriptures disagree so fundamentally? What is there that each may learn from the other? Have they in their own mutually conflicting ways held to dimensions of the gospel that, if brought and *held together* in some way by the Spirit who reminds and teaches us about the words and ways of Christ (John 14.26), would complement each other and lead us into a deeper level of truth?[11]

There have been many signs of that happening, at least on a theological level. The decision of the Second Vatican Council in 1964 to speak of Mary in the context of the Church broke a lot of the ground that had been hardened over the years. Much to the surprise of other Churches looking into the Council from the outside and, indeed, to many of those within the Roman Catholic Church itself, the bishops chose not to produce a major statement about Mary, emphasizing her unique place in the scheme of salvation, and perhaps even proposing a new doctrine about her. Rather, they located her in their teaching about the Church, positioning her as a believer among believers, albeit one with a distinctive part to play in the life of the Church.[12] Serious space for better understanding between the Churches has been further opened up by the writings of John Paul II, Benedict XVI and Francis since the years of the Council.[13] Protestant theology has responded cautiously, but there have been some notable attempts to reappraise its traditional suspicion of Mariology, not least because it has remembered that Luther, Zwingli and other reformers were much more positive in their views of Mary than later Protestant tradition.[14] Indeed, Martin Luther's sermon on the Magnificat and Pope Francis' sermons on Mary seem to breathe the same spiritual air – a love of Mary and a clear affirmation of her place in the life of the Church on the one hand, while underlining at every point that, in Francis' words, 'Mary always brings us to Jesus.'[15] All this makes me wonder whether Mary, having been, as it were, a cause of disunity in the past may be an instrument of unity in the future.[16] And I am interested in the way that the most dynamic spheres of affection and activity among different Christians and Churches in the twenty-first century have to do with a common instinct for *life* – the life of persecuted Christians wherever they are, the life of the most vulnerable, whatever their condition, the life of the planet, the environment for life that God has given to every living thing. The gift of life, as we have already seen, is intrinsic to the life of Mary, whose 'unique vocation' is to bear the Life of the world.[17]

Speaking more personally, there are three theological insights that have helped me to come to a fuller appreciation of Mary and the part she plays in the life of the Church, individually and corporately. Like Melanchthon, my theological and spiritual antennae have always been alert to any claims for Mary that encroach on God's purposes that belong solely to Christ and to the way he completely and sufficiently fulfils God's revealing and redeeming work. 'What does Christ do if Mary does all this?' Melanchthon said in the face of the titles assigned to Mary in late-medieval theology and the part she seemed to play in Christian piety.[18] The 'deadly mixture of superstition, heresy and commercialization', as the great church historian, Jaroslav Pelikan, described the sort of Mariology Melanchthon would have encountered, has not been confined only to that period and place.[19] It is right to defend the sole mediatorial person and work of Christ, and Luther's principle, that 'it is better to take away too much from her than from the grace of God', is a good check.[20] However, there are two things that Mary does for us that even Jesus cannot do. Mary gives birth to him as his mother – Jesus could not bring himself to human birth without her. Mary shows us how to be a disciple of her son – Jesus can teach us how to be disciples but he cannot be a disciple of himself. Mary can and has.[21]

The second insight that moved my thinking about Mary follows on closely. Mary loved Jesus with the fierce and fearless intensity of a mother's love, and she was loved by Jesus from his earliest days with a love that would be always beyond the power of human words to convey. I have two icons in the little chapel in my house where I am privileged to pray each day. They are the work of a skilled and prayerful iconographer among the clergy with whom I serve in the Diocese of Coventry. One is of Mary. Unusually for icons of Mary, it depicts Mary by herself and not with Jesus. It is clear, though, from her gesture that Jesus is close by. Her hands direct you to an icon of Christ on the opposite wall and her look of love in that direction carries your eyes from her into the eyes of her son, who somehow looks both to her and to you as you look at him. The love between a mother and a child belongs to its own realm and is utterly personal to that particular relationship, and that is true for the love between Jesus and his own mother. But there is a quality of loving and being loved, of seeing and being seen between Mary and her son that draws us into the gaze between them, and touches our hearts to love and to receive love, to see and to allow ourselves to be seen in a way that is consistent with her loving of Jesus and Jesus' loving of her, and yet is unique to our own particularity.[22]

The third insight follows on again. I remember being awe-struck when I first began to realize that Jesus invites us to share deeply in the divine trinitarian relationships of loving between Father, Son and Spirit. Jesus prays that we may be where he is, bound by the Spirit into the oneness of Father and Son, joining Jesus as he says in the Spirit, *Abba*, Father (John 17.20–24; Gal. 4.6). It is only more recently, though, that I have begun to see better how Jesus invites us to share widely in his human relationships, with all the servants and saints of God, including his mother. The scene that John describes at the cross of Christ captures the heart of this experience, and poignantly so. 'When Jesus saw his mother and the disciple whom he loved standing beside her, he said to his mother, "Woman, here is your son." Then he said to the disciple, "Here is your mother." And from that hour the disciple took her into his own home' (John 19.26–28).

Mary is given the disciple whom Jesus loved as her own, to love him as she loves Jesus. The disciple is given Jesus' mother to be his mother and to take into his own home. There is more to be said about this passage, and we will return to it in later chapters. For now, I want to stay with the simplicity of the gift of Jesus' relationships becoming our relationships. Through our relationship with him we find ourselves in a net-work of relationships that would not have been ours without him. As we receive Jesus into our hearts, so we take each other into our homes and find a place with them, 'including Mary the mother of Jesus' (Acts 1.14) in a common 'pilgrimage of faith'.[23] Our relationship with God is rooted in our relationship with others in a household of faith in which we say together, 'Our Father'.

Taking Mary into the home of my life in Christ and in his Church began for me with the more simple, ordinary and instinctive human recognition than these three more considered theological judgements. Every person expects other people to respect their mother. A way of respecting others is by respecting their mothers. In that sense, to honour Jesus and to love him, is to honour his mother, and to love her. Although finding the right spiritual and theological place for Mary in my own home and heart has been a journey requiring a good deal of thought and study, conversation and prayer, I know I have been much helped by my own direct experience of mothers and mothering over four generations. The larger part of this book about Jesus' mother was written during a period of sabbatical leave from the normal round of a bishop's work. On the first day of the sabbatical when I was counting up the books about Jesus' mother that I wanted to read, our daughter-in-law went into labour. A few hours later, a son was born to her as a brother to two sisters. A few days later, I saw the joy in his mother, a deep contentment that seemed not only to overcome the strain and pain of giving birth but also to have brought a measure of healing to the grief of an earlier miscarriage. Tears of loss now somehow subsumed in tears of joy.

A few days after the birth of one grandchild, we heard that another grandchild had suffered her first serious accident after just a year of life and would need some surgery. In the scale of things, it was not a bad injury, but it was hard for her and for those who loved her, especially – as I could tell from her anguish – the child's mother. Another few days later my niece gave birth to her second child. For all sorts of reasons following the birth of her first, it was decided that a caesarean would be the best route into the world for this new life. Conscious, though, of the way that that sort of delivery would restrict her movements and make it more difficult for her to care for her elder child, my niece declined the offer of a less risky delivery. She was ready to endure the potential dangers and damage to herself that a vaginal birth could bring. The child was born safely, though the labour was long and hard, and not without its cost to the mother's body. A few months later, I witnessed the terror on the face of another daughter-in-law when her toddler went missing on the beach. The separation was short but its impact was long-lived. We all reacted, including, of course, the child's father but it was her mother who felt most the wound of sudden separation which, though short, cut deep in her heart and lives long in her mind.

My wife and I have five children. I was there at their births. I was there as they grew and faced life's challenges. I have been there as they have been ill or injured. I have known the particular suffering that comes to a father of children through parenthood for over three decades. But I have also seen the agony on their mother's face when a child is distressed, witnessed this mother weep when a child is ill and heard her wail when a child's life is under threat. And I have known that a sword has pierced her body and soul in a visceral way which, love my children as I do, I have been spared. Over these years, I have seen a woman carry a child within her womb and in her arms. I have watched a woman's body changing before my eyes as new life is formed within her. I have stood alongside a woman pushing life into the world with all her strength. I have seen that spark of fierce instinctive love flash across a woman's face when she sensed her child was in danger. And I have known such strength in a mother which means that nothing will stop her, certainly no thought of herself, from being there at her child's point of greatest pain (John 19.25–27). I have known that nothing would hold her back from rejoicing in the child's greatest achievement, praying for a glorious future (Acts 1.12–14).

Throughout my life I have experienced the constant loving of my own mother, now well into her 90s, and I wonder often how my life will be when she, whose body gave me the chance to breathe my first breath of life, breathes her last. I knew also the loving of her mother, my grandmother, who believed in me when I did not believe in myself, and I remember that dear lady saying that she had once been told, and found it to be true, 'That children will break your back when they are young and break your heart when they are old.' I realize that all these experiences of mothers and mothering have been gifts that not everyone has received, and I recognize that reflecting on the blessings Jesus knew from his mother may expose the deficits in mothering that some may have experienced in their own lives. Not all mothers live out the calling of motherhood and some fail badly. But as I reflect on Jesus' mother through the pages that follow, and on what we can learn from her about life itself and how to live it well, I thought it right to acknowledge the good gifts I have received from the mothers who have been closest to my life. I hope that this inner disposition towards the goodness of mothers in human life, with the particular strength they bring and the suffering they carry, rooted in their bodies and manifest in their souls, fits me to consider well the place of Mary in the life of Jesus and in our own lives. I hope too that readers will make their own allowances for any points at which my own experience of mothers is unhelpfully colouring my conclusions, or leads me towards the sort of idealization of motherhood by men that women can find oppressive. But I confess to being somewhat in awe of the mystery of mother-hood, and the work of God through it; and I am keen to learn more about the vocation to mothering that it can teach us all. I hope that discovering more about the place of Mary in Jesus' life will help us to see her place in the life of the Church of Christ more clearly and to receive more deeply Jesus' gift to us, his disciples, as he says, 'Here is your mother' (John 19.27).

The following five chapters trace the story of Mary's life in so far as it intersects with Jesus' life. As I have said, my aim is twofold. First, to reflect on Mary's life so as to learn more about the life that she bore into the world: the life of Jesus, the life that is life itself, the Life of God lived out in human life. Second, to learn from the story of Mary's life and all that she teaches about life with her son, and of how life may be lived more truly and fully. The journey of each chapter through the stages of Mary's life will conclude with a rudimentary attempt to apply the ethic of life we can see through Mary, *the bearer of life*, to different areas of human living, and to the sort of social and political policies that will best support such life. So, for example, the next chapter looks at the beginning of Mary's life and the beginning of Jesus' life. Here, as with other chapters, we will meet areas of theological complexity, some of which have caused a measure of theological controversy as Christians have come to very different assessments of Mary's signifi-cance. All this will need to be carefully navigated in a way that helps to steer a course towards the overall theme of *life*, and avoids being overwhelmed by arguments that, though inter-esting and important, are not of themselves the main purpose of this book. Chapter 2 then concludes with an application of an 'ethic of life' to an area of social policy, in this case to the beginning of life and vexed questions about the termination of the life of the unborn.[24] The ethical reflection at the end of the present chapter roots all of the later reflections in the fundamental affirmation of life as a gift from God, a gift to be received well and lived fully. It recognizes that, despite the uni-versal desire for life, indeed for a good life, the Christian ethic of life often runs counter to cultural assumptions, established expectations of society and the way governments organize the affairs of their nations. Ephrem the Syrian put it well in the fourth century in one of his hymns addressed to Jesus, 'The womb of Your Mother turned the world upside-down. The maker of the universe entered as a rich man and left it as a beggar. The mighty came in and emerged as the lowly.'[25] While not naive about either the complexities involved in applying an 'ethic of life' to actual situations and practical matters of policy in a compromised world, or the challenges in pressing for their adoption in the corridors of human power, the ethical reflections draw strength from the words spoken to Mary by the angel – 'Do not be afraid ... For nothing will be impossible with God' (Luke 1.30, 37).

Chapter 3 moves on to the stage of Mary's life where she gives birth to Jesus, parents him through his formative years and learns to be a disciple of Jesus as well as his mother. Its concluding ethical application focuses on policies and practices that serve children, especially their education. Chapter 4 travels with Mary further along the way of Jesus' life, looking at how, through his teaching and healing, dying and rising, Jesus forms a community around him in which Mary plays her part. Its ethical focus is on peace and, in particular, policies for the eradication of nuclear weapons. Chapter 5 explores Mary's life with the risen Christ in the life of the early Church through the Spirit whom they knew as 'the Spirit of life' (Rom. 8.2). This chapter takes us further into the in-between time and space after the resurrection of Christ and before his *parousia*. There is much to ponder as we reflect on Mary's part in the life of the Church and the work of Christ in this period of grace: for as she once waited with Joseph and Elizabeth for Jesus' first *parousia* to be revealed to those round about her, she now waits, with all God's faithful servants and saints, for the second *parousia* of Jesus when he shows fully and finally the 'strength with his [God's] arm' to the whole world and establishes the kingdom of which 'there will be no end' (Luke 1.51, 33). The ethical exploration at the end of the chapter is on the care of the environment, and what it means to tend and till the earth God has given to us and to which God has chosen to come to dwell for ever (Rev. 21.1–4).

The book draws to a close in a more devotional key by way of a meditation on Mary as companion, sister and mother. It reflects on the invitation to receive Mary, to live fully with her in the life of the Church and to attend to her abiding word to do whatever her son tells us to do (John 2.4), so that his life will be received as the life of the world (John 6.51).

'How can it be?': Ethics of (impossible) life

Life is a universal category. By definition, everything living has life. Every creature, human beings among them, has a common interest in life, in sustaining life and in promoting what is good for their share in that life. In this way, that which I have called 'an ethic of life' is a fundamental ethical category that concerns each person, regardless of religious belief, and connects us with all living things. Together we have a common quest for life that is good and brings benefit to us all. As we said at the beginning of this chapter, for those who believe in God as creator, life is a gift given by the source of life. Christians believe this source of life is the God of love who entered into the fabric of created life with such intensive involvement that 'the form of God' was born in 'human form' (Phil. 2.6–7). God comes to us in Jesus Christ to bring us into a fullness and abundance of life that has the quality of eternity about it (John 10.10). This 'eternal life' is given to those who are 'born from above' (John 3.15–16, 3) through the Spirit who comes to us through the Son who is 'born of a woman' (Gal. 4.4) among us.

Little wonder that Mary said to the angel, 'How can this be?' (Luke 1.34). Perhaps her mind was only on the implications for herself of the conception and birth of Christ in and through her, just as we can very easily think only of the impact of Jesus' life and teaching, his presence and power, his word and work upon us and our own ways of living. Perhaps, though, she knew instinctively that what was promised to happen within and through her would have implications for all things, for all life, for all times. Her child would be 'the Son of the Most High' who, in doing 'great things' for her, was bringing down 'the powerful from their thrones' and lifting up 'the lowly' wherever they are (Luke 1.32, 46–52). This was the sort of kingdom that Jesus announced in his words and made evident in his works, as the hungry were 'filled with good things' and the promises of blessing to Abraham were fulfilled (Luke 1.53–55). It is the kingdom for which Jesus taught his disciples to pray, the doing of God's will on earth as it is in heaven.

In this way, Mary's Magnificat functions in Luke's Gospel in a similar way to John's prologue. There John tells us in majestic theological prose about the eternal reality of God who, in Jesus Christ, enters the sphere of human history. The rest of John's Gospel shows us what the dwelling of God among us looks like and the difference it makes to human life. In Luke's Gospel,

Mary's Song, with its sublime theological poetry, sets out the character of God and the work that God will do. In the rest of the Gospel Jesus does the sort of things that Mary's manifesto pictures God doing: he brings mercy to those who fear God, scatters the proud who deceive themselves, and sends the rich empty away. In both John and Luke, the Word becomes flesh to 'bring good news to the poor' (Luke 4.18) and 'grace upon grace' (John 1.16) for all.

This is why Christians believe in one God who, as Father, Son and Holy Spirit, is the Creator of life, the Redeemer of life and the Consummator of life, bringing the life created and redeemed by God into the fullness and goodness of life that God intends. The God whom Christians worship as *thrice holy*, is the God whom we praise as *thrice Life-Giver*. Christian ethics is the expression of God's life-giving purposes in the conditions of the age in which we live our lives. It is the response to the ancient call of God to 'choose life' (Deut. 30.19). But it is not straightforward to do so. 'It was loathsome and I loved it. I was in love with death,' said Augustine, the son of Monica, not meaning that he loved death itself but rather that he seemed to love the ways of thinking and acting that caused death.[26] That, according to a good deal of Christian thought that has taken a cue from Augustine's honesty, is a common, indeed universal human experience. We want life but we have a propensity to damage life, even to destroy life. And what is true for individuals is true for collections of people in society, even as those societies appear to advance in their service of life. So much of our scientific progress, for example, preserves and promotes life and yet at the same time it creates a capacity to bring great harm.

'How can it be *since* I am a virgin?' said Mary to the angel. How can it be that we can offer an ethic of life in a world that has a proven propensity for love of death rather than an unfettered freedom to choose life, a world that, in the prophecy of Isaiah, so often makes 'a covenant with death' (Isa. 28.14–18)? Mary believed the words of the angel that 'nothing will be impossible with God' (Luke 1.37) for herself,

Elizabeth, the lowly, the hungry, and all those in need of God's mercy. She heeded the words of the angel spoken to her, to Joseph and the shepherds, 'Do not be afraid' (Luke 1.30; 2.10; Matt. 1.20); words repeated by the risen Christ in the vision of the Seer: 'Do not be afraid; I am the first and the last, and the living one. I was dead, and see, I am alive for ever and ever' (Rev. 1.17–18a). Mary chose, courageously, to receive the gift of life that would reshape the curve of human history by reforming the human will and to say herself, 'Here am I' (Luke 1.38). Inspired by her witness, the experiments in an ethic of life that conclude each chapter will try to apply to particular matters fundamental Christian convictions: that life is a gift we are invited to receive in its fullness, that it is a life to be lived together and that it is a life not only to be lived *with* others but *for* others. Those sections are not without their own 'sinces' – recognition of the conditions of the world that make living out an ethic of life very complex and very provisional. But, as Pope Francis indicates, the cost that mothers in every age suffer when death is chosen over life presses urgent ethical demands upon us.

> I have learned much from those mothers whose children are in prison, or lying in hospital beds, or in bondage to drugs, yet who, come cold or heat, rain or wind, never stop fighting for what is best for them. Or those mothers who, in refugee camps or even the midst of war, unfailingly embrace and support their children's sufferings. Mothers who literally give their lives so that none of their children will perish.[27]

We have seen such women demonstrating on the streets of Kabul soon after the Taliban came to power in 2021, chanting 'I am a mother, when you kill my son, you kill part of me'; and we have heard their cries from the basements of Ukrainian cities, grieving at the endless cost of war caused by the arrogance of men.

Perhaps it was because of the stories that he heard from his own mother, and the passion for life lived well that she shared with him, that Jesus learned to believe what he said to his disciples when they dismissed his vision of life as unrealistic and unreasonable: 'For mortals it is impossible, but not for God; for God all things are possible' (Mark 10.27). The resurrection of Christ and the coming of God's Spirit upon them later persuaded Jesus' followers that God had spoken and acted in such a radical way in Jesus that the prophetic hope for God to do 'a new thing' (Isa. 43.19) was being fulfilled in him *and through them* as they followed him in his way. That is why the words and deeds, the lifestyle and worldview of the early Christians caused those who encountered them to say that 'These people who have been turning the world upside down have come here also ... They are all acting contrary to the decrees of the emperor, saying that there is another king named Jesus' (Acts 17.6–7). In so doing, in speaking and acting in the name of the 'Author of life' (Acts 3.15), in standing in the temple telling 'the people the whole message about this life' (Acts 5.20) and in proclaiming among the Gentiles 'the repentance that leads to life' (Acts 11.18), they were speaking and demonstrating the word and action of God, the giver of life who annuls the 'covenant with death' (Isa. 28.18).[28]

Christian faith shares an ethic of life with all human traditions and an instinct for life with all living things. But it brings to that common quest the distinctive perspective of God's word and action in Jesus Christ which demonstrate that it is possible for God's will to be done in the messiness of the earth as well as in the holiness of heaven. It will always challenge the decrees of Caesar that put life to death with the command of God who raised Jesus to life and gives the Spirit of life to those who place their hope in him and seek to 'renew the face of the ground' (Ps. 104.30). Although it is not unrealistic about the pervasiveness of human sin, and although it recognizes that the struggle for life is not only against the weakness of the human will but 'against the rulers, against the authorities, against the cosmic powers of this present darkness' (Eph. 6.12), Christian faith sets its hope on the greater power of God that has made humanity alive in the risen Christ and 'disarmed the rulers and authorities' (Col. 2.13–15). Its ethic of life may have an intensive application in the lives of those who confess Christ as Lord – those called to be salt and light of the world (Matt. 5.13–14) – but the achievement of Jesus Christ as Lord of the world affects the life of the world in all its extensity.[29] Therefore, what Christian faith says about life and the living of it well concerns the world and all its peoples. The impossible events on which the Christian ethic of life is founded and sustained – the incarnation of God, the resurrection of Christ and the gift of God's Spirit to all flesh – pertain not only to the life of Christians and the community of the Church but to the life of the world and the community of creation. 'For nothing will be impossible with God' (Luke 1.37).

Notes

1 Gregory Narek, 'Litany for the Assumption of the Blessed Holy Bearer of God', in *The Festal Works of St. Gregory of Narek: Annotated Translation of the Odes, Litanies, and Encomia*, ed. and trans. Abraham Terian (Collegeville, MN: Liturgical Press, 2016), p. 147.

2 Hannah Arendt, *The Human Condition*, 2nd edn (Chicago, IL: The University of Chicago Press, 1998), p. 314, provides an insightful analysis of the universal human interest in sustaining life within the context of the life processes of every species:

> The reason why life asserted itself as the ultimate point of reference in the modern age and has remained the highest good of modern society is the modern reversal [of much that it had received from the past] operated within the fabric of a Christian society whose fundamental belief in the sacredness of life has survived, and has even remained completely unshaken by secularization and the general decline of Christian faith. In other words, the modern reversal followed and left unchallenged the most important reversal with which Christianity had broken into the ancient world, a reversal that was politically even more far-reaching and, historically at any rate, more enduring than any specific dogmatic content or belief. For the Christian 'glad tidings' of the immortality of individual human life had reversed the ancient relationship between man and the world and promoted the most mortal thing, human life, to the position of immortality, which up to then the cosmos had held.

3 See Stephen J. Shoemaker, *Mary in Early Christian Faith and Devotion* (New Haven, CT: Yale University Press, 2016), for an accessible account of early Christian devotion to Mary and the background to the *Theotokos* title.

4 For example, Mary is described as 'Mother of Life' in apolytikon and kontakion for the Feast of Dormition in the Orthodox Liturgy – see Andrew Louth, 'Mary in Modern Orthodox Theology' in *The Oxford Handbook of Mary*, ed. Chris Maunder (Oxford: Oxford University Press, 2019), p. 233 – and in the Vesper Hymn for the Feast of Annunciation, 'Rejoice Mother of Life', Kyriaki Karidoyanes Fitzgerald, 'Mary the *Theotokos* and the Call to Holiness' in *Mary Mother of God*, ed. Carl E. Braaten and Robert W. Jenson (Grand Rapids, MI: Eerdmans, 2004), p. 85. A similar designation can be found in Roman Catholic theology and piety. See for example Joseph Cardinal Ratzinger, *God and the World: Believing and Living in Our Time*, trans. Henry Taylor (San Francisco, CA: Ignatius Press, 2002), p. 294: 'She [Mary] becomes the Mother of the One who is life and gives life, Mother of life and of the living.'

5 This includes sermons preached on the Feast of the Solemnity of Mary, Mother of God in 2015, 2017, 2019 and 2020 which can be found at https://tinyurl.com/3j6vjhsp, accessed 16.1.2023.

6 Philip Melanchthon, 'Apology of the Augsburg Confession', cited in Timothy George, 'The Blessed Virgin Mary in Evangelical Perspective', in Braaten and Jenson, *Mary Mother of God*, p. 114.

7 St Epiphanius, 'Panarion', cited in Fitzgerald, 'Mary the *Theotokos* and the Call to Holiness', p. 97.

8 Nicene-Constantinople Creed of 381 CE.

9 Irenaeus, *Against the Heresies*, 3.21.1 in *The Ante-Nicene Fathers,* ed. Alexander Roberts and James Donaldson, 10 vols (Peabody, MA: Hendrickson, 1994).

10 See my *Holding Together: Gospel, Church and Spirit – the essentials of Christian identity* (Norwich: Canterbury Press, 2008), which seeks to develop an ecclesial (or catholic) form of evangelicalism that is open to the Spirit. Chapter 5, 'Meeting Mary', makes an attempt to look at Mary in this way.

11 See Jesus' teaching on the Holy Spirit in John's Gospel, especially John 14.25–26, 16.12–15.

12 Second Vatican Council, 'Lumen Gentium: Dogmatic Constitution on the Church', chapter VIII, in *The Documents of Vatican II*, ed. Walter M. Abbott (New York: Herder and Herder, 1966), pp. 85–96.

13 See Pope John Paul II, '*Redemptoris Mater*' in *The Encyclicals of John Paul II*, ed. J. Michael Miller (Huntington, IN: Our Sunday Visitor, 1996), pp. 354–411. For Benedict XVI, see Joseph Cardinal

Ratzinger, *Daughter Zion: Meditations on the Church's Marian Belief*, trans. John M. McDermott (San Francisco, CA: Ignatius Press, 1983), where he is critical of forms of Marian devotion that 'destroy the correlation between truth and life' and which 'lead to a poisoning of the intellectual-spiritual organism, the results of which are incalculable' (p. 11); and Hans Urs von Balthasar and Joseph Cardinal Ratzinger, *Mary: The Church at the Source*, trans. Adrian Walker (San Francisco, CA: Ignatius Press, 2005). For Francis see his addresses at General Audiences in November 2020 and March 2021 which can be found at http://www.vatican.va/content/francesco/en/audiences.index.html#audiences.

14 See, for example, Heiko A. Obermann, *The Virgin Mary in Evangelical Perspective* (Minneapolis, MN: Fortress Press, 1971); Carl E. Braaten and Robert W. Jenson, eds, *Mary Mother of God* (Grand Rapids, MI: Eerdmans, 2004); Beverly Roberts Gaventa, *Mary: Glimpses of the Mother of Jesus* (Minneapolis, MN: Fortress Press, 1999); Beverly Roberts Gaventa and Cynthia L. Rigby, eds, *Blessed One: Protestant Perspectives on Mary* (Louisville, KY: Westminster John Knox Press, 2002); Tim Perry, *Mary for Evangelicals: Toward an Understanding of the Mother of our Lord* (Downers Grove, IL: InterVarsity Press, 2006).

15 Pope Francis, 'Prayer for the Marian Day on the Occasion of the Year of Faith: Address of Holy Father Francis', https://tinyurl.com/ycyr37wx.

For Martin Luther's understanding of Mary, see Martin Luther, 'The Magnificat, 1520–1', in *Works of Martin Luther: with introductions and notes*, Vol. 3, ed. Henry E. Jacobs, trans. Albert T. W. Steinhaeuser (Philadelphia, PA: A. J. Holman, 1930), pp. 103–65. See also his discussion of the Hail Mary in Mary Jane Haemig and Eric Lund, eds, *Little Prayer Book, 1522, and a Simple Way to Pray, 1535: The Annotated Luther Study Edition* (Minneapolis, MN: Fortress Press, 2017).

16 Such hopes were expressed before the Second Vatican Council by the pioneering Roman Catholic ecumenist Abbé Paul Couturier and were lived out in his relationship and theological collaboration with his Protestant friend, Pastor Jean de Saussure and other Protestant leaders and pastors such as Max Thurian of Taizé. See Geoffrey Curtis, *Paul Couturier and Unity in Christ* (London: SCM Press, 1964), pp. 281–7.

17 The Anglican–Roman Catholic International Commission, *Mary: Grace and Hope in Christ* (London: Morehouse, 2005).

18 George, 'The Blessed Virgin Mary in Evangelical Perspective', p. 114.

19 Beverly Roberts Gaventa, '"Nothing Will Be Impossible with God": Mary as the Mother of Believers', in Braaten and Jenson, *Mary Mother of God*, p. 17.

20 Luther, 'The Magnificat', p. 136.

21 See my *Seeing Jesus and Being Seen by Him* (London: SPCK, 2016). Herbert McCabe makes a similar point: '[Mary] is what being redeemed is all about, she shows what it means to be redeemed.' Herbert McCabe, 'The Immaculate Conception', in *God Matters* (London: Continuum, 1987), p. 213.

22 These ideas are worked out more fully in my *Seeing Jesus*.

23 Mary's 'pilgrimage of faith' plays an important part in the Second Vatican Council's 'Lumen Gentium' and is picked up in later Roman Catholic thought, including by succeeding Popes, e.g., John Paul II (with Joseph Ratzinger's influence, later Benedict XVI), in '*Redemptoris Mater*'; Pope Francis, 'Homily of his Holiness Pope Francis, Vatican Basilica, Sunday 1st January 2014', https://tinyurl.com/4bh6k2h8, accessed 16.1.2023.

24 For a fuller development of the ethics of life drawn from the life of Jesus, see Michael Banner, *The Ethics of Everyday Life: Moral Theology, Social Anthropology, and the Imagination of the Human* (Oxford: Oxford University Press, 2013).

25 I use the translation quoted in Muna Tatari and Klaus von Stosch, *Mary in the Qur'an: Friend of God, Virgin, Mother*, trans. Peter Lewis (London: Gingko, 2021), p. 93.

26 Augustine, *Confessions, Volume I: Books 1–8*, ed. and trans. Carolyn J.-B. Hammond, Loeb Classical Library 26 (Cambridge, MA: Harvard University Press, 2014), II.4 (pp. 74–5).

27 Pope Francis, 'Homily of his Holiness Pope Francis, Vatican Basilica, Sunday 1st January 2017', https://tinyurl.com/yc4shbmv.

28 For a fuller treatment of the radical character of Christian ethics and for its rooting in the Christian doctrine of God's being and action, see Michael Banner, *Christian Ethics and Contemporary Moral Problems* (Cambridge: Cambridge University Press, 1999).

29 I draw here on Dan Hardy's concept of 'intensity' and 'extensity'. See Daniel W. Hardy, 'Truth, the Churches and their Mission' in *Finding the Church: The Dynamic Truth of Anglicanism* (London: SCM Press, 2001), pp. 127–41.

2

Chosen

O Son of the Bounteous One, whose love so willed
that he should reside in a poor girl's womb,
grant me utterance and words
that in due wonder of you I may speak.

O you who are discerning come, listen and give ear
to this action so entirely filled with wonder;
sing glory to him who had bent down
to give life to Adam who had sinned and died.
('The Angel and Mary', Ephrem the Syrian)[1]

'Favoured one': Chosen in grace for life

'This garden was created by a genius and ruined by a fool,' said
Lynne, a gardener. It was as if it existed but had lost its true
life. It was green and growing but was devoid of other colour
and odourless, a shapeless mass of vegetation where only the
toughest shrubs seemed to survive. I was at a loss on how to
restore its true life, to release the fullness of life that had been
suppressed for all these years. Lynne took on the challenge.

The Bible pictures the origins of life following a similar
pattern using strokes of elegant storytelling with restrained
energy and ordered drama in ways that go on captivating
poets and artists, philosophers and theologians. God speaks
and breathes life into being, forming it into light and water and
earth and animal life of every kind culminating in the making
of humanity in the image and likeness of God. The 'genius', as
Lynne called him, who originally planted my garden worked
with what was *there* – the space, the earth, the climate, the life

forms. God created out of what was *not there* – out of noth-ing. God is the Gardener who created 'in the beginning': at the genesis, the birth, of everything that has existence. Creation is the gift of life from the Giver of life. It is an act of abundant, overflowing, generative love. It is gift. It is grace. It is goodness in movement. God chose to bring 'things that are not' (1 Cor. 1.28) into being in a design of grace that would be, for God, a long and costly road. This is no one-off action. It is a com-mitment to bring creation into being and to shape its life into a fullness that reflects the beauty and wonder of God's own divine life.

'Ruined by a fool,' said Lynne. She could see something of the original pattern and purpose of the garden but she knew full well that it had fallen far from all that the first gardener had planned. I had mistaken the contractor who came weekly to keep it in order for a gardener who would love it into life. So, with the story of creation. The gift of creation given to humanity to receive and care for, to till and tend is grasped as a possession to own and control. Having reached out to take and taste that which belongs only to God – grasping for 'equality with God', as Paul would put it (Phil. 2.6) – the sights of predatory humanity would be on the gift of life itself, to treat it as its own to do with as it may. So, God 'placed the cherubim, and a sword flaming and turning to guard the way to the tree of life' (Gen. 3.24) to preserve it as a gift of God to be received and not a right to be possessed.

Even though God does not leave humanity without signs of mercy but clothes them in 'garments of skins', life 'east of the garden of Eden' (Gen. 3.21, 24) is hard. Decay erodes and death stalks. Its first stench hits us in the murder of Abel, and the refusal of Cain to acknowledge that he is his brother's keeper (Gen. 4.8–9). Here we see in painful starkness the problem humanity now faces. Death has been chosen over life. Sin has become embedded into the fabric of creation. The gift of life has been rejected. Amid the darkness of despair, though, there is a shaft of hope's light, a word of promise hidden in a word of judgement:

'I will put enmity between you and the woman,
and between your offspring and hers;
he will strike your head,
and you will strike his heel.'
(Gen. 3.15)

It was a word to a woman and an assurance to creation. It
was a word fulfilled in a woman for the salvation of creation.
Mary and her offspring are introduced into the story of salvation from as soon as our need is known. Gregory of Narek,
a tenth-century Armenian poet, imagined Eve, who took the
fruit that would lead to death, coming close to Mary as Mary
waited to bear the fruit that would bring life to the world:

The lost Eve,
Deprived of life,
Stood still
Next to the Virgin.
Her feet were aching,
Her waist bent,
Limping through life.
Lost compared with the Virgin.

With her shrivelled arms,
With tears she implored:
'Life-giving Saviour,
Give life to the lost'.[2]

Even in the tragedy of the fall from grace with its loss of
life and descent into death, there is a hint of the 'mystery of
[God's] will', the 'plan for the fullness of time, to gather up all
things in [Christ], things in heaven and things on earth' (Eph.
1.9–10). It is a mystery that stretches back even further, before
the beginning of time. It is a plan before the '*In the beginning*'
of the first verse of the Bible. God 'chose us in Christ before the
foundation of the world to be holy and blameless before him in
love' (Eph. 1.4). The only way our life could be secured would

be by being bound closer to the life of God, the source of life. Intrinsic to God's choice of us in Christ is God's choice of the woman who would bear Christ into the world as our life. That is why the birth narrative of Matthew's Gospel revolves around the fulfilment of the ancient prophecy:

'Look, the virgin shall conceive and bear a son,
and they shall name him Emmanuel',
which means, "God is with us."'
(Matt. 1.23, citing Isa. 7.14)

The gospel of our Lord Jesus Christ is that God is so *for us* that God is *with us* in human history and we are with God.

Matthew's Gospel begins with a genealogy to establish the credentials of Jesus as 'the son of David, the son of Abraham'. But he does so by highlighting four women around whom there was more than, as Beverly Roberts Gaventa delicately puts it, a sense of 'ambiguity and impropriety':[3] Tamar, Rahab, Ruth and the one Matthew calls only 'the wife of Uriah'. Interpretations abound of why Matthew frames the origins of Jesus' life in a way that did not follow the usual conventions. This much seems clear: that he wanted to highlight both the role of women in the generation of life and the way God works through unpredictable people and pregnancies that may even seem to threaten the purposes of God. And so, at the conclusion of his genealogy, he places the spotlight on Mary and her relationship to Jesus Christ: 'Jacob begat Joseph the husband of Mary, from whom was begotten Jesus the one called Christ'.[4]

The staggering claim that God has come to be with us by being conceived in Mary's womb gave the early theologians, hymn writers and liturgists of the Church much to contemplate as they followed Matthew in searching out the place of Mary in the promise of God to redeem Israel and to renew the creation. These have been further developed particularly in Catholic and Orthodox theology, and we will look at these more closely later when we consider Mary's response to the news that she had been chosen to conceive and carry 'the son of the Most High' (Luke 1.32). For the moment, though, I would like to draw on the proposal of the Lutheran theologian, Robert Jenson, that Mary is 'Israel concentrated' as the space for God to dwell.[5] Jenson maintains that if God is to have dealings with the creation that God has brought into being – which by definition is different from God and 'the uncreated space he himself is' – then God needs space within creation to relate to that which is not God and to be with it.[6] God chooses Israel as that space, relating to the world through Israel, being with this people in so far as they will receive him, and inhabiting places, especially the Ark of the Covenant, where God chooses to dwell among them. God finds this space in faith-filled Mary as she receives the fullness of the gift of God's presence and becomes, as the Akathistos Hymn of the Orthodox Church puts it, 'Space of the Spaceless God'.[7] In this space, God the Word becomes flesh, so that God could live among us (John 1.14). That is why John Donne, Anglican poet, wrote of Mary, 'Immensity cloysterd in thy deare wombe.'[8]

'You will conceive in your womb': Chosen in grace for new life

Lynne, like the 'old gardener', worked the earth as it was. She cleared the ground and suppressed seeds grew again. She let the light in and the life forms returned. She cut back the overgrowth and let the blossom bloom. Jesus worked the earth of the old creation, but his coming brought a new creation. The word and breath of God that brought all things into being now speaks and breathes in such a way as to enter that created sphere to take on the fabric of humanity and to dwell among us. In order to succeed in the work for which God's Word was sent, God's Word is sown into 'the foundation of matter', penetrating the earth as it grows into human life in the flesh of Mary's body.[9] Jesus Christ, 'the Son of the Most High' (Luke 1.32) is conceived of a virgin not because the Bible decries humanity's normal ways of procreation – childless Elizabeth has conceived through intercourse, as Hannah and Sarah did before her – but because something radically new is needed here that interrupts creation's course with a new genesis, a new beginning. A direct action of God's Word to implant itself in the fabric of human life and society is required for this work of new creation. 'Of course,' as the Roman Catholic theologian, James Alison, puts it, 'there is a biological mystery here: where did the necessary extra chromosome come from which alone enables a male child to be conceived?' 'And the only answer I know,' he goes on to say, 'is a negative one: not from any human paternity, or from within any human structure of desire, parentage, male possessiveness, need to control or to propagate. Rather it came in the way that Creation comes: as something out of nothing.'[10]

'How can this be,' asks Mary, 'since I am a virgin?' (Luke 1.34). The angel's answer is that it comes to be because of God. A new creation of the 'things that are not' (1 Cor. 1.28) is to be conceived in her, born through her, and nurtured by her. The Holy Spirit who brooded over the first creation will now overshadow Mary and the Son of God will come to life in her. The creative power of God that once made humanity from the dust of the earth now remakes human life in Mary's womb. Thus, the angel says:

'Rejoice,
you who enjoy God's favour!
The Lord is with you.'
(Luke 1.28, NJB)

Mary is not the only one who has 'pondered what sort of greeting this might be' (Luke 1.29). Systematic theologians and biblical scholars, preachers and pastors, Churches and communions have long debated them. Translators have vied for theological accuracy, knowing that great theological weight would hang on their decision, and ecclesiastical approval or opprobrium would follow. I have chosen to go with the New Jerusalem Bible's translation because I think it is sensitive both to the original Greek text and to the history of interpretation of its meaning across the Churches.[11]

The angel's greeting is best seen as a whole. *Chaire*, literally 'rejoice', is the way Gabriel greets Mary. It calls to mind earlier greetings to God's people where God's presence is promised to them.

> Sing and rejoice, O daughter Zion!
> For lo, I will come and dwell in your midst,
> says the LORD.
> (Zech. 2.10)

The angel is saying more than 'Hail', as traditional Roman Catholic translations have put it, and more than 'Greetings', as Protestant versions have more blandly rendered it. There is good news in the greeting. There is joy of the coming kingdom that will have no end. There is the exaltation to be had when God comes to dwell among the people that caused David and 'all the house of Israel' to leap and dance 'before the Lord with all their might' (2 Sam. 6.5, 14–16). Later, when the wonder of the angel's words has begun to sink deeper into her, Mary's soul sings, her spirit rejoices, and the Church through the ages echoes her praise.

Kecharitōmenē, the angel goes on to say in a formulation that John Wycliffe and William Tyndale in their early translations of the Greek New Testament into English – perhaps over conscious of the Latin Vulgate's translation *gratia plena* – render 'full of grace'. The Douai translation did the same for English-speaking Roman Catholics from the late sixteenth century. The King James Version went in a different direction, and one generally followed by later Protestant translations, when it chose to say not that Mary was 'full of grace' but rather that she was the 'favoured one'. Behind the linguistic choices lay major theological questions: had Mary been so formed and shaped by the grace of God that she was the obvious choice to bear the beloved Son of God – so holy that she was the right habitation for this holy child (Luke 1.35)? Or was Mary less the subject of grace, herself full of grace, and more the object of grace to be shown grace unbounded in this moment? Was she so favoured by the surprising, lavish, undeserved favour of God – the *unmerited grace of God*, to use a term loaded with theological freight over the centuries – that God reached out to her and chose her not because of anything that might be said to belong to her but because God has looked with the freedom of divine favour upon her and loved her?

When caught in the tangles of debates within Western Christianity, I often find it helpful to look to the East, and especially to the ancient sources preserved in the living traditions of Oriental Orthodoxy. The hymns of St Ephrem, still sung by Syrian Orthodox Christians, and the poetry of St Gregory of Narek, dear to the spirituality of Armenian Orthodoxy, offer a rich seam of reflection on Mary that brings fresh perspective on old arguments. I have used snippets of their wisdom to begin each chapter of the book. In one of his most enchanting hymns, Ephrem imagines an extended dialogue between Gabriel and Mary. Gabriel is almost overwhelmed by the news that he has been told to impart to Mary. The best advice the angel who dwells before God can give the young woman in whom God has chosen to dwell, is to:

Cry out 'Holy, holy, holy',
just as our heavenly legions do, adding nothing else,
for we have nothing besides this 'Holy',
this is all we utter concerning your Son.[12]

Holiness belongs to God. We have nothing besides this holiness, this unutterable beauty of the goodness of God, and Mary is right to respond, 'Great is his mercy and not to be measured, far beyond what lips can describe.'[13]

Gabriel's attention remains on the third element of the greeting. Mary is to rejoice; she enjoys God's favour because *the Lord is with her*. This is the blessing that will be hers – the blessing of God's presence within her, growing in her, soon to be given through her.

He will come to you, have no fear,
he will reside in your womb, ask not how.
O woman full of blessings, sing praise
to him who was pleased to be seen in you.[14]

This is the purpose of God since 'before the foundation of the world': to bless us in 'Christ with every spiritual blessing in the heavenly places'. This is 'the good pleasure of his will, to the praise of his glorious grace that he freely bestowed on us in the Beloved' (Eph. 1.3–6). And here we see that plan playing out in Mary with astonishing physicality. By God's favour – the action of God's grace – God's own self will dwell in Mary and she will be filled with the fullness of God, grace beyond measure. The God of life who is so *for Mary*, comes to be *with Mary*, so that the God of life who is so *for us* may come to be with us and give us all – with Mary – the life that we have lost.

Just as from the small womb of Eve's ear
Death entered in and was poured out,
so through a new ear, that was Mary's,
Life entered and was poured out.[15]

'Sing glory', the angel implores Mary, 'to him who had bent down to give life to Adam who had sinned and died' and prophesies that 'height and depth shall sing out to him ... for he, the Lord of all, has come down and dwelt in a virgin, to make all things new'.[16]

The holiness of God, the blessings of God, the life of God coming to humanity to be with us and to transform us: these are the great themes of Gabriel's greeting to Mary. They are reflected in Elizabeth's greeting to Mary when the younger cousin visits the elder after the angel had left her.

'Blessed are you among women,
and blessed is the fruit of your womb.
And why has this happened to me,
that the mother of my Lord comes to me?'
(Luke 1.42–43)

Mary is full of the blessing – the grace – of the presence of the Lord. Elizabeth's child leaps within her womb at the sound of Mary's voice anticipating the joy of all creation as its redeemer takes the form of human life in Mary's womb to make all things new.

There is an additional theme in Ephrem's poetry that is intrinsic to our understanding of the life that God brings to the world through Christ. Part of Mary's perplexity was her puzzlement as to why God wanted her, 'a mere poor girl' when 'the world is full of kings' daughters'. Gabriel's response was clear.

It would have been easy for him to dwell in a rich girl,
but it is with your poverty that he has fallen in love,
so that he may become one with the poor
and enrich them when he has been revealed.[17]

There is good evidence that Mary was by no means privileged in her background or protected from the strains of human life, eking out a subsistence from the earth. It is likely that Luke depicted this girl, who even when married to Joseph could only afford the sacrifice of the poor when she presented her first-born in the temple, as one of the *Anawim*, the poor of Israel (see Lev. 12.8). It is even more clear that at least some early Christians felt the need to improve her social status. The second-century text commonly known as the *Protoevangelium of St James* tells the story of Mary's conception and birth before giving its own version of Jesus' conception and birth.[18] This alternative infancy narrative has influenced the imagination of the Church on many levels and, in turn, provoked several counter reactions. We will return to it later in the chapter when we reflect on God's work in the life of Mary before the annunciation. Here I want to focus on the way its account of Mary raises her social, economic and religious status. It is the source from which we first hear of Mary's parents, Joachim and Anna. Joachim, we are told, is 'very rich' with flocks of sheep and herds of cattle. Anna, who was childless, is so awestruck by the gift of Mary to her, as well as by the gifts of the child herself, that she gives Mary over to the temple to be cared for in the sacred space of its precincts. So significant and special is Mary in the eyes of society and religion that the widowers of Israel are summoned to offer to marry her and maintain her virginal purity.

All of this is a long way from Luke's account, which does not even attempt to provide for Mary the sort of claim to personal credentials that he gives to Zechariah and Elizabeth (see Luke 1.5–6). Luke is content, rather, to emphasize that Mary was visited by the angel not in the environs of Jerusalem's temple, as in the *Protoevangelium*, but in the small town of Nazareth, in the inferior region of Galilee.[19] Although influential in many spheres, the *Protoevangelium*'s alternative attempt to raise Mary's status clearly did not impress Ephrem in the fourth century who preferred to speak of how the fire of God's Spirit 'reached the destitute girl, to fill her with wealth'.[20] This was exactly the point that Martin Luther wanted to preserve – and to recover – in the sixteenth century. Luther's commentary on Mary's Magnificat continually underlines Mary's ordinariness. Luther argues that this 'poor and plain citizen's daughter', with no wealth, wisdom, power, position, reputation, was not a predictable choice for the purposes that God had for her.[21] But that is the point for Luther. That is the gospel. That is the way of God – to choose and to exalt the lowly.

Luther was writing as a pastor to a particular person, in this case, as we saw earlier, John Frederik, the 17-year-old son of the Elector of Saxony, whose future responsibilities would include the right to elect the Emperor of the Holy Roman Empire as well as to rule the Kingdom of Saxony. It was at a critical point in Luther's life, just after he had been warned in a Papal Bull that he faced excommunication unless he recanted many of his views. It was at a hinge moment in European history in terms not only of the future of the Reformation but also of the sort of society that would evolve as the modern period began to dawn. Luther commended the Magnificat to the young prince whose choices would have massive sway on the lives of people in Saxony and much further afield. He encouraged him not only to heed Mary's warning about the dangers of the pride of human hearts but also to adopt the social programme of which she sings: 'For unless a lord and ruler loves his subjects, and has a chief concern not how to live at ease, but how to uplift and improve his people, his case is hopeless; he rules but to his soul's perdition.'[22]

Mary's Magnificat lays out a messianic manifesto of the sort of life for which her son will pour out his life for others during his ministry and then, when his hour had come, lay down that life for the life of the world. The life of the kingdom of which 'there will be no end' (Luke 1.33) is the life that the world would see breaking into its own history through the words and works of Jesus Christ. The descendants of Eve, 'limping through life',[23] would be lifted up with this woman who now stood tall in praise with head and voice raised to rejoice in the 'great things' that God had done for her, and was soon to do for 'Abraham and to his descendants for ever' (Luke 1.55).

'Here am I': Consenting (by faith) to life

Another woman, Julian of Norwich, many centuries later told of her intense encounter with Jesus Christ in a series of revelations.

> I received in some measure touch, sight, and feeling of three properties of God in which the strength and significance of the revelation consists; and they were seen in every revelation … The properties are these: life, love and light. In life there is a marvellous familiarity, in love there is a noble courtesy, and in light there is endless kindness.[24]

Familiarity, courtesy and kindness are the marks of Mary's encounter with the word and will of God in Ephrem's extended hymn. Ephrem imagines the sort of conversation that may have taken place as Mary, 'perplexed by his words' questioned Gabriel on what was happening to her, and how it would take place, and why. Courtesy is a deep theme running through Julian's reflections. She tells of the courteous love that allows her to glimpse something of the passion of Christ, 'our courteous Lord'. She believes that 'the greatest fullness of joy we shall have … is the marvellous courtesy and friendliness of our Father who is our maker, in our Lord Jesus Christ who is our brother and our Saviour'.[25] Courtesy runs throughout the 54 verses of Ephrem's hymn. The angel gives space for Mary to ask her questions, and there are many of them. Gabriel is ready with his answers, each one tuned to the particular anxieties to which Mary gives voice. Even when Gabriel assures her that 'My Lord is true', Mary presses the angel on 'How can this be', when 'no man has ever known me, nor any ever slept with me?' It is when Gabriel speaks of the love that has compelled God and the promise of God's Spirit to reside over her that she says:

> In that case, O angel, I will not answer back:
> if the Holy Spirit shall come to me,
> I am his maidservant, and he has authority;
> let it be to me, Lord, in accordance with your word.

God created by command: '"Let there be light"; and there was light' (Gen. 1.3). God chooses to re-create by consent: 'let it be with me according to your word' (Luke 1.38), says Mary. That did not mean that Mary's questioning was over. Luke tells us later she 'treasured all these things in her heart' (Luke 2.51), and there is every indication that she continued to weigh them and make sense of them. Indeed, Ephrem imagines the questioning continuing in the annunciation even after Mary's decision to accept the angel's message and to open herself to receive the gift that God was waiting to give. But there has been a shift. Mary had 'believed that there would be a fulfilment of what was spoken to her by the Lord' (Luke 1.45). She had offered herself in obedience to God: 'Here am I' (Luke 1.38).

She had declared herself – in words the translations generally soften – *he doule kuriou*, the slave of the Lord. Her allegiance was to God. Her belonging was with God. Her life was under 'the rule of grace' in God's household: not a slave to sin 'which leads to death' but obedient to the one who gives life (Rom. 6.15–17).[26] Mary's questions go on but now they are questions from faith. Mary has breathed the fresh air of decision and given her consent on earth, with all the hosts of heaven holding their breath till Mary gives her word to God's Word.

Divine courtesy and human consent permeate the annunciation and they run their course through the history of Christian theology as theologians and churches calibrate the relationship between the initiative of God's grace and the response of human faith. We will return to those questions shortly but, before leaving the scene of the encounter between Mary and the angel, I would like to touch upon a suggestive theme proposed in more contemporary theology by Karen O'Donnell. Drawing on her own story of pregnancy and, more so, the pain she experienced through her 'multiple reproductive losses' and the scars they left, O'Donnell writes movingly about the trauma of conception.[27] She speaks of trauma involving a rupture to the *body's integrity* (something new and potentially threatening happens to the body), to *time* (time becomes disrupted in some way and memory disturbed) and to *cognition* (so overwhelming is the experience that it is beyond the immediate capacities to understand, even to describe).[28] O'Donnell interrogates Christian theology through the lens of trauma and its several ruptures. She shows how 'Christianity has always been a religion of the body.'[29] God takes on a human body to be born, to live and to die. Individual bodies gather into the one body of the Church and eat together with the risen and exalted Christ who feeds them with his body. Intrinsic to the body of Christ is the body of Mary, and so O'Donnell defines the root of Christian faith as the 'Annunciation–Incarnation event'. Mary's consent notwithstanding, the annunciation, O'Donnell contends, was traumatic for her because of the rupture to her body, and to time and cognition, that it involved.

O'Donnell goes on to show how Mary's visit to her cousin Elizabeth straight after the angelic visitation brought a measure of recovery to her, and we will see wisdom in that insight when we look more closely at that moment in Mary's story. At this point I want to underline with O'Donnell the *bodiliness* of Mary's experience of the annunciation. Her response to the angel's words was experienced and expressed bodily. Her perplexity was felt bodily. Her questioning was voiced bodily. Her consent was made bodily and the consequences took place bodily. Her memory of everything that happened to her and to her body was bodily. And the consequences were, of course, bodily. Bodies matter. Mary's encounter with the grace of God manifested itself in her body and her obedience to the grace of God was proved through her body: she voiced her consent and moved her body to go not to her home, and to Joseph who would become her husband, but to Elizabeth who she knew had also encountered the grace of God in a seemingly impossible way. God acts in the life of the world. God's action impacts every human life bodily, indeed, every form of life in its physicality. Christian existence is the new reality of life lived in response to God's intense interest and involvement in the life of the world and is lived out in bodily practices: in ongoing decisions voiced by the body to say *yes* to God and in a participation with others in a bodily community that meets, sings and eats together as it reimagines the world according to the life of God's kingdom, praying unceasingly, 'Your will be done on earth, as in heaven.'

O'Donnell reminds us that there is a cost to consent, a cost that is paid bodily. Dietrich Bonhoeffer came to that sort of realization as a pastor and theologian in 1930s Germany during the inexorable rise of Nazi Socialism. His famous *Nachfolge (Following)*, published in English as *The Cost of Discipleship*, begins with these words: 'Cheap grace is the deadly enemy of our Church. We are fighting today for costly grace.'[30] Bonhoeffer took a lead role among the extraordinary minority movement within the German Protestant Church that stood up against 'the tyrannical despiser of humanity', refusing to give way to the culture of death that was enveloping the German people (corrupting the Church in the process, deflecting its allegiance from Christ to another lord) and threatening the world.[31] Bonhoeffer railed against those who claimed to believe in the unbounded, undeserved grace of God while singing their hymns more loudly to cover the sound of the wailing of the Jews as the trains carrying them to the death camps passed by. The grace that took the Son of God to the cross is the grace that summons us to follow Christ in the 'extraordinariness of the Christian Life' obedient to Christ's call, whatever it might cost.[32] Hence, Bonhoeffer said, 'Only those who obey, believe', just as he said, 'Only those who believe, obey.'[33] Belief in and obedience to Christ are bound together in the reality of discipleship in the world.

Bonhoeffer illustrated his principle in Matthew's version of the story of the Rich Young Ruler who came to Jesus to ask how he could fully and truly live, how, in his words, he could have 'eternal life' (Matt. 19.16–26). Jesus reminded him about the commandments and how the way 'to enter into life' was by believing that only God 'is good' and by living in God's way. The young man pressed Jesus further. 'Which ones?' he asked, as if God's commandments were a list from which we could choose, rather than an ethic of love and responsibility to which we are called in every aspect of our lives. Jesus, courteously, pointed him towards the commandments to love one's neighbour. But this was not enough for the questioner, confident as he was that all these commandments were being kept. 'What do I still lack?' he asked. Jesus could see that he was evading God's word and that he needed to be confronted with the call of God in such a way that he could no longer hide behind the self-assurance of his piety. 'Sell your possessions ... then come, follow me.' As the young man walks away, and as Jesus explains how hard it is to enter the kingdom of heaven – to take hold of the life that really is life (1 Tim. 6.19) – the disciples ask, 'Then who can be saved?' Reflecting on Jesus' answer, that, 'For mortals it is impossible, but for God all things are possible,' Bonhoeffer concluded that, 'The answer Jesus gives showed the disciples that they had understood him well. Salvation through following Jesus is not something [we] can achieve for ourselves – but with God all things are possible.'[34] Mary engaged the angel in a series of questions not to evade but to discern. Even so, there came the time for decision. 'For nothing will be impossible with God,' announced the angel and Mary, believing that 'there would be a fulfilment of what was spoken to her by the Lord' declared, 'Here am I, the servant of the Lord' (Luke 1.37, 45, 38). The impossibility of responding to God in fullness of faith and openness of obedience had been made possible by the God of grace who had favour on Mary and filled her with 'the gift of God' (Eph. 2.8). Mary consented to the gift of life.

'The gift of God' is the central theme of John Barclay's monumental study of Paul's understanding of the grace of God and how our response to God is related to God's grace. Barclay's findings take us deeper into the work of grace in Mary's life. Having carefully analysed the Jewish understandings of grace circulating in the environment in which Paul wrote, Barclay makes the distinction between, on the one hand, *unconditioned* gift and, on the other, *conditional* gift. He contends that the distinctive characteristic of Paul's understanding of the gift of God's grace is that it is given without regard to the worth of the recipient. Barclay describes this as the '*incongruity of grace*'. The criteria by which the ancient world, including the ethnic and Torah-based norms of Judaism itself, judged a person's worth were overcome by the extravagant, unbounded gift of God's grace. 'The gospel stands or falls with the incongruity of grace,' Barclay says when assessing the logic of Paul's letter to the Galatians.[35] At the same time, though, Barclay maintains that Paul shared with many others the contemporary Jewish understanding of God's grace: the belief that God's gift was given in the expectation that it would not be *passively received* and, as it were, just sit there in some sort of treasury of gifts, but that it would be *actively received* in such a way that it would be expressed in a new life that was itself generated by the generosity of the gift and the character of the gift-giver.

CHOSEN

Therefore, Barclay also says, 'The good news stands or falls with the realization [that is, the expression], in thought and practice, of the incongruous gift.'[36] On the basis of Barclay's findings, we can say that Bonhoeffer was true to fundamental Pauline convictions about, first, the invitation to believe that the gift of God's saving life is given to all, regardless of any assessment of our worth in the social, cultural, economic, religious, or moral norms of any age; second, the call to live in a new way congruous with the Giver of grace; and, third, that the capacity to respond in the way the gift requires is itself a gift within the gift – 'mercy is for Paul not just restorative, but *creative*: it brings into being what was otherwise impossible'.[37]

Where does this leave Mary and the classic tension to which we referred earlier between, on the one hand, more Catholic notions of Mary being 'full of grace' – a human subject active in grace – and, on the other, more Protestant notions of Mary as shown 'favour' by God – an object of grace? These are not esoteric questions belonging to remote spheres of theological speculation. They are practical questions that affect how the renewed life into which God calls us is received and lived out in the world.

Martin Luther is of help here. He drew on Paul's delineation of human beings as spirit, soul and body (1 Thessalonians 5.23). Mary's spirit – the spirit that later 'rejoices in God my Saviour' (Luke 1.47) – was simply one of faith. She believed in the word of God's grace. Even though lowly and of no cultural, social or economic status, God had chosen her to conceive the one who would 'reign over the house of Jacob for ever'. Even though a virgin, God had chosen her to bear 'the Son of the Most High' (Luke 1.32–33). Even though herself in need of a saviour, she would nurture the holy one. Mary's response was the perfect expression of evangelical faith, trusting only in the gospel of grace and, relying on nothing of herself, refusing to be deflected by the assessments of others.

Mary's soul – the soul that would later 'magnify the Lord' – was also of real interest to Luther. 'O how simple and pure a heart was hers, how strange a soul was this.'[38] He was struck

37

by the way Mary's soul exalts not in any sort of status of her own, even though she was the one in whom such great things had happened. The quality of Mary's soul after the annunciation is a measure of her soul before the annunciation. Julian of Norwich recounted how, in one of her revelations, 'Christ brought to mind our Lady':

> I saw her in a spiritual manner but in her bodily likeness, a simple and humble girl, young in years, in the form that she was when she conceived. God also revealed to me in part the wisdom and the truth of her soul, and in this I understood the reverent contemplation with which she beheld our God who is her maker, marvelling with great reverence that he was willing to be born of her who was a simple creature of his own making. For it was this that she wondered at: that he who was her creator was willing to be born of her who was created. And this wisdom and faith, recognizing the greatness of her maker and the littleness of her created self, caused her to say humbly to the angel Gabriel, 'Behold me here, the handmaid of the Lord'.[39]

If the truth of Mary's spirit was that she was ready to put her faith in the incongruity of God's grace, then the 'truth of her soul' was that she was ready, in Luther's words, to 'be caught up, as it were unto Him' and say her *yes* to God so that through the life and work of the 'Son of the Most High' conceived in her, the world might be brought into congruity with the way of God's grace: 'for nothing will be impossible with God'.[40] All of this raises the question of the preparation of Mary for the announcement of the good news, the gift of God to be born in her for the life of the world. It could never be the case of Mary being ritually worthy (as the *Protoevangelium* would have preferred), or morally worthy (as some forms of Catholic thought have contended), or worthy by the absence of ethical worth (as some forms of Protestant thought have proposed), or worthy through gender-based exploitation (as some forms of feminist thought have suggested), or worthy through her experience of the Spirit (as some forms of charismatic thought have imagined), or *even* worthy by economic oppression (as some liberationists have proposed). Mary remains – and knows that she remains – an object of grace. In Barclay's terms, her faith – like ours – is 'a declaration of bankruptcy, a radical and shattering recognition that the only capital in God's economy is the gift of Christ'.[41] Nevertheless, the incongruity of grace affirmed and accepted by Mary does not preclude God so working in Mary's life prior to the encounter with the angel to enable her to respond in faith and obedience to the angel. 'The truth of her soul' was expressed, as we have seen, in the action of her body: speaking and singing; visiting Elizabeth and receiving her greeting; forming with Elizabeth and their unborn children a new community of the extraordinary, seemingly impossible, reign of God; returning to Nazareth carrying her child of three months who was now beginning to show himself to the world through the enlargement of her body.

We are touching here on a doctrine that is especially disputed among the Churches, that of the immaculate conception of Mary which maintains that Mary was 'from the first moment in the first instance of her conception ... preserved immune from all stain of original sin'.[42] Although as an Anglican I feel no need to defend a doctrine defined by Pope Pius IX in 1854, and although I agree with Orthodox belief that it is not right to make this particular interpretation of Mary's origins an article of faith, I have come to respect it and to be ready to listen to what it is seeking to say, searching for what lies behind it. I can see better than I once could why Luther could commend Mary for her faith in the entirely undeserved grace of God and also say that Mary 'was without sin'.[43] I can appreciate more of how the doctrine can serve and clarify the grace of the gospel rather than undermining or obscuring it by 'another gospel' (Gal. 1.6–9).

Proposals for the immaculate conception affirm God's originating interest in Mary that began at the earliest point. 'For we are what [God] made us,' said Paul, 'created in Christ Jesus for good works, which God prepared beforehand to be our way of life' (Eph. 2.10). God's choice of Mary, and of all Christ's people, was made 'Even before they had been born or had done anything good or bad' (Rom. 9.11). That is the root of God's choice of Mary. The doctrine goes on to say that God's interest in Mary took a form at her own conception that was distinctive to her calling. There was argument in the eighteenth-century Evangelical Revival that, although making no mention of Mary, may help to shed some light on the doctrine from an unexpected source. When Charles Wesley penned his great hymn, 'Love Divine, all loves excelling', it included the line, 'Take away the power of sinning.' Joseph Fletcher objected on the grounds that to ask God to take away our *power* of sinning would be to ask God to divest us of the freedom of our human nature. John Wesley, with his overall influence on the Methodist movement, could see that Charles was reaching after something important – after all, John was committed to the 'renewal of love' or what became known as Christian Perfection.[44] Nevertheless, he took Fletcher's point and so the verse was dropped. Later, though, in some hymn books (regrettably not Anglican ones) a new line was suggested and so evangelicals across the world have heartily sung for decades that God may 'Take away the love of sinning.'

My understanding is that the purpose of the doctrine of the immaculate conception is not to remove the power of sinning but rather to deliver Mary from the love of sinning; and this, according to Muna Tatari's and Klaus von Stosch's analysis of Ephrem and the Syrian Fathers, was very much their view: 'The decisive factor for them is less about the cleansing from original sin and much more about freedom from sinning.'[45] It was not that Mary was preserved from the temptation to sin but that she was freed from the captivity of sin. It was not that her will was denied its freedom but that it was not curved unbendingly towards sin. Like Eve, Mary was not created with an incapacity *to sin* but with a capacity *not to sin* – the stain of humanity's irresistible propensity to sin was removed. Unlike Eve, she chose to live in this capacity and not to fall captive to sin. Rather than saying, 'No, it will not be to me according to your word, here I am the servant of myself – the slave of my own desires who insists on choosing the fruit that delights my eyes,' Mary says, 'Yes, let it be to me according to your word – here am I, the servant of the Lord who receives the fruit that God gives to me, the fruit of my womb, even though I fear the cost of such obedience.' Conceived in grace, formed by grace, shaped by the gift of God, Mary chooses to live as God desires, dependently on God, obediently to God and so openly to God that she *receives* – and does not *reject* – the life of God. So behind the doctrine of the immaculate conception, and all the arguments it set in place even centuries before the Reformation, is God's desire and plan to secure the *yes* – 'Here am I, let it be to me according to your word' – that was the necessary precondition of both the fullest *yes* of humanity uttered by the Saviour, 'not my will but yours be done' (Luke 22.42) and the eternal yes of God to humanity in which all the promises of God are founded and fulfilled (2 Cor. 1.20).[46]

Mary's *yes*, therefore, is a *yes* that comes not from her own powers but wholly from the prior grace of God that has been watching over Mary, preparing her spirit for this moment of faith, preparing her soul for this call to obey and preparing her body to utter its *yes*. Not a stuttering, half-hearted, 'yes-but' sort of *yes*, but a confident, full-throttle, nothing-held-back sort of *yes* that says with an astonishing, courageous, risk-taking openness to God,[47] 'Here am I, the servant of the Lord.' She says *yes* to life, *yes* to the source of life, *yes* to the Spirit of life, *yes* to the child who conquers death, *yes* to the life of the 'kingdom that will have no end', *yes* to the hungry being 'filled with good things', *yes* to the impossible ethic of life becoming truly possible: a *yes* so filled with faith in the favour of God that fear is overcome, a *yes* that anticipates the *yes* of her son, upon which her own salvation, with all the world, depends. It is a *yes* imagined well in the cover picture of this book – faith reaching out to God, receiving the life of God; love responding to the grace of God; hope standing tall in the stature of human responsibility trusting in the promise of God.

'Blessed are you among women, and blessed is the fruit of your womb': Considering life with Mary

Mary, we are told, 'pondered' God's word to her through the angel and she 'treasured all these things in her heart' through Jesus' childhood (Luke 1.29, 2.51). In the final section of this chapter, I want to follow her example and reflect on the events we have described and what they tell us about Mary, about her son and about the life God has for us through Jesus' saving work. We will take our cues from the scene in Luke immediately following the annunciation when 'Mary set out and went with haste to a Judean town in the hill country' (Luke 1.39). There were a series of greetings as soon as Mary, after a considerable journey, stepped inside the house of Zechariah: Mary to Elizabeth, the child within Elizabeth to the child within Mary, and Elizabeth to Mary. Then there was a question, 'Why has this happened to me, that the mother of my Lord comes to me?' Mary, the (much) younger cousin is renamed by Elizabeth as 'the mother of my Lord'. That is how Mary is described by John in his Gospel: Jesus addresses Mary as 'Woman' but where John narrates her place in the story of Jesus it is as 'his mother'. It was important in the early life of the Church to secure the reality of Mary's authentic motherhood. Femininity and flesh were dubious things in the religious and philosophical culture, generally dubbed as Gnosticism, swirling around the Mediterranean world at the time. In the apocryphal and relatively early Gospel of Thomas, for example, Jesus said, 'When you see one who was *not* born of woman, fall on your faces and worship. That one is your Father.'[48] Even though Paul says almost nothing about Mary directly, what he does say is critical: Jesus *was* born of a woman (Gal. 4.4). Not only was the motherhood of Mary vital for establishing that Jesus was fully human – that, as the (Orthodox) Liturgy of St James puts it, 'God took flesh' from Mary – it also rooted Jesus in the realities of ordinary human life, in families and food, communities and economies, births and deaths, and so on.

It is unhelpfully easy to detach Mary's song from its immediate setting in the story. Our Bibles give it its own heading
and our liturgies turn it into the Church's canticle of praise.
But Luke links the song to the visit with an 'and': Elizabeth
pronounced Mary as blessed because she believed the word of
the Lord *and* Mary extolled, 'My soul magnifies the Lord, and
my spirit rejoices in God my Saviour.' The child to be born of
Mary was the one through whom God's purposes of salvation
for all people – Mary included – would be achieved. As we
have seen, Luther's commentary on the Magnificat shows how
at the point when Mary might have exalted herself, she repeat-
edly exalts God alone. All generations will call her blessed
but that is because God has done great things for her. It is
God's name that is holy. God's work in Christ is 'to reconcile
… *all things*, whether on earth or in heaven, by making peace
through the blood of his cross' (Col. 1.20). The mysterious
irony of Mary soon to deliver the one who would deliver her
has not been lost on the poets of the ages, from fourth-century
Syrian Ephrem to contemporary Britain or America:[49]

Breath, mouth, ears and eyes
he is curtailed who overflowed all skies,
all years. Older than eternity,
now he is new. Now native to earth as I am, nailed
to my poor planet, caught
that I might be free, blind in my womb
to know my darkness ended,
brought to this birth for me to be new-born,
and for him to see me mended
    I must see him torn.[50]

In debates among medieval theologians one of the principal
objections to notions of Mary's immaculate conception was
that it detached Mary from the salvation that Jesus was still
to bring through his death and resurrection. In order to give
the proposal for Mary's unique conception any credibility it
was necessary for its advocates to be very clear that although

she may have been redeemed from the wilfully destructive and damning effects of original sin *before* the cross of Christ, that act of grace was not apart from the cross but *because of* the cross. Hans von Balthasar, a more recent advocate, expressed it in this way: 'She is "pre-redeemed" so that she can give birth to the Redeemer.'[51] Mary was as much in need of redemption *through* Christ as the rest of the human race because 'she belongs to the offspring of Adam [and so] is one with all those who are saved'.[52] Furthermore, whatever work of God's incongruous grace through Christ took place in the earliest stages of Mary's life and however deeply the transformative grace of God sanctified Mary's spirit, soul and body as mother of Christ, she would need, in the words of the Second Vatican Council, to 'advance in her pilgrimage of faith' and learn with others to be a disciple of Christ the Saviour and Lord in what Paul calls 'the obedience of faith' (Rom. 1.5, 16.26).

With her consent, Mary is made the mother of Jesus Christ. In her the life-giving Word is conceived and formed and, through her, given birth into the world to bring creation to new birth through his saving life, death, resurrection and ascension. Through her 'obedience of faith', Mary becomes a disciple of her own son, hearing him promising life in its fullness, seeing that life come to the sick, the lame, the rejected, witnessing him bring life to the dead, rejoicing as he defeats death and sends his life-giving spirit. 'Blessed are you among women and blessed is the fruit of your womb,' exclaimed Elizabeth – full of the Holy Spirit, full of God, Luke tells us – as she met her young cousin lifted now into the dignity of 'the mother of my Lord'. 'And,' she went on to say, 'blessed is she who believed that there would be a fulfilment of what was spoken to her by the Lord' (Luke 1.45).

There is a subtle difference in Luke's use of words in these two acclamations. In the first he draws on the same verb for Mary and her child (*eulogeo*) when Elizabeth declares that they are blessed. It is a word used for a wide range of purposes, from a way of speaking well of someone to an ascription of praise to another person or to God, to an expression of praise and thanksgiving to God or a prayer seeking God's goodness for someone or some situation. It is often associated with the Eucharist and was used commonly in relation to the gift of a child (1 Cor. 10.16). The Lord is with Mary. She has been blessed with the gift of the Lord. She has been so favoured, so blessed, that she is full of grace; God is growing within her. This 'unique vocation' to be the 'mother of my Lord' belonged to Mary alone, and in this state of motherhood, Mary is uniquely blessed by God.[53] Elizabeth could see, though, that Mary shared a state – a way of being and living – that belonged to all of those who, with her, would believe. *Makaria*, Elizabeth exclaimed, drawing on a word that Luke – and Matthew – would make much of later to describe the joy of those with the sort of attitudes or dispositions that would allow them to experience the reality of the kingdom of God. Mary, Elizabeth discerns, is the first of the *makarioi*. Others will follow her in believing as well in the other dispositions that Luke and Matthew regard as the marks of a disciple. This way of living is also a state of grace. It is the gift of grace to live in a new relation to God. That is what grace is: the gift of relationship with God given in creation by God's Word and Spirit, now given in the redeemed and renewed, the reconciled and restored relationships of the new creation. This new life is embodied – literally – in two women in a world where men control the levers of power, shape a world of injustice and form the cultures that through the centuries have favoured conflict and allowed death to reign. Not so their sons, for here, as Luise Schottroff says, 'two pregnant women beat the drum of God's world revolution'.[54] Its song sounds in what Bonhoeffer called, shortly before Christmas at the close of the year in which Hitler came to power, 'the most passionate, the wildest, one might say the most revolutionary Advent hymn ever sung'.[55]

Bonhoeffer goes on to say that with 'all the tones of the women prophets of the Old Testament that now come to life in Mary's mouth', Mary's Magnificat returns Elizabeth's declarations on the blessings bestowed on her by God, and the blessedness she experiences from those blessings, in a blessing to God.[56] She celebrates the life that the God of grace will bestow on the world as every generation receives his mercy, as the powerful proud are displaced and the lowly lost are lifted up, as the hungry are filled with good things, and the rich exploiters sent away empty. God's promises of old are fulfilled and creation declared once more to be good, so that God may dwell on earth.

> Heaven on earth and earth in heaven,
> Descent into depths and ascent unto heights,
> New heaven, heaven adorned with Sun's Light –
> The good news from above spread on earth.[57]

Resonance restored between earth and heaven as the life of one is lived in the other runs through the poetry of the annunciation through the ages. 'For in this rose contained was heaven and earth in lytle space', wrote someone in the fifteenth century whose name we no longer know.[58] 'Each reflects the other's face,' wrote Edwin Muir in the twentieth, 'Till Heaven in hers and Earth in his / shine steady there.'[59] It is a theme that has captured visual artists, especially of the Renaissance, and none more than in Botticelli's *Cestello Annunciation*, as bodies move and hands reach out in intensity of encounter, signs of heaven already visible on the kneeling woman leaning forward to touch such grace. Lost resonance is a recurring theme in the writings of the German sociologist Hartmut Rosa, who contends that the pace, technology and economics of modern human life have so equipped us with capacities for controlling the world that we have become alienated from it and so from each other. Rosa's long and rich monograph, entitled simply *Resonance*, ends with these words.

> We are operating in what has become the dominant *mode of coping with despair*, in which we encounter the world of people and things as mute, cold, indifferent, or hostile. Making it speak or even sing again is not within our power alone, but nor is it simply out of our hands. We can begin today to work on the quality of our relationship to the

world: individually on the subject pole of this relationship, mutually and collectively on the world pole. *A better world is possible*, and it can be recognized by its central criterion, which is no longer domination and control, but listening and responding.[60]

We can see this world beginning to be possible in the listening and responding of Mary and Elizabeth to God's gift of grace. But they both knew that the herald of the coming age and its Messiah would come only through the birth pangs and heavy weight of labour. There would be a cost to the restoration of resonance between human beings and the world in which they live and with God who gave them life. Swords would take heads and pierce souls; and there would be a cross, with a mother standing near.

Life in its beginning – Case study 1: Abortion

In a chapter that has given so much attention to the beginnings of Mary's life and the life of her son, not only to the biological beginning of Mary and of the incarnate Christ but to the origin of Mary's life in the redemptive intention of God and to the eternal election of Jesus Christ in the will of God, it is difficult not to focus this ethical reflection on God's gift of life at its beginning, and consequential questions concerning the termination of that life by the human will. However, I do so with real caution, conscious, on the one hand, of the genuine moral and theological complexity of such matters and, on the other, of the personal traumas and dilemmas experienced by people, especially women whose bodies, souls and spirits are integrally bound up with the extraordinarily difficult decisions involved. I am especially conscious of the risks in writing on abortion as a man. That is not only because of the obvious distance that being a man places me from the bodily involvement faced by a woman in these realities. It is also because I suspect that the bodily experience of women provides for a much more subtle, sensitive and nuanced understanding of child, mother and society than the polarization of the debate into 'pro-life' and 'pro-choice' allows, and would allow for a more wholesome and widely reasoned deliberation than the current polemicized and politicized debate if only it were given the opportunity.[61] Nevertheless, as tempting as silence is, it would be a form of avoidance, and strategies of avoidance are one of my main concerns.

My aims in this short reflection on an ethic of life in relation to the beginning of life are limited. First – and this applies to other reflections at the end of subsequent chapters – to discipline myself not only to think theologically and ethically about life in a general, overarching way, but to follow that through into specific, ordinary conditions of human life with all their personal difficulties and moral dilemmas which, in turn, require social policy on the part of governments and, in this case, medical action by health professionals. Second, to draw some rudimentary conclusions from Mary's experience of conception and pregnancy to inform Christian perspectives on responsible practices. Third, in that connection and within this very complex area of social policy into which it is difficult for pastors to speak, to follow the principle of Hannah Arendt, who said, 'What I propose, therefore, is very simple: it is nothing more than we think about what we are doing.'[62] So, essentially, I want to ask whether my own British society is thinking about what it is doing in its practices of abortion and whether it is satisfied that its legal frameworks and their implementation are correct and justifiable.

From everything we have considered about Mary's life – God's choice of her before the beginning of time, God's interest in her life from conception, God's purpose for her to bear the life of God's son and then the momentous events of Jesus' own conception – I find myself bound to say that human life begins when conception is established. I say when conception is *established* not to confuse this clear principle of connection between conception and human life (though I recognize, in one sense, it does), but out of respect for the way both biological reality (for example, the loss of a high proportion of single cell zygotes and multiple cell blastocysts before implantation) and traditional Christian reflection (for example, proposals on the quickening of the soul) attest to some sort of process in the formation of the stability of the human embryo beyond the earliest stages of conception. However, at the same time I should also say that I am not persuaded that arguments about when human personhood begins are of much value. Human beings are always in the process of *becoming* and there are serious risks in definitions of the personhood of an embryo, with all its God-given potential for fullness of human life, by socially constructed designations that inevitably change. It is safer, and more objective, to determine the status of the embryo not by human assessment but according to God's gift of life and, therefore, as a life belonging to God and, in so being and becoming, infinitely loved by God and worthy of great respect and care.[63]

In finding myself having no choice except to be *for life*, I should add that, in being for the life of the *child*, I am also for the life of the *mother* and for the life of the *society* in which the life of the child is conceived and which shapes the decisions of the woman who conceives that child. Again, Mary's life and her pregnancy may have something to teach us. God seeks Mary's consent to bear Jesus not only because of the divine courtesy of the grace of God but because of how important it is that the new life she is being asked to bear should be received by her in the freedom of her will, albeit she finds the news greatly perplexing at first. Perhaps there is a sense in which Mary's consent mirrors the need for the life of the child to be welcomed by the maternity of the mother.[64] It certainly tells us that the life of the woman is bound intimately to the life of the child and that God cares for her life beyond measure, loving her infinitely too. Mary's Magnificat lays out a manifesto for the sort of world that God's coming to us in Jesus Christ was already beginning to make possible. Her song recognizes the strength of the forces – the grip of the powers and principalities – to oppress the lowly, deny the hungry and entrap the poor.

The social and economic conditions in which life is conceived and which determine the environment in which decisions are made, *together with* the moral ecology which shapes social behaviours, are of deep concern to the grace of God and its effects are the cause of God's endless compassion. The lowly whom Mary prophesies will be lifted up includes the women of every generation who have been humiliated by the prevailing economic, social and moral conditions of their time and to whom the God of life promises justice and freedom. So with 99 per cent of abortions taking place in developing or third world countries, with 62 per cent of women in Britain saying that financial factors played a part in their decision to terminate and 57 per cent of women in receipt of Universal Credit or Tax Credits who know about the UK's two-child limit on welfare provision saying that it played an important part in their decision about whether or not to continue with a pregnancy, and with girls as young as 11 being pressurized into sexual experimentation by boys and inculcated into a culture that so glamorizes sex that it neglects its power to conceive new life, questions about the responsibility of societies and all their institutions need to be asked alongside any discussion about the responsibility of individual women.[65]

Abortion law in the UK, its interpretation and implementation, raises a number of questions about responsibility for each of us, including policymakers. Behind those also lie questions about the responsibility of those who become pregnant and of the partners involved, who may face difficult decisions. The 1967 Abortion Act which, in essence, remains in place, has only ever been applied to England, Scotland and Wales, not to Northern Ireland. Since 2010, abortion law has been formally devolved to Scotland and Northern Ireland but not to Wales. However, in 2020 the UK Parliament intervened in Northern Ireland to change its legal framework from a more restrictive position to a more permissive one, relative to the rest of the UK. My attention will be mainly on abortion law in England and Wales.

One of the main purposes of the 1967 Abortion Act was to

give women access to safe and legal means to terminate a pregnancy under carefully regulated circumstances. Indeed, one of the main motivations of David Steel, the architect and sponsor of the Bill, was to render back-street abortions, with all their dangers, history. Essentially the Act allowed for abortion in circumstances where there was risk to the woman's life, risk of serious damage (or permanent injury) to her mental or physical health, risk to the physical or mental health of existing children in the family or substantial risk that the child 'would suffer from such physical or mental abnormalities as to be seriously handicapped'. Termination was originally allowed up to 28 weeks of gestation. The Human Fertilisation and Embryology Act 1990 lowered the limit to 24 weeks. There have been numerous unsuccessful attempts to change the law in one direction or the other, the most recent of which included a proposed (defeated) amendment to the Police, Crime, Sentencing and Courts Bill in 2021 which would have lifted the restriction on abortion at any time, and would have allowed for gender to be a qualifying reason.[66] The recent changes to Abortion Law in Northern Ireland remove the time limit on abortions in cases of risk of the foetus dying before birth or being born with a severe physical or mental impairment.[67]

According to the Office for National Statistics, 25.2 per cent of pregnancies in England and Wales in 2021 (214,256) ended in abortion, a rise from 24 per cent in 2018, and the highest number since the Abortion Act was introduced.[68] Figures increased in women in their late 30s and 40s, although they did decline in women under 18. Women in deprived areas are more likely to have an abortion and since 2013 abortions among women with two or more previous live births has increased by 22.2 per cent. Since 1967 there have been 9,550,135 abortions in England and Wales carried out under the terms of the Act.[69] The more restrictive law in Northern Ireland is estimated to have involved 100,000 fewer abortions than would have been the case if it had been under the same jurisdiction as England and Wales.[70] In 2021, 98 per cent of abortions were performed under ground C: 'that the continuance of the pregnancy would involve risk, greater than if the pregnancy were terminated, of injury to the physical or mental health of the pregnant woman'. Of these, 99.9 per cent were due to a risk to the mother's mental health.

These figures raise a number of questions that a responsible society cannot avoid, and one which Christians, shaped by their faith's fundamental ethic of life, cannot fail to ask. Has the Abortion Act, designed to provide access to safe terminations for women in particular and carefully regulated circumstances, become instead an alternative means of birth control? Has it kept pace with the increasing sophistication of medical technology which allows unborn children to survive out of the womb before 22 weeks; and are we content with the medical procedures used for late-term abortions, including injections of medicine to stop the fetal heartbeat?[71]

Similarly, are we entirely content with the decision of legislators to make 'abortion pill treatment at home' permanently available – a procedure permitted and used widely during the Covid-19 pandemic – which allows women to self-administer terminations at early stages of gestation following telephone consultations and assessments? Do they provide the appropriate level of psychological and medical diagnosis and care intended by the Abortion Act?[72] Has the clause allowing terminations of pregnancies of those at risk of 'such physical or mental abnormalities as to be seriously handicapped' been interpreted in a much more open way than the law intended, running counter to society's entirely proper re-evaluation of the concepts of 'handicap' and 'disability', such that the protection and flourishing of the differently-abled are now a matter of vigorous concern in a way that they were not previously? More specifically, was Heidi Crowter, from my own city of Coventry, right or wrong to take legal action against the Government because foetuses designated at risk with Down's syndrome – her own identity – are included in that definition; and are Heidi and those who support her right or wrong to look at the practice of Iceland and Denmark where abortion has led to almost no Down's syndrome children being born?[73]

I realize that my own perspective on the side of *life* – one that I think is unavoidable for Christians – may have skewed the way I have posed these questions. But I return to my basic aim, fashioned on Hannah Arendt, of simply asking whether, here in England, at least, we are really *thinking about what we are doing* in the deliberate termination of a quarter of pregnancies. I also return to my initial comments about the complexity – moral, social, economic, familial, personal – of all these matters and their deep sensitivity, and so I draw to a close with the salutary words of William Stringfellow.

> The ethical discernment of humans cannot anticipate or usurp the judgement of God, but is an existential event, an exercise of conscience – transient and fragile. To make such an affirmation involves a radical reverence for the vocation of God and an equally radical acceptance of the vocation to be human.[74]

I am of the view that the 'exercise of conscience – transient and fragile' as it is – requires Christians to insist that, at the least, society through its processes of deliberation, including especially the debates and decisions of its parliamentary policy and lawmakers, considers its practices of abortion, clarifies its thinking and examines whether the law as it stands is appropriate and, if it is, whether it is being properly enacted by its medical and legal practitioners.[75] By so doing we can demonstrate to each other that, whatever our belief systems, we have 'accepted the vocation to be human', with all its responsibilities to care for life, and especially for the life that cannot defend itself, while at the same time being ready to draw close, with Mary, to those for whom pregnancy is perplexing, even threatening.

Notes

1 St Ephrem, 'The Angel and Mary', in Sebastian P. Brock, *Sogiatha: Syriac Dialogue Hymns*, Syrian Church Series 11, ed. Jacob Vellian (Kottayam: St Joseph's Press, 1987), p. 14.

2 Gregory of Narek, 'Ode for the Theophany' in *The Festal Works of St. Gregory of Narek: Annotated Translation of the Odes, Litanies, and Encomia*, ed. and trans. Abraham Terian (Collegeville, MN: Liturgical Press, 2016), p. 215.

3 Beverly Roberts Gaventa, *Mary: Glimpses of the Mother of Jesus* (Minneapolis, MN: Fortress Press, 1999), p. 33.

4 Translation by Beverly Roberts Gaventa in Gaventa, *Mary*, p. 39.

5 Robert W. Jenson, 'A Space for God' in *Mary Mother of God*, ed. Carl E. Braaten and Robert W. Jenson (Grand Rapids, MI: Eerdmans, 2004), p. 56.

6 Jenson, 'A Space for God', p. 51.

7 Jenson, 'A Space for God', p. 51.

8 John Donne, *The Complete English Poems of John Donne*, ed. Constantinos A. Patrides (London: Everyman, 1985), p. 430.

9 Hans Urs von Balthasar, 'The Catholicity of the Church' in Hans Urs von Balthasar and Joseph Cardinal Ratzinger, *Mary: The Church at the Source*, trans. Adrian Walker (San Francisco, CA: Ignatius Press, 2005), p. 162.

10 James Alison, 'Living the Magnificat with Rossini and Mary' in *Living the Magnificat: Affirming Catholicism in a Broken World*, ed. Mark D. Chapman (London: Mowbray, 2007), pp. 13–32. Raymond Brown makes a similar point when he says, 'The begetting is not quasi-sexual as if God takes the place of a male principle in mating with Mary. There is more of a connotation of creativity ... Mary is a virgin who has not known man, and therefore the child is totally God's work – a new creation.' Raymond Brown, *The Birth of the Messiah* (New Haven, CT: Yale University Press, 1999), p. 314, quoted by Tina Beattie in *God's Mother, Eve's Advocate: A Marian Narrative of Women's Salvation* (London: Continuum, 2002), p. 229.

11 The weight of ecclesiastical pressure is perhaps indicated by the decision of the revisers of the New Jerusalem Bible to revert to a more classical Catholic translation of *Chaire kecharitōmenē*: 'Rejoice full of grace! The Lord is with you' rather than the translation 'Rejoice, you who enjoy God's favour! The Lord is with you', used in the 1985 New Jerusalem Bible.

12 St Ephrem, 'The Angel and Mary', p. 20.

13 St Ephrem, 'The Angel and Mary', p. 20.

14 St Ephrem, 'The Angel and Mary', p. 18.

15 St Ephrem, 'Church' 49:7, quoted in Sebastian P. Brock, *The Luminous Eye: The Spiritual World Vision of Saint Ephrem the Syrian*, rev. edn (Collegeville, MN: Liturgical Press, 1992), p. 33.

16 St Ephrem, 'The Angel and Mary', p. 14.

17 St Ephrem, 'The Angel and Mary', p. 19.

18 For the text of the *Protoevangelium*, see Ronald F. Hock, *The Infancy Gospels of James and Thomas: With Introduction, Notes, and Original Text featuring the NEW Scholars Version Translation* (Santa Rosa, CA: Polebridge Press, 1995).

19 See Isaiah 9.1; 1 Maccabees 5.15; Matthew 4.13–16; Luke 22.59; John 1.46, 7.41; Acts 2.7.

20 St Ephrem, 'The Angel and Mary', p. 15.

21 Martin Luther, 'The Magnificat, 1520–1' in *Works of Martin Luther: with introductions and notes*, Vol. 3, ed. Henry E. Jacobs, trans. Albert T. W. Steinhaeuser (Philadelphia, PA: A. J. Holman, 1930), p. 112.

22 Luther, 'The Magnificat', p. 164. During the Peasants' War of 1524–5 Luther distanced himself from the full outworking of the radical nature of the Magnificat that was embraced by those revolting against their rulers. This was because of the Lutheran cause relying on the protection of local rulers at this time. For the rest of his life, Luther would be a defender of the social status quo.

23 Gregory of Narek, 'Ode for the Theophany', p. 215.

24 Julian of Norwich, *Revelations of Divine Love*, trans. Barry Windeatt (Oxford: Oxford University Press, 2015), p. 162.

25 Julian of Norwich, *Revelations of Divine Love*, p. 49.

26 John Barclay's description of the character of God's gift in Christ fits Mary's response well. See John M. G. Barclay, *Paul and the Gift* (Grand Rapids, MI: Eerdmans, 2015), p. 497.

27 Karen O'Donnell, *Broken Bodies: The Eucharist, Mary, and the Body in Trauma Theology* (London: SCM Press, 2019), p. 2.

28 It is interesting to compare O'Donnell's contentions for the trauma of the annunciation with Tina Beattie's reflections on both the virginal conception and the virginal birth (that is, the miraculous birth through which Mary's virginity is maintained): 'God's son comes gently into the world. Never, from the moment of conception, does he do violence to the body of a woman.' Beattie, *God's Mother*, p. 33. I do not think, however, that even the doctrine of the 'perpetual virginity' of Mary would undermine the traumatic impact that Mary's experience of conceiving, carrying and delivering would have had on her.

29 O'Donnell, *Broken Bodies*, p. 1.

30 Dietrich Bonhoeffer, *The Cost of Discipleship*, trans. R. H. Fuller (London: SCM Press, 2001), p. 2.

31 Dietrich Bonhoeffer, *Ethics*, vol. 6 of Dietrich Bonhoeffer Works, ed. Clifford J. Green (Minneapolis, MN: Fortress Press, 2009), p. 85.

32 This is Bonhoeffer's subtitle to his chapters on the Sermon on the Mount in his *The Cost of Discipleship*.

33 Bonhoeffer, *Discipleship*, p. 25. Punctuation added to aid the meaning in English.

34 Bonhoeffer, *Discipleship*, p. 40.

35 Barclay, *Paul and the Gift*, p. 370.

36 Barclay, *Paul and the Gift*, p. 387.

37 See also Bonhoeffer, *Ethics*, p. 86. Barclay, *Paul and the Gift*, p. 327.

38 Luther, 'The Magnificat', p. 138.

39 Julian of Norwich, *Revelations*, p. 7.

40 Luther, 'The Magnificat', p. 117.

41 Barclay, *Paul and the Gift*, p. 383.

42 *Catechism of the Catholic Church*, rev. edn (London: Burns and Oates, 1999), para. 491.

43 Martin Luther, *Hauspostille 1544*, D. Martin Luthers Werke, Kritische Gesamtausgabe, 52. Band (Weimar: Verlag Hermann Böhlaus Nochfolger, 1915), p. 39.

44 For fuller attention to Charles Wesley's hymn and John Wesley's thought, see my *Holding Together: Gospel, Church and Spirit – the essentials of Christian identity* (Norwich: Canterbury Press, 2008), pp. 74–8.

45 Muna Tatari and Klaus von Stosch, *Mary in the Qur'an: Friend of God, Virgin, Mother*, trans. Peter Lewis (London: Gingko, 2021), p. 70.

46 See the sermon Walker Kasper gave at the 2008 Catholic and Anglican joint pilgrimage to Lourdes: https://tinyurl.com/4ahx4c42, accessed 16.1.2023. It was part of the 'Mary and the Unity of the Church' ecumenical conference.

47 Courage is a theme that runs throughout Ann Loades' writing about Mary, which she contrasts with attitudes of obedience and submission which have received more attention in the theological tradition. See Ann Loades, *Grace is not Faceless: Reflections on Mary* (London: DLT, 2021).

48 G. Th. 15, in *The Nag Hammadi Library in English*, ed. James M. Robinson (New York: Harper & Row, 1981), p. 120.

49 I am grateful to the poet who penned these evocative lines:

Did you know
that your baby boy has to come to make you new?
And this Child that you delivered will soon deliver you.
('Mary, did you know?' Mark Lowry)

50 Luci Shaw, 'Mary's Song' in *Accompanied by Angels: Poems of*

the Incarnation (Grand Rapids, MI: Eerdmans, 2006), p. 29. Reprinted by permission of the publisher.

51 Hans Urs von Balthasar, 'The Marian Mould of the Church' in *Mary: The Church at the Source*, pp. 138–9.

52 Second Vatican Council, *Lumen Gentium: Dogmatic Constitution on the Church* (Vatican City: Vatican Council II, 1964), chapter VIII, para. 53.

53 The Anglican–Roman Catholic International Commission, *Mary: Grace and Hope in Christ* (London: Morehouse, 2005), p. 3.

54 Luise Schottroff, *Lydia's Impatient Sisters: A Feminist Social History of Early Christianity*, trans. Barbara Rumscheidt (Louisville, KY: Westminster John Knox, 1995), p. 191, quoted in Elizabeth Johnson, *Truly Our Sister: A Theology of Mary in the Communion of Saints* (London: Continuum, 2003), p. 260. I am grateful to Elizabeth Johnson for her exposition of Mary's visit to Elizabeth and her song (pp. 258–74), including her reference to Bonhoeffer's 1933 Advent Sermon quoted below. For a few of the many other studies of the Magnificat from a distinctively feminist perspective, see Rosemary Radford Reuther, 'Mistress of Heaven: The meaning of Mariology', in *New Woman, New Earth: Sexist Ideologies and Human Liberation* (New York: The Seabury Press, 1975), pp. 36–62; Tina Beattie, 'The Magnificat of the Redeemed Woman', *New Blackfriars* 80 (1999), pp. 443–50; and Ivone Gebara and Maria Clara Bingemer, *Mary, Mother of God, Mother of the Poor*, trans. Philip Berryman (Maryknoll, NY: Orbis Books, 1989).

55 Sermon preached by Bonhoeffer on the Third Sunday of Advent in 1933, in Dietrich Bonhoeffer, *The Mystery of Holy Night*, ed. Manfred Webb, trans. Peter Heinegg (New York: Crossroad, 1996), p. 6, quoted by Johnson in *Truly Our Sister*, p. 267.

56 Bonhoeffer, *The Mystery of Holy Night*, p. 6.

57 Gregory of Narek, 'Ode for the Church' in *The Festal Works of St. Gregory of Narek*, p. 101.

58 See Andrew Burnham, *Heaven and Earth in Little Space: The Re-enchantment of Liturgy* (Norwich: Canterbury Press, 2010), p. vii.

59 Edwin Muir, 'Annunciation', in *Collected Poems* (London: Faber and Faber, 1960), p. 117.

60 Hartmut Rosa, *Resonance: A Sociology of Our Relationship to the World*, trans. James C. Wagner (Cambridge: Polity Press, 2019), p. 459. See also Rosa's *The Uncontrollability of the World*, trans. James C. Wagner (Cambridge: Polity Press, 2020), and *Social Acceleration: A New Theory of Modernity* (New York: Columbia University Press, 2013).

61 See Tina Beattie, 'Whose Rights, Which Rights? – The United Nations, the Vatican, Gender and Sexual and Reproductive Rights', *Heythrop Journal* 55 (2014), pp. 979–1112, for a sensitive attempt to unite voices, especially women's.

62 Hannah Arendt, *The Human Condition*, 2nd edn (Chicago, IL: The University of Chicago Press, 1998), p. 314.

63 See Michael Banner, *The Practice of Abortion: A Critique* (London: DLT, 1999), which argues that the notion of life belonging to God is a key Christian contribution to ethics of abortion.

64 See Beattie, *God's Mother, Eve's Advocate*.

65 These figures come from BPAS, 2020, *Forced into a Corner: The two-child limit and pregnancy decision making during the pandemic*, https://tinyurl.com/2p9dpwsy, accessed 16.1.2023.

66 This amendment (NC55) can be found at https://tinyurl.com/55t 6s6at, accessed 16.1.2023.

67 For an explanation of the changes to abortion law in Northern Ireland see Elizabeth Rough, 2021, 'Abortion in Northern Ireland: Recent Changes to the Legal Framework', *House of Commons Library*, https://tinyurl.com/ye238vbe, accessed 16.1.2023.

68 See https://tinyurl.com/yt9t53um, accessed 16.1.2023.

69 This figure is calculated by adding the 214,256 total for 2021 to the figure for 1967–2020 of 'over 9,335,879' given in https://tinyurl.com/357ufxz3, accessed 16.1.2023.

70 See https://tinyurl.com/yc4ery8m, accessed 16.1.2023.

71 For information on the procedures used in late term abortions see: Royal College of Obstetricians and Gynaecologists, 2010, *Termination of Pregnancy for Fetal Abnormality in England, Scotland and Wales*, https://tinyurl.com/y9waxba4, accessed 16.1.2023; Anna K. Sfakianaki, Katherine J. Davies, et al., 'Potassium Chloride-Induced Fetal Demise: A Retrospective Cohort Study of Efficacy and Safety', *Journal of Ultrasound in Medicine* 33 (2014), pp. 337–41.

72 For more information on the decision to introduce 'at home abortions' and the adherence to the Abortion Act see *Guidance in Relation to Requirements of the Abortion Act 1967 for all those responsible for commissioning, providing and managing service provision*, available at https://tinyurl.com/5xvvr3jw, accessed 16.1.2023.

73 See Sarah Zhang, 'The Last Children of Down Syndrome', *The Atlantic* (December 2020), https://tinyurl.com/469wt3fk, accessed 16.1.2023.

74 William Stringfellow, *An Ethic for Christians and Other Aliens in a Strange Land* (Eugene, OR: Wipf and Stock, 2004), p. 57.

75 Whatever one's views about the principles and practices of abortion, I think there is merit in the 2022 US Supreme Court's decision to remove the decisions from wranglings over the interpretation of the Constitution by lawyers to the elected representatives of the people. I am grateful to my colleague in the Diocese of Coventry, Mark Bratton, for his analysis of the Court's judgement.

3

Called

The virgin gave birth,
The virgin gave birth,
The virgin gave birth,
To the life of humankind,
To the one coequal with the Father,
The blessed Savior, the Giver of Life.
('Ode for the Theophany',
Gregory of Narek[1])

'Born of a woman': Giving birth to life

'He is the God who asks to be born of a woman,' writes the
Roman Catholic theologian Tina Beattie.[2] This is the courteous
God described in the last chapter who con-descends – descends
to be *with us* in the original meaning of the word – stooping
low enough to enter humanity under the bar of human consent. 'God is with us,' Matthew insists (1.23) – *Emmanuel*, the
prophecy fulfilled. Now, 'when the fullness of time had come',
as Paul says in his one short but sufficient reference to Mary,
'God sent his Son, born of a woman' (Gal. 4.4). This gift to the
woman is 'of the Holy Spirit': the Spirit at work in Mary's life
before the annunciation, revealing to her the reality of God's
grace and enabling her now, in all the intensity and perplexity
of her encounter with the angel, to receive the gift that God
was ready to give.

The source of life who *is* life takes on human life through the
body, the flesh of Mary. The 'living one' (Rev. 1.18) takes on
human form for the salvation of the world: 'the Word of God

the Father who is Life by nature, rendering the flesh united to him capable of endowing with life,' as Cyril of Alexandria put it in the fourth century. The Spirit of life works with the energy of Mary's body to fashion the flesh of God – God in full humanity – from the cells of her body.[3] 'Who will spin which threads for the veil: the gold, the white, the linen, the silk, the violet, the scarlet, and the true purple?' ask the priests in *Protoevangelium of James* when they determine to 'make a veil for the temple of the Lord'.[4] And fittingly, the story goes on to tell us, 'the true purple and scarlet threads fell to Mary. And she took them and returned home.' An exercise of historical imagination it might be, but as an image of Mary weaving a home for God among mortals, it has much to say. 'Of her flesh he took flesh,' poets have echoed through the ages, marvelling at the astounding biological processes uncovered by scientists in our own day that enable the onset of new life, with connections in the brain taking place at a rate of a million per second.[5]

The birth narratives make it clear that through Mary Jesus was conceived and born into the reality of human life with all its social interactions and political – even geopolitical – contexts. It is likely that questions hung over Mary. They began with Joseph, her betrothed. Perhaps it was fear of the incessant questions, even if only communicated through quizzical looks, that caused Mary to seek sanctuary with Elizabeth and Zechariah a long way from home. Joseph (who also came to believe the angel and welcomed Mary as his wife), Elizabeth and Zechariah (who welcomed Mary and her child into their home), John, their son (who welcomed Jesus from the womb), together with the relatives and the people of his home town (who found it more difficult to welcome his ministry), show us that Jesus was born into and grew up in family and community life, with the joys and tensions it brings. Families and communities are always located in wider social, national and international settings. Luke's account of Jesus' birth begins by locating Jesus' family in the political and administrative systems of the Roman Empire. Augustus is emperor. Quirinius is a local governor. A census is scheduled. An imperial decree had been issued, interstate bureaucracy was in action, and people – including pregnant Mary and Joseph, her betrothed – were required to comply, whatever its impact on them. Life-threatening destitution was a constant companion.

Caesar's decree was not quite what Paul meant when he wrote that 'God sent his Son, born of a woman, born under the law' (Gal. 4.4), but the law of the state is not unrelated to the law of God. Both are in some sense responses to the reality of human and societal evil. The sinfulness of the world from an individual to an institutional level would have been evident throughout the pregnancy and birth of Jesus but it is the evil of Herod and the machinery of mindless violence he puts in motion that underlines the depth of human depravity and the lengths to which it will go to pervert the purposes of God. Herod, the abuser of children, the pursuer of a family, determined to eradicate this young child, the wielder of power that forces vulnerable people to flee to another land to live there in fear of what they might find when they return, was cast in a mould familiar to human history. We have seen it in our own time.

Herod, his aides who comply and his systems that control, embody the culture of death to which the world seems inexorably drawn in what Pope Francis has called 'an attack against life'.[6] In the plaintive words of the sixteenth-century 'Coventry Carol',

> Herod the king in his raging
> Set forth upon this day
> By his decree, no life spare thee
> All children young to slay
> All children young to slay.[7]

No wonder Matthew sees the slaughter of these innocents as another stage in the fulfilments of Jeremiah's words that:

'A voice was heard in Ramah,
wailing and loud lamentation,
Rachel weeping for her children;
she refused to be consoled, because they are no more.'
(Matt. 2.18)

Rachel, the wife of Jacob, was so distraught at her childlessness that it was as death to her (Gen. 30.1). Centuries later, the mothers of Ramah wept with the same sense of agonizing loss when Babylonian armies swept through their communities, wreaking havoc, forcing God's people into exile. The same sound was heard in Bethlehem, as mothers wept and 'refused to be consoled, because [their children] are no more' (Matt. 2.18). It is the sound I heard as I was preparing to write this chapter. Visiting Armenia, I was taken by an Orthodox bishop to the Military Cemetery in Yerevan. I knew it would be hard and I was grateful to be able to pray together with the bishop in the cemetery chapel before we walked among the dead. But I was still not ready for the hundreds of new graves with faces of young people etched on their headstones, still less for the sight of a mother clinging to one of them, holding on to the image of her son, weeping inconsolably, refusing to be comforted. Mothers through the ages weep and wail where the forces of injustice, violence and war deprive their children of life. They refuse to be comforted, hungering and thirsting for righteousness, protesting against the pride that causes such destruction, determined that the powerful people who cause death will be brought down from their thrones. Rachel still weeps in Ramah and Bethlehem; and God, 'born of a woman' (Gal. 4.4) is still in our midst.

When Paul says that Jesus was 'born under the law', his mind is on the Jewish law and the 'works of the law' that belonged to Jewish life and identity. He is positive about the law. It was the guardian of the people of God until the promise of life to Abraham was fulfilled (Gal. 3.15–29). The law is an outworking of grace, a gift to promote good life among God's people, shape their character as a people and preserve their place in the purposes of God. Even though she risked the threat of the law when she consented to a pregnancy before her marriage, Mary lived faithfully within the law of God's covenant, following the practices of the faith. As we will see later, with Joseph she presents Jesus in the temple 'according to the law of Moses' (Luke 2.22) and they ensure that Jesus regularly takes part in the Passover celebrations in Jerusalem. Jesus is brought up to love the law, and the righteousness for which it strives. Mary plays her part as a Jewish mother in growing the habits of the law in her son. Jesus learns that the purpose of the law is to protect, preserve and promote the life that God gives, and he commits himself to fulfil the law, to accomplish its purposes (Matt. 5.17–18). The righteousness that he brings – the righteousness of the kingdom of heaven – will require an obedience 'to the point of death ... on a cross' (Phil. 2.8) under the apparent curse of the law, just as it had required an obedience of Mary to his conception beyond the apparent strictures of the law. In 'the fullness of time ... God sent his Son, born of a woman, born under the law ... to redeem those who were under the law, so that we might receive adoption as children' (Gal. 4.4–5), writes Paul. However, 'the new covenant in [Christ's] blood' does not abrogate the old, 'for the gifts and the calling of God are irrevocable' (1 Cor. 11.25; Rom. 11.29). It is rather that the obedience of Christ opens the Gentiles to the life that belongs to the promise of God. Through the obedience of a faithful Jew, born and raised in a faithful Jewish family, God's promise that 'in [Abram] all the families of the earth shall be blessed' (Gen. 12.3) will be fulfilled.

Jesus said that he came to fulfil the prophets as well as the law and, as we have seen, Matthew's Gospel is especially keen to show how Jesus' conception and birth bring the words of the prophets to fruition. The same theme is evident in Luke, even if less explicitly, and the women in his Gospel, especially Mary, play a key part in the unfolding of God's promises. Elizabeth is filled with the Holy Spirit, enabling her not to be shocked at the disgrace of her young cousin's premature pregnancy but to rejoice that she carries 'the mother of my Lord' (Luke 1.43).

Elderly Anna, a prophet of God, fasting and praying through day and night in the temple, pours out praise to God when she sees the child Jesus in the arms of Mary and Joseph, and speaks words of prophecy over him. 'The image of Mary in the New Testament is woven entirely of Old Testament threads,' says Joseph Ratzinger (later Pope Benedict), echoing the mindset of the fathers of the Church's early days and the approach of the Christian East still in our own day to Mary.[8] He writes movingly about Isaiah's prophecy to Israel fulfilled in Mary:

> Sing, O barren one who did not bear;
> burst into song and shout,
> you who have not been in labour!
> For the children of the desolate woman will be more
> than the children of her that is married, says the LORD.
> (Isa. 54.1)

Mary, Benedict claims, although younger and most probably full of the fertility lost to Sarah, Rachel, Hannah and Elizabeth, represents not only the line of Israel's childless women to whom God gave life but, in her virginity, and the powerlessness of that state to bear life, Mary embodies even more our utter dependence on God to give life. In this very 'surrender to barrenness', she fulfils Israel's calling to give itself over to the life of God and to bear that life in the world.[9]

'For God so loved the world that he gave his only Son', John's Gospel tells us (3.16). The beginning and end of God's work is the love of God. God so loves the world that God gives life to the world. The demonstration of that love and the means by which God effects the purposes of God's love is the gift of God's Son, 'born of a woman'. Bonhoeffer puts it this way:

> God overrules every reproach of untruth, doubt, and uncertainty raised against God's love by entering as a human being into human life, by taking on and bearing bodily the nature, essence, guilt, and suffering of human beings. God becomes human out of love for humanity.[10]

And as he says elsewhere in his great work *Ethics*, it is in the reality of the 'conception and birth of Jesus Christ [that God] has taken on humanity bodily'.[11] It is a conception and birth that reverses the order of God's relationship with the world. The Creator of life is conceived in Mary. The sustainer of life grows cell by cell in Mary. 'The Author of life' (Acts 3.15) is given birth by a mother; and none of this without cost. 'Who is this calcium-consumer inside me? And who is this bone-sacrificer I have become?' asks Natalie Carnes in her *Confession*, a beautiful theological meditation on motherhood mirroring Augustine's great work by the same name.[12] We might also imagine God asking, 'Who is this life-provider on whom I depend? And who is this life-receiver I have become?' A human body carries the presence of God in whom the cosmos is held.

Mary in the *Protoevangelium* weaves the temple's veil with scarlet as well as with purple thread. Was a similar thought in the mind of the writer as in T. S. Eliot's 20 centuries later when he wrote 'The Journey of the Magi'?

This set down
This: were we led all that way for
Birth or Death? There was a birth, certainly,
We had evidence and no doubt. I had seen birth and death,
But had thought they were different; this Birth was
Hard and bitter agony for us, like Death, our death.[13]

'In the midst of life we are in death,' says the medieval liturgical text carried over into the Church of England's Funeral Service in its 1662 Prayer Book. I have known its truth in the births I have witnessed in person and the others I have waited for at a distance. Birth remains dangerous, even today. Mothers know its risks for themselves and feel it even more for their children. To what extent it shrouded Mary's birth-giving in the conditions of the first century, risks heightened even more by resident animals and visiting shepherds, we shall not know. Surely, though, Tertullian is closer to the event in his graphic scenes of pain and physicality than the traditions evolving at the same time in the second and third centuries that protect Mary's body from any sort of damage.[14] What we do know is that Mary knew, as every mother knows, that the child she delivered would one day face death himself. She would soon be told to prepare herself for the suffering of her son and the sword that would pierce her own soul. The God who, John tells us, 'gave his only Son', is the God who, Paul tells us, 'gave him *up for all of us*' (John 3.16; Rom. 8.32). In giving the Son to birth, God gave up the Son to death. And his death is not only 'our death', as Eliot says and Mary felt, but, with Mary, our birth into life and our salvation.

'She treasured all these things in her heart': Forming the life of the born

The first 1,000 days of a child's life, from conception to around two years old, are critical to their development.[15] The body, especially the brain, is developing at an astonishing pace. Attachment between the baby and caregivers is a determinative influence on the social and emotional development of the child. The pregnant mother's level of stress can pass on messages to the unborn child about the world and the dangers it represents, and the link between a mother's body and her child continues through lactation and other means of contact.[16] Jesus' 1,000 days were disrupted and uncertain, many of them spent on multiple journeys between Nazareth, Judea's hill country, Bethlehem, Jerusalem and Egypt. Every age has looked to Mary with thanksgiving for the care she provided for her child but the understanding of the importance of the formative experience of life – in womb and world – provided by contemporary biological and social knowledge increases that sense of respect and appreciation for all that Mary and Joseph were able to provide for Jesus physically, socially, psychologically and spiritually, especially under such harsh conditions.

Joseph played a key part, not to be underestimated. He took

Mary as his wife when there was good reason to walk away. 'He went to be registered with Mary,' as Luke tells us (2.5), without detailing the demands that the journey and the search for accommodation would have made upon him. We hear from Luke as well about the role of Joseph in fulfilling the requirements of the law, soon after Jesus was born, and about the prophecy over the child he witnessed in the temple. Matthew tells us more about the critical decisions and life-saving action he took to enable his family to escape to Egypt, and the spirituality and practicality they showed. Joseph's obedience to God during these dramatic days continued through to the decision to return to Israel when those 'seeking the child's life [were] dead' (Matt. 2.20). We will return to some of these scenes shortly and to the parenting of Joseph and Mary. At this point, though, we focus on the bodily relationship between the infant Jesus and his mother, and the way Mary brings life to Jesus through their sensory interaction.

There are many ways in which a mother and child are bound together by touch. The child being formed bodily within the mother's body, literally taking flesh from her, makes them, in one sense, intimately connected. From another angle, though, once the amniotic sac is in place for the developing foetus, their distinct bodies only make direct contact when the pregnancy comes to an end. The child leaves the warmth of the womb and the bodies of mother and baby touch as the child moves through the birth canal into the light of day. Whether or not Mary was the first to take the new-born Christ into her hands at birth, her flesh had already been the first flesh to touch the flesh of God and her body the first to hold God's body. All this and other ways of touch between a mother and child are intimate and profound. Among them I would like to reflect upon Jesus' – and Mary's – experience of breast feeding, not least because it involves all the other senses, particularly tasting and smelling.[17]

The only direct reference we have to Mary breast feeding Jesus is the woman in the crowd in Luke's Gospel who calls out to Jesus, 'Blessed is the womb that bore you and the breasts that nursed you!' (Luke 11.27). To be sure, she may only have made an assumption that Mary had once suckled Jesus, just as I too am assuming that Mary fed Jesus from her breast. Such assumptions can be hurtful to women who find they cannot breastfeed their children for whatever reason, or when their milk does not last. Bodies are depleted by poverty, journeys can add to the toll, and the stress of homelessness in a strange town would not help her body to function as Mary would have hoped. I think it is reasonable, though, to assume that Mary was able to take Jesus to her breast and to go on doing what she had been doing nine months previously – giving life to Life. The *Virgo Lactans*, Nursing Madonna, is a present though not prevalent image in medieval western art and eastern iconography, including in Armenia. Gregory of Narek draws upon the imagery in his writings, such as in his *Encomium on the Holy Virgin*, where he says,

> You nourished with milk and nurtured on earth the true Son of the Father of Light and sheltered with your caring arms the One who contains all.[18]

In these depictions, including Armenian versions, Mary is usually enthroned in heaven joyfully feeding her son arrayed in royal robes. But not always. In the war-torn region of Nagorno Karabakh there is a remarkable fifteenth-century Khachkar (a large stone cross) in the village of Handaberd with a small carving at its base of a woman suckling her child.[19] Iconography is not a strongly developed tradition in Armenian Christianity. More ancient in the history and deeper in the spirituality are the Khachkars, scattered across the South Caucasus, many of them now in Azerbaijani hands after wars of the twentieth and twenty-first centuries, and many of them threatened or defaced. Some have been destroyed for ever. Khachkars tell a theological story. At the top is heaven and at the bottom earth. Between the two, as the path from one to the other, is the cross. It is a life-giving cross, foliage spreads from it, and fruit too, often grapes, filling every remaining space with abundant life.

The Handaberd Khachkar follows these conventions but the central image in the space traditionally reserved for the earth is occupied by a mother, simply dressed, feeding her child. She is not, though, serenely smiling, absorbed in her own world of intimacy with her child. Her face looks pained and pre-occupied. Breast feeding makes all sorts of demands upon a woman's body and soul. I know it often brings discomfort and is seldom without pain of some sort. It costs to give life to another. It is possible the Khachkar was commissioned to commemorate a family's child who had died – and there is certainly a look of deep sadness on the mother, not unlike the inconsolable grief of Rachel. Of course, to all who saw the image it would bring to mind also Mary feeding Jesus, or rather Jesus feeding from Mary, for the child reaches out to her breast to receive its milk. Gregory describes it as 'life-giving milk'. Its setting here in the Handaberd Khachkar sends one to the cross, where grieving Mary stands nearby and where soon blood and water will flow from the stricken body of Christ and bring life to the world.

Often during breast feeding mothers will kiss their child. There is more going on here for the body than expression of emotion. The kiss enables the mother to gauge the child's health. Her lips will detect pathogens on the child's body that then trigger her body to produce the necessary antibodies so that her milk will protect and heal her child. Christina Rossetti's 'A Christmas Carol (In the bleak mid-winter)' imagines angels and archangels thronging the air at Jesus' birth, 'But,' she says,

> ... only his Mother
> In her maiden bliss
> Worshipped the beloved
> With a kiss.[20]

When the woman in the crowd called out 'Blessed is the womb that bore you and the breasts that nursed you!' Jesus responded, 'Blessed rather are those who hear the word of God and obey it!' (Luke 11.28). By no means need this be seen as Jesus disparaging his mother or playing down her role in his early life. Jesus was echoing the affirmation of his aunt, that Mary is blessed through her belief, 'that there would be a fulfilment of what was spoken to her by the Lord' (Luke 1.45). The fathers of the Church liked to talk about how Mary first conceived 'through the ear' (*conceptio per aurem*) in contrast to Eve who, they said, sinned through the ear. It is an image depicted very dramatically and somewhat playfully in a late fourteenth-century carving over the doorway to Mary's Chapel in Würzburg that has God the Father speaking through a mouthpiece into a pipe that is directly attached to Mary by an earpiece in the shape of a dove and along which the infant Christ can be seen sliding towards his mother.[21] It shows how Mary heard God's word and yielded herself to it – 'Let it be with me according to your word.' When she 'worshipped the beloved with a kiss', she adored the baby to whom she had given birth and to whom her body was bound, knowing that this child was 'the Son of the Most High' whose kingdom will have no end (Luke 1.33). When the little boy had become a grown man, we read of another kiss. This time it was Judas who kissed Jesus, Judas whom Jesus called a friend, even then (Matt. 26.48–49). Jesus' life depended on the life-giving of a mother. His life was enriched by her loving, as it was by the relationships with his friends that also brought him life. In the mystery of the incarnation, the life of Mary and the life of Judas depended on the life-sustaining work of the eternal Word of God now made flesh in Jesus. In the reality of redemption, their capacity to receive the new life that Jesus was bringing – the life that would overcome the death that had beset the world under the dominion of sin – would depend on their belief in Jesus and their readiness to obey.

Mary's kiss – her touch – brought life and love to Jesus so that Jesus could bring life and love to us, and it brought life to her, touching and transforming her world with the grace of God. Her speaking to Jesus and his hearing of her, gave Jesus the words to bring to us the word of life. The ear develops quickly in the womb, much more rapidly than the eye. Four

and a half months into the pregnancy the ear is fully developed. The capacity of the ear for recognition is greater than
that of the eye. Jesus would have heard his mother's voice from
the womb and come to recognize her tones, drawing comfort,
strength and security from the sound of her voice. His identity would be shaped by her words and his ability to speak
hastened by the quality of her speech to him. The affirmation
of her words before he had any ability to understand their
linguistic content would not only communicate her love to him
but also become the means by which the love of God would be
impressed upon him. In time, it would be through her words
that Jesus would learn more of the Fatherhood of God and of
his unique place in God's purposes.

Sight plays its part in development too, and I have written
elsewhere about the significance of Mary's gaze of love upon
Jesus, of his return of love as he looks at her. We are invited
to step into that gaze and love Jesus with a love that, though
different from Mary's unique love as a mother, has its own
intensity that belongs to the particular characteristics of our
relationship to him. Stepping into the gaze of love between
mother and son so that we can see Jesus truly, we find ourselves being seen by Jesus and loved by him fully. What I had
not appreciated when I wrote about the exchange of sight
between Jesus and his mother is what I have now learned from
the writing of my own son, and that is the way seeing would,
of course, have involved smiling.[22] We can be on sure ground
in saying that Jesus experienced the transformative effect of
smiling on human life – the joy in beholding another – through
his mother. Perhaps it was seeing her smile that made him
ready to believe what his ears later heard: 'You are my Son,
the Beloved; with you I am well pleased' (Luke 3.22).

The hearing and seeing between mother and child are an
exchange of love, of giving and receiving, of giving back and
returning that form the child as a relational being.[23] In time this
concentrated attachment, in which the mother is the primary
focus of the child's attention, widens to take in others, believing that they too can be trusted to bring solace and safety,

support and strength. Mary navigated that process of attachment and detachment through all of Jesus' senses well, and Narek was right to rejoice in her role:

O Mother of the Creator
Bearer of the One beyond reach:
you cuddled the One who cannot be contained,
supported the Almighty,
fed the One who works miracles,
clothed the One who adorns with glory,
caressed the One blessed on high.
Lo, for all these, and in keeping with your true word,
we bless you with unrestrained lips,
O Mother of Jesus.[24]

The Orthodox theologian Dumitru Stăniloae describes Mary's love as 'human love [that] has become fervent, has reached its high point, by being concentrated in a motherly heart and manifesting itself through it'.[25] In saying something particular about Mary, Stăniloae is also saying something more generally about mothering. In a not entirely dissimilar way, Beverly Roberts Gaventa draws on the writings of the influential feminist philosopher, Sara Ruddick, and her notion of 'maternal thinking'.[26] It is not only mothers who think and act maternally. As we noted in Chapter 1, other women do so in their relationships, attitudes and actions, and men do as well when they seek to nurture life. Jesus would have experienced this maternal thinking from others as well as his mother. Indeed, Mary's mothering of Jesus would have been shared with women in the family and the community and, in that wider sense of life-giving relationships, with many men, Joseph in particular.

We can see how Jesus loved with the fervent love of a mother throughout his ministry. Matthew brings this most clearly to light when Jesus laments over Jerusalem, saying, 'How often have I desired to gather your children together as a hen gathers her brood under her wings, and you were not willing!' (Matt. 23.37). Luke tells us he wept. Inspired by this and other scenes,

St Anselm, medieval theologian and Archbishop of Canterbury, called Jesus 'my Mother', and prayed:

> May your fearful one be comforted by you;
> despairing of himself, may he be strengthened by you,
> and through your perfect and unending grace,
> may he be made new by you.[27]

In John's description of Jesus' last supper with his disciples, he describes one of them – 'the one whom Jesus loved' – resting on his bosom (John 13.23, KJV). It is an image that calls to mind the opening of John's Gospel where he tells us that Jesus Christ, 'the only begotten Son', is 'in the bosom of the Father' (John 1.18, KJV). The closeness that comes from feeding a child from the breast, and the gift of life and love it gives, is defined not so much by the particular human action of breast feeding with its biological and relational parameters but by the life-giving reality of God and our creation in the image and likeness of God.

We are treading the tightrope here described in Chapter 1. Mothering is more than the physical conception, birth and care of a child. It is a way of being to which we are all called, female and male, after the mothering of God. But I want to take nothing away from the unique experience of women who do bring new life to birth through their bodies. And in trying to learn from that experience of all women who give birth and care for their young, and the concentration of human loving it manifests, we can also affirm the point Stăniloae wanted to underline. That is, in the words of the Anglican–Roman Catholic International Commission's 'Agreed Statement on Mary', her 'unique vocation' to be *Theotokos*, the God-bearer, the bearer not just of a human life but of *Life* itself (Godself) in human form.

Before leaving the early years of Jesus, there are two other scenes from the Gospels to explore. Both of them show Mary and Joseph active in co-parenting, the one supporting the other as they both celebrate and protect their child. We have touched

on them both before. The first is Luke's account of Joseph and
Mary travelling with Jesus from the simple lodgings in Bethlehem to the grandeur of Jerusalem's temple 'to present him
to the Lord' (Luke 2.22–39). Luke shows us how carefully
and thoroughly Jesus' parents complete 'everything required
by the law of the Lord'. They have their child circumcised at
the right time. They name him Jesus. They come to the temple not only for Mary's purification after giving birth as the
law required but for *their* purification – perhaps Joseph had
been more closely involved in the delivery than most fathers of
the time. They offer a prescribed sacrifice for the purification
ritual, albeit the option for the poor. They present their son to
God so that, 'according to the law', they could redeem their
child from priestly service in the temple, for as their first born,
he belonged to the Lord (Ex. 13.2).

In a sign of the activity of the Spirit, Luke tells us that
Simeon was 'guided by the Spirit' to enter the temple and that
when he saw the child, he knew that the promise of the Holy
Spirit – 'that he would not see death before he had seen the
Lord's Messiah' – was being fulfilled. He took Jesus into his
arms and praised God that his own eyes, though old and probably failing, had indeed seen the promised salvation. The scene
is one of unbounded joy as the elderly priest *receives* the gift
of salvation into his arms and *presents* the child to the Lord,
giving God praise. Luke tells us that even Mary and Joseph
who have already seen and heard great wonders over recent
months 'were amazed'. Ephrem, some centuries later, was also
astounded by the story, and tried to search out its layers of
depth.

But Simeon the priest when he had received Christ in his arms
so that he might present him to God, understood when he
beheld him that he was not offering Christ but was himself
being offered. For the Son is not to be offered to his Father by
a servant; rather the servant is offered by the Son.[28]

As we have seen before, Ephrem is fascinated by the reversals of the incarnation: the Giver of life is given life by Mary. Here, though, he shows that the reversal itself involves the re-expression of the theological order in redemptive form. On one level, the eternal Son is offered to the Father by a human priest, but on another deeper, truer level, the priest is being offered to the Father by the eternal Son. By taking on human life, God's beloved Son has become the priest of all humanity who, in the words of the Church of England collect, 'was this day presented in the Temple in substance of our flesh [so that] we may be presented to you with pure and clean hearts by your Son Jesus Christ our Lord'.[29]

The amazement of Mary and Joseph probably took on a different feel when, after he had blessed both of them, Simeon addressed Mary directly, speaking of the opposition that Jesus would receive and of the sword that 'will pierce [her] own soul too'. The relationship between the suffering of Christ and of Mary, and of what it might tell us of the relationship between Christ's sufferings and his followers, individually and collectively, is a complex one that we will explore in the next chapter. For the moment, I simply want to acknowledge the suffering that comes to parents along with their joy. The next scene will show that in more graphic detail. But before we leave the temple, Luke would have us see that after the prophecy of pain comes another prophecy of praise, this time from the very elderly woman, mentioned earlier. Her name was Anna and she was a remarkable example of faithful, disciplined devotion to God. For decades she had worshipped, fasted and prayed. Now she praised God for the child and prophesied over him 'to all who were looking for the redemption of Jerusalem' (Luke 2.38).

We reflected earlier on the horror of Herod's infanticide and the inconsolable suffering it would have caused mothers, families and communities in and around Bethlehem. For Joseph and Mary, the brutal egoism of a ruling despot forced them to flee to another land, sharing the dangers and risks, the fear and uncertainties of millions of migrants and refugees over the centuries, including the over 100 million people estimated by the UN Refugee Agency to be displaced by persecution, conflict and violence as I write.[30] I met some of them in Armenia and Georgia from Nagorno Karabakh, Abkhazia and Chechnya, lands far away from western attention for most of the time. They tell the same stories as the refugees I have met in Jordan and Iraq, Egypt, Nigeria and in my city of Coventry which has given asylum to thousands from across the world, including many from Ukraine. Children are always the centre of the struggle for life with mothers and fathers fiercely protecting and preserving the lives of their offspring.

Matthew's portrayal of Joseph is inspiring, and I have heard other fathers speak of their own tenacity in their stories of displacement. Joseph combines a spiritual openness to God with astute reading of the political realities and a determined practicality. He managed to navigate the threatening journey and somehow find employment as a migrant worker; his commitment to care for the life of 'the child and his mother' was unyielding, throughout. Mary is silent in the narrative but Matthew's repeated reference to 'the child and his mother' creates a strong sense of the deep bond between them (Matthew 2.13, 14, 20, 21). It calls to my mind the Stalingrad Madonna, an evocative image of a woman enfolding her child in her clothing – in herself – to be found in the Kaiser Wilhelm Memorial Church in Berlin, in Coventry Cathedral and also in Volgograd, as former Stalingrad is known today. It was drawn on the back of a military map by Kurt Reuber, a German soldier, medic and pastor during the worst battle in human history. Amid the hate-filled darkness and death of war at its worst, Reuber determined that Christ's birth would still be celebrated even in the carnage. So, he drew a mother silently shrouding her child, protecting this valuable life as far as she could from the sin and evil of the world, and carols were sung around it. Reuber scrawled 'Licht, Leben, Liebe' around the edge of the drawing – light, life, love – and the mother with her child gave hope that somehow through the silent suffering of a mother, new life would be given to the world.

'There he made his home': Being nurtured in faith, hope and love

Matthew and Luke tell us that Jesus spent the remaining years of his childhood in Nazareth, living in the home of Joseph and Mary.[31] They offer none of the detail, most of which is exotic and eccentric, that can be found in apocryphal gospels. We hear only of the incident recounted by Luke when Jesus was 12 years old. Luke prefaces that story with the comment that 'The child grew and became strong, filled with wisdom; and the favour of God was upon him' (Luke 2.40). Jesus' physical growth is accompanied by mental and spiritual growth as he develops in wisdom. At the end of the narrative of the 12-year-old in the temple, Luke reinforces the same double development: 'And Jesus increased in wisdom and in years, and in divine and human favour' (Luke 2.52). In the Infancy Gospel of Thomas, Jesus seems to arrive ready-made, already conscious of his unique identity and confident about exercising his spiritual powers. He has no interest in learning from his parents and even in the temple interrogates the elders and teachers, explaining the law to them.[32] In Luke though – and Matthew's silence on Jesus' childhood makes the same point – Jesus, like other children, learns from his community and, Luke implies, from Mary.

The annual Passover Festival to which Joseph and Mary, in company with other pious Jewish families, took their growing child begins to lift the lid on Jesus' growing sense of identity, as well as telling us more about their parenting, particularly the relationship between Jesus and his mother (Luke 2.41–52). When his parents discover that their son is not with others in the travelling party heading back to Galilee over the four-day journey, they rush back to Jerusalem and find him in the temple. We hear that the people who heard Jesus 'sitting among the teachers, listening to them and [contrary to Thomas' account] asking them questions' were 'amazed at his understanding and his answers'. His parents' response was astonishment. For the first time since she sang her song, we hear Mary's voice as she asks, 'Child, why have you treated us like this? Look, your father and I have been searching for you in great anxiety.' We then hear the voice of Jesus for the first time, saying, 'Why were you searching for me? Did you not know that I must be in my Father's house?' It is a revealing exchange. Simeon's prophecy is being fulfilled. Even Mary's 'inner thoughts' (Luke 2.35) are being brought to light. There is a piercing of her own soul not only in the emotional anxiety that she had endured searching for her missing child, extreme as that would have been, but also as Joseph – the one she calls Jesus' father and who shared her angst over these days – hears Jesus speak of an overriding calling to another Father's house. The salvation that Simeon saw in the infant Jesus and of which Mary knew from Gabriel's and Elizabeth's words was taking the shape of sonship in an even more profound, intimate and natural way than Mary had imagined.

Luke tells us that Jesus returned to Nazareth and was obedient to his parents. His home remained with them, their family and community bound together in a network of human relationships. His home was also with God, and with the community that God would build around him. Mary's obedience to the gift of motherhood she has been entrusted with will be tested by how freely she is able to liberate Jesus into the fullness of his identity as 'Son of the Most High' and into the calling of his kingdom that will have no end. It will be a long and painful journey for Mary, as it is for any mother, any parent. The loss that cut through Mary on the journey as she heard that her child was nowhere to be seen was compounded in the temple when she heard him talk of wanting to be seen primarily as the son of another Father. Luke is pointing to the cross on which Mary's son will hang following that other Father's will. Luke also suggests, though, that Mary's readiness to treasure 'all these things in her heart', rather than dread them, will fit her well to the challenges that lie ahead for her as she goes on helping Jesus to grow in wisdom and in God's favour, and the pressures that he would face as both 'the carpenter's son' and the beloved Son of God, in whom both fathers were well pleased (Matt. 13.55, 3.17).

Luke's account shows that Mary's and Joseph's parenting of Jesus took place within a community of 'relatives and friends' (Luke 2.44). This entirely accords with what we know of first-century Palestinian family life, especially in rural and peasant settings. Staying alive when living at subsistence level was a constant challenge, made no easier by the taxes of an occupying force and the whims of the puppet Roman tetrarch from the unreliable Herodian dynasty. It required skill and knowledge, organization and ingenuity, hard individual work and constant mutual support, the sharing of property and of tasks. It provoked prayer. It evoked reflection on God's past faithfulness and trust in God's present provision through daily, weekly, and annual religious rhythms in the home, in the synagogue, and in village and Jerusalem. It called for celebration of the gift of life, thanksgiving for God's mercy to generations of lives lived under God's care, praise for the promise of fuller life in the justice of God's kingdom. Women played a critical role in the fabric of this social environment where the domestic was impossible to distinguish from the economic and religious. They would have decisive influence on the children of the extended household in every way. Carol Meyers describes how 'the day-to-day interactions of mothers with children in the household were of foundational significance in passing most aspects of Israelite culture from one generation to the next'.[33] Elizabeth Johnson explains both how women 'created the atmosphere breathed in by these young lives' and how mothers had a special responsibility for the care of their young, boys as well as girls, at least up to the point when the boys were old enough to accompany their fathers in work beyond the family compound.[34] Luke shows how it was entirely normal for Mary and Joseph to entrust their child to the wider parenting of 'relatives and friends' while at the same time making clear that their child remained their own to whom they were bound in love and care.

The New Testament gives us some indication of Jesus' family. Luke tells us of Mary's cousin Elizabeth and her husband Zechariah. John mentions Mary's sister or sister-in-law.

Matthew has a particular interest in Joseph, Mary's husband. Matthew and Mark refer to Jesus' brothers and sisters, naming the former but not the latter: James, Joseph, Judas and Simon (Matt. 13.55; Mark 6.3, 3.31). We also read of Jesus' brothers in the upper room accompanying Mary after the resurrection (Acts 1.14) and we know of the leading role played by James, 'the Lord's brother' (Gal. 1.19) in the Jerusalem Church. A good deal of attention was given in the early centuries of the Church and, more recently, over the last two centuries, to the exact relationship they had to Jesus. Were they siblings who shared the same mother and father, as would appear to be case from a straightforward reading of the text? Were they children of Joseph from an earlier marriage, given that Joseph, who probably died some time between Jesus' visit to Jerusalem as a 12-year-old and the beginning of his public ministry around the age of 30, was likely to have been older than Mary, and that ancient tradition attests that he was a widower when he married her? Were they cousins of Jesus who were called *adelphoi* (brothers) and *adelphai* (sisters), in a way that was customary in first-century Palestine in much the same way as it is in twenty-first-century situations through much of the world today, for Mary is never called their mother? Broadly, three views of the scriptural evidence were held in the first few centuries of the Church, with Tertullian expounding the first, Jerome the third and those influenced most by James' *Proto-evangelium*, the second. Interest in such questions was not only historical. Theological weight soon became attached to them because of the question of whether Mary's virginity remained only until after Jesus' birth (as is suggested but not required by Matthew 1.24–25 and Luke 2.7) or whether it continued permanently. In other words, was Mary only *parthenos* – Virgin – until the birth of Jesus or was she *aeiparthenos* – Ever-Virgin?

Rather like the Roman Catholic doctrine of the Immaculate Conception of Mary (also held without as much theological definition in the East), I do not feel bound to accept the dogma of Mary's Perpetual Virginity held by Rome and the Eastern Churches. However, neither am I inclined to reject it in the manner of modern Protestantism which, contrary to Luther, Zwingli, Calvin, Cranmer and other mainline reformers (and, later, John Wesley), regards the idea as self-evidently inconsistent with scripture.[35] As ever, there are real questions of scriptural interpretation to navigate. I find myself close to fourth-century Basil of Caesarea. On the one hand Basil was clear that 'normal conjugal relations' between Mary and Joseph after Jesus' birth 'would not have affected the teaching of our religion' because it does not 'affect the doctrine of the mystery [of the incarnation]'. On the other, he was respectful of the views and testimony of those who 'do not allow themselves to hear that the Mother of God (*Theotokos*) ceased at a given moment to be a virgin'.[36]

The most modern and interesting interrogation of the doctrine of Mary's perpetual virginity has been by feminist scholars, especially Roman Catholics. Some have dismissed the doctrine out of hand, seeing it as a denial of women's sexuality and another patriarchal attempt to suppress female desire. They argue that it arose as the Church gave way to Greek (and gnostic) downgrading of the physical. Playing out the consequences of these views in attitudes to sexuality, the Church became more and more captivated by the idea of celibacy. Notions of Mary's perpetual virginity followed, with sex denigrated as inherently sinful and always to be avoided by the pure, rather than, in keeping with Hebrew tradition, a celebration of human bodiliness and a gift that brings the fruit of life. Mary, the one woman a male-led Church extols, is usurped by men into an impossible ideal for women of virgin *and* mother.

Other feminist theologians have taken a more sympathetic view. Tina Beattie, for example, is critical of some of the justifications given for the doctrine, detecting attempts to diminish the liberative power of Mary by concepts of moral virtue and femininity that belong neither to the scriptural text nor to the deeper truths underlying the doctrine. At the same time, though, she defends the doctrine on a number of grounds, one of them being that:

If Mary is a virgin only for as long as it takes to produce God's
son, and after that she becomes Joseph's wife in a sexual relationship, then retrospectively Mary will be seen to have been
nothing more than an object of exchange between God the
father and Joseph her husband. Her virginity does not have
intrinsic value for her personhood but only in functional
terms as part of the necessary apparatus of the incarnation.[37]

Mary's personhood is defined not by her relationship to men
– and by the expression of their sexuality in intercourse and
through bearing their children – but through her relationship
with God, her desire for God's will and her readiness to receive
the relationships and responsibilities God gives to her. Beattie
compares Mary with Eve, suggesting, like the fathers of the
Church before her, that Eve's virginity was lost through listening to the word of the serpent. Its guile deflected her relationship
with God – with the freedom, dignity and equality that it gave
her – and, in so doing, incorporated her 'into an economy of
knowledge that makes her a victim of man's power'.[38] Mary's
virginity for Beattie is a demonstration of God's redemption of
sexuality from the effects of the fall, freeing women from male
domination, restoring the equality between men and women,
and liberating sex from both corrupted desire and repressive
societal duty. In this way a contemporary feminist is not so
far from those women of the early and medieval Church who
insisted that their God-given womanhood called them to con-
secrated virginity in God's service rather than to the desires of
individual men or the demands of patriarchal society.

Discussions, historical and theological, about Mary's virginity will continue, but what is clear is the point made by Elizabeth
Johnson that Mary's mothering of Jesus was very unlikely to
have taken place in the one-child family depicted in art and
iconography, but rather in a setting surrounded by other
children, whether full- or half-brothers and sisters or cousins,
close or more distant, each vying for her time.[39] The intensity
of the relationship between Mary and Jesus in John's Gospel,
and Luke's suggestions of the formative influence of Mary on

Jesus' growth in wisdom and God's favour, are all the more interesting in the light of that full family life. It seems likely that Jesus drew on his observations of his mother in some of his parables, perhaps most clearly when he compared the kingdom of heaven with 'yeast that a woman took and mixed in with three measures of flour until all of it was leavened' (Matt. 13.33). Bread sustained life and women spent much of their time and energy making it. Jesus would have spent hours with his mother as she joined other women in producing this basic foodstuff that played such an important part in preserving the life of the family. Through her work he made connections not only with God's work of creation but with the coming kingdom of God where the leaven of redemption would bring a new sort of life to the world. Jesus taught his disciples to pray, 'Give us this day our daily bread', and I wonder whether he learned the heart of that prayer from his mother, from her example if not actually from her own words.

For some time, I have proposed that Jesus' teaching on the beatitudes grew out of his experience of Mary's motherhood. The closest I have found to other commentators making the same connections is in a moving meditation on Mary as a 'figure of the church' by the French Protestant pastor Jean de Saussure. Saussure was a good friend of the leading and groundbreaking Catholic ecumenist, Abbé Paul Couturier and the saintly Abbé was deeply drawn to the pastor's reflections on the way the beatitudes show us how 'to subsist only by thy [God's] grace'.[40] We saw in the last chapter how Mary is the first to be described as *makaria*, a word that translators have found difficult to translate into English. There we described it as the joy of those with the sort of attitudes or dispositions that allow them to experience the reality of the kingdom of God – a living in grace through the gift of a rightly ordered relationship with God and God's ways. In Matthew's Gospel, Jesus' teaching on the beatitudes comes near the beginning of Jesus' public ministry. We have heard that Jesus travelled through Galilee teaching in synagogues, 'proclaiming the good news of the kingdom' and bringing the healing of God to 'all the sick' (Matt.

4.23–24). Now we hear some of the content of that preaching and the life of the kingdom that Jesus proclaims. In a scene that mirrors Luke's account of the child Jesus in the temple, the adult Jesus sits not with the teachers but as a teacher, setting out the characteristics of those who would follow him in the way of the kingdom (Matt. 5—7). The beatitudes breathe the same air as many of the prophecies of Isaiah and the psalms of Israel, and Jesus, like the psalmist, says,

> Come, O children, listen to me;
> I will teach you the fear of the LORD.
> Which of you desires life?
> (Ps. 34.11–12)

Here is the way to life for those who desire life: the renewed life of the kingdom of God, the fullness of life promised by God and made possible by the Spirit of life at work in God's people. It is the sort of life that Jesus saw lived out in his mother, recipient of the Holy Spirit, bearer of life. 'Blessed are the poor in spirit, for theirs is the kingdom of heaven,' Jesus begins (Matt. 5.3). Poverty of spirit is the first and fundamental disposition of the people of God. 'How blest are those who know their need of God,' as the New English Bible puts it. It is 'the one needful thing' (Luke 10.42): to know one's need of God and to admit one's entire dependence on the grace and goodness of God. It is the heart of Christian faith, and finds its expression in the best of Christian theology and spirituality throughout the ages and cultures, from the spiritual disciplines of ascetic monasticism in the East to the Reformation's doctrine of justification by faith in the West. 'How can this be?' (Luke 1.34), asks Mary. How can God's will be fulfilled in me? How can God's salvation reach me? How can I stretch myself to God to serve God in the way I desire? 'The Holy Spirit ... the power of the Most High will overshadow you,' said the angel, '*therefore* the child to be born will be holy; he will be called Son of God' (Luke 1.35). Mary's poverty of Spirit – her recognition of her utter helplessness before God – was answered by the *therefore* of the gospel. Mary believed 'that there would be a fulfilment of what was spoken to her by the Lord' (Luke 1.45).

'Blessed are those who mourn, for they will be comforted,' Jesus went on to say (Matt. 5.4). At some point before his ministry began Jesus would most probably have seen his mother mourn the death of Joseph and face the dangers that becoming a widow would bring to her and her family. There would have been other deaths as well in the community and the family – John, her nephew, among them – some of them cruel like John's. When Mary saw the effects of the proud, the powerful and the rich upon the lowly, excluded and poor, she would have mourned for the 'oppressed' and 'broken-hearted', the 'captives' and 'the prisoners', and yearned for the coming of 'the year of the LORD's favour' (Isa. 61.1–2). Perhaps Jesus found himself drawn to the prophecies of Isaiah and the calling of the Suffering Servant partly because of his mother's vision of a society that brings life to all, and the cost that he knew it brought to her. She would be among those given a 'garland instead of ashes, the oil of gladness instead of mourning' (Isa. 61.3) even though her grief would one day be greater than it had ever been before.

'Blessed are the meek, for they will inherit the earth,' Jesus continued, echoing the psalmist (Ps. 37.11). The meek are not the weak. Whatever the appearances – personal, social, economic, political – the meek are the strong who trust in God and the confident who wait for God. They are humble and gentle and kind. They may be lowly in the world's terms but they are exalted by God. The earth belongs to them for it is only the meek who can care for it as a gift of God. In a rare self-description, Jesus uses the same word of himself. 'I am *praus* (meek, gentle) and *tapeinos* (humble or lowly) in heart (Matt. 11.29).[41] Jesus would have learned about Moses, who was described in similar terms (Num. 12.3), and learned from him. He would have also watched his mother and, perhaps, heard her talk and sing of the lowliness that God raises up. He would have learned from her that in the kingdom where life is lived in God's way, the 'servant shall prosper ... shall be exalted and lifted up, and shall be very high'. But he would also have learned from her life and the stories she told that the birth pangs of the kingdom may cause God's servant to be 'despised and rejected by others ... and as one from whom others hide their faces' (Isa. 52.13–53.3).

'Blessed are those who hunger and thirst for righteousness, for they will be filled', said Jesus (Matt. 5.6). Later he called his disciples to 'strive first for the kingdom of God and his righteousness' (Matt. 6.33). The life of God's kingdom is the life of righteousness. The life where people live in the right way – according to the law of God's life – and where right prevails throughout the life of the whole community. The kingdom of God is justice for all. Jesus' messianic manifesto is beginning to unfold. His messianic community is to embody this yearning for the just and gentle rule of God in its common life and to work passionately for the coming of the life of God's kingdom in people and their families, in communities and the nation, in Israel and among the nations. Jesus had seen such hunger and thirst for the ways of God in his mother whose heart was not only for her son, her family and her community, but for all those – the lowly, the hungry, the poor – who depended upon 'the promise [God] made to our ancestors' (Luke 1.55).

'Blessed are the merciful, for they will receive mercy' is the beatitude Jesus commends at the midway point in Matthew's account (Matt 5.7). 'Be merciful', says Jesus in Luke's Gospel, 'just as your Father is merciful' (6.36). Paul exhorts the Ephesian Christians to 'be kind to one another, tender-hearted, forgiving one another, as God in Christ has forgiven you' (Eph. 4.32). In one of the most intense moments of God's revelation to the Hebrew people, God 'passed before' Moses and 'proclaimed',

> The LORD, the LORD,
> a God merciful and gracious,
> slow to anger,
> and abounding in steadfast love and faithfulness,
> keeping steadfast love for the thousandth generation,

forgiving iniquity and transgression and sin,
yet by no means clearing the guilty.
(Ex. 34.5–7)

The dispositions of Jesus' disciples are the characteristics of
God. Their experience of the kingdom of God will be in proportion to their embodiment of the ways of God. Mary knew
that when she sang about how God's 'mercy is for those who
fear him from generation to generation' (Luke 1.50). Jesus
had seen in his mother the form that the fear of God takes in
human life – honesty and humility, belief and obedience, joy
and praise, faith, hope and love – and she had shown him what
it means to receive and to enact God's mercy.

'Blessed are the pure in heart, for they will see God,' Jesus
assures his disciples (Matt. 5.8). Psalm 24 would have echoed
in their minds. Those with 'clean hands and pure hearts' will
'ascend the hill of the LORD' and 'stand in his holy place', those
who do not 'lift up their souls to what is false' or 'swear deceit-
fully'. They are the ones who will 'receive blessing from the
LORD'. From the fullness of the Church's belief in the incarnation of God in Jesus Christ and the reflections on Mary that it
sets in motion, this beatitude, and the psalm that may lie behind
it, are a remarkable summation of the one who 'found favour
with God' (Luke 1.30). Mary saw God made flesh – divine Life
in human life. From the perspective of Jesus through the years
growing up in her company, we can safely say that he saw in
her the pureness of a heart set on the purposes of God and
shaped by the grace of God.

'Blessed are the peacemakers, for they will be called children
of God' said Jesus (Matt. 5.9), perhaps with the psalmist's
mandate for all God's people to 'seek peace' (34.14) in his
mind. Righteousness and peace are two sides of the same work
of God. Another psalm pictures them kissing each other wherever the purposes of God are fulfilled (Ps. 85.10). Jesus will
tell his disciples to bring peace to the homes they visit. He will
speak peace to the storms raging on the Sea of Galilee and in
a woman's heart. On the brink of his death, he will weep that

Jerusalem does not know the things that make for peace. Risen from the dead, he will pronounce peace upon his disciples as he sends them into the world (Luke 10.5–6; Mark 4.39, 5.34; Luke 19.42; John 20.21). Mothers play an instinctive part in peace-making. They know too well the cost of conflict and the pain of the violence that comes in its wake. There can be little doubt that Jesus would have witnessed Mary at work bringing peace in the interactions of family life in the extended household in which they lived. As we will see in the next chapter, it is possible that we see an example of Mary's peace-making in the incident recounted by Mark when Jesus' family 'went out to restrain him' (Mark 3.21–22). The *shalom* of God – the peace that God intends for creation – was the overarching beat of her song.

'Blessed are those who are persecuted for righteousness' sake, for theirs is the kingdom of heaven,' promised Jesus as the beatitudes draw to a conclusion (Matt. 5.10). Simeon had warned Mary that Jesus would be 'a sign that will be opposed' (Luke 2.34). As she helped Jesus to understand more fully the calling of the 'Son of the Most High' and bringer of the kingdom, perhaps she reminded him of the words of the prophet they would have heard together in the synagogue, 'Listen to me, you who know righteousness, you people who have my teaching in your hearts; do not fear the reproach of others, and do not be dismayed when they revile you' (Isa. 51.7). Jesus amplified this final beatitude by applying it not only to the cause of God's righteousness but to himself: 'Blessed are you when people revile you and persecute you and utter all kinds of evil against you falsely *on my account*' (Matt. 5.11). It would not have taken much insight for Jesus to know that prophets cannot expect much honour from their home town, and that some of the antipathy directed against him would deflect on to his family, his mother included. If Mary told him about the sword that Simeon said would 'pierce [her] own soul too', or if she told him something about the reaction of people to her pregnancy, there is added poignancy to Jesus' words. As she may have said to him, 'Do not be dismayed when they revile you,' so he now said the same to her, and to all who with her believe and obey. 'Rejoice and be glad,' Jesus says, for your reward is great in heaven. 'Rejoice!' – the angel's greeting to his mother – for great indeed was her reward on earth as in heaven.

When soon after Jesus' conception Elizabeth called Mary *makaria* – blessed – she was 'filled with the Holy Spirit' (Luke 1.41). Like her cousin, soon to sing her song of prophecy of the kingdom of God, and Zechariah, Simeon and Anna whose words in the Spirit would speak of Jesus' place in God's coming kingdom, Elizabeth's greeting to Mary in the Spirit has the hallmarks of Christian prophecy: taking what belongs to Christ and declaring it to us and so making known 'the things that are to come' (John 16.13). And like the prophets of old, Elizabeth speaks on two planes, the present and the future. On one level, her prophecy is a discernment of what has happened, an uncovering of what has come to pass for the sake of creation's future. Mary has believed God's word and received God's Son. On another level, it is an unfolding of the future. Mary will embody the characteristics of Jesus' disciples in her own prophetic presence and they will learn from her something of what happens when a life is lived near Jesus, learning from him the ways of God. Holding the present and future together is the prophetic recognition lived out in Mary's believing, praising and loving, that 'nothing will be impossible with God' (Luke 1.37). In the next chapter we move on to consider Mary's part in Jesus' ministry. Her role in his birth and childhood, in his formation for life and release into adulthood, was to prepare him to hear the voice of heaven saying, 'You are my Son, the Beloved' and to receive the Spirit descending upon him (Luke 3.21–22); and then to say his own, 'Here am I, the servant of the Lord; let it be with me according to your word' (Luke 1.38). Her work was done well.

Life as learning – Case study 2: Ethics for education

'Let it be with me according to your word' (Luke 1.38). Mary welcomed the gift of a child, receiving this new life as a gift from God to be formed within her and nurtured by her for the fullness of life that God had for this young child. Mary's acceptance of the gift of the child was at the same time God's embrace of human childhood. In Jesus, God knew the life of a child *as* a human child, including the love and care of a mother and of Joseph, who became his earthly father. Human childhood, elevated into divine experience, assumed an infinite worth.

When Jesus' disciples asked him the sort of question that seemed to be often on their minds – 'Who is the greatest in the kingdom of heaven' (Matt. 18.1) – Jesus beckoned a child towards him and put the child 'in the midst of them'.[42] A child in the midst of adults: they were to give this child their full attention, for here, in this small child they would see greatness. Jesus went on to say that 'whoever welcomes one such child in my name welcomes me' (Matt. 18.5). The child carries the name of Jesus, and in welcoming the child, they welcome Jesus.

There is a lot going on in this encounter and exchange. The child for Jesus seems to represent the radical inversion of status that is found in the kingdom of God where 'the first will be last' (Matt. 20.16). In this way the child is an answer to the disciples' preoccupation with their own status. They are not to seek the standing of the highest but to assume the place of the lowest. They are not to take on the attitude of those who have authority over others (and therefore a confident self-sufficiency) but rather the position of those who are dependent on the goodness of others (and are more ready to rely on the provision of God). But the child for Jesus is not just an object to be displayed for the learning of adults. Children are subjects in their own right, with their status raised by Jesus. In a story in Matthew's next chapter, when children who were being brought to Jesus were being turned away by Jesus' (adult) disciples, he said firmly, 'Let the little children come to me, and do not stop them; for it is to such as these that the kingdom of heaven belongs' (Matt. 19.14). Both dimensions – the child as the illustration of authentic discipleship in God's kingdom and the child as last in the world but first in the kingdom of God to whom the kingdom's good gifts belong – are brought together in some chilling words of Jesus between the two stories where he warns that it would be better for those who 'put a stumbling-block before one of these little ones' to have 'a great millstone ... fastened around [their] neck' and be 'drowned in the depth of the sea' (Matt. 18.6).

What might an ethic of life look like that placed the child *in the midst of us*, calling us to focus our ethical attention on the child and challenging us to interrogate all of our social policies – economic, finance, welfare, health, immigration and migration, environment, education and, indeed, our defence and foreign policies – by how far they serve children and the legacy that older people are leaving for younger people? What would it look like to engage with the questions that children and young people put to those whom society traditionally vests with power and authority, and for the elders to acknowledge the understanding of the youngers, ready to be 'amazed' at their own answers to the dilemmas of humanity and the dangers facing the earth (Luke 2.46–47)? An ethic of life will be concerned, of course, with the fullest life for all, but it will always give priority to those whose life is vulnerable, and whose voice is silent or muted. Jesus reminds us that children were vulnerable in ancient societies. Our own experience tells us that children and young people remain vulnerable in modern societies, including western democracies. Having no voting power of their own, they are reliant on adults to keep them *in the midst* of political decision-making about the present which will bear heavily upon their future as well as their present.

Countless children live in poverty of one sort or another in the UK. Financial poverty is a reality for millions of children. Agreeing the most accurate measurements is a complex and contested matter but it is accepted that somewhere near 4 million children were living in poverty in 2020–21.[43] Although an improvement on the previous year – probably thanks to support provided through the Covid-19 lockdowns – they were soon to increase through the cost-of-living increases that came in the wake of Covid intensified by the war in Ukraine with all its knock-on effects. The threat of further economic insecurity caused by climate change and geopolitical tensions, with the risks they bring of war and conflict on a wider scale, hang like a foreboding cloud over the young of the UK as they do over the children and young people of other societies. Financial poverty involves food, energy, housing, and other forms of physical poverty, all of which can be causes of hygiene and health poverty. There are also forms of emotional poverty that press down upon children, eroding year-on-year their sense of well-being, stifling their prospects and stealing their futures.[44] There is the poverty of reliable relationships, with children denied the attention they deserve through parental absence and neglect or simply through parental incapacity caused by family breakdown and other family dysfunctionality, the strain of work or the pressure of not being in work. Poverty of care, with its physical and emotional manifestation, is experienced by children in families that are doing their best against impossible odds to do right by their children, in families where adults abuse their responsibilities to children, and in the social care systems that take on the children whom families have failed but where the provisions of the State too often also fail them, especially teenagers for whom most of its systems and structures were not designed.[45] And there is spiritual poverty with children deprived of narratives that make sense of life, rituals that give shape to life and opportunities to hear about the God who has given them life and offers them unending love throughout their lives and to encounter Jesus Christ, the one who put children at the centre of human concern.

Radical and far-reaching approaches are needed across society and through government policy to address the symptoms and the causes of child poverty. Political will at the highest level of government and cross-government action is necessary to effect long-lasting change through coordinated social policy in family support, early years and childcare provision, housing, employment, social security and education, combined with close cooperation with people on the ground in the different localities of the UK's life, including charities, churches and other religious organizations.[46]

Given Jesus' experience as a learner of the ways of the kingdom of God through the wisdom of his mother, and conscious that those who follow in his way are called disciples (*mathetai*) – learners, I will focus on the role of education in lifting children into fuller life. The educational policy of successive governments has been essentially functional. Its eyes have been on the structures by which schools are organized and governed and on the systems by which the learning of children can be focused, monitored, improved and tested, and those responsible for their education held to the highest account. All this is of value and is not be disparaged. Effective structures of leadership, governance and support for schools are necessary if they are to be effective learning environments. Competence in English and maths, knowledge across key areas of a coherent curriculum, and a range of skills are all important. Suitability for employment in today's economy and in the economy of tomorrow is required. Standards of behaviour are vital for successful schooling and for work as well as other aspects of life.

Nevertheless, by the example of Mary who receives the gift of a child as the centre of her vocation to God and by the criterion set by Jesus when he put a *child in the midst of us* and said that the kingdom of heaven belongs *to such as these*, there has been something missing from our educational policy of successive governments that are usually too short term in their policy-making. The deepest deficit in contemporary educational policy is a compelling vision for education, an understanding of what education is *for* that reaches after the character of the kingdom of heaven and sets its sight on the purposes for each human being and the society of which they are part. Where there is no vision for education that is deeply grounded in the life that God wills for humanity, it can easily become enlisted in the service of other gods. In our own culture it is the money god who reduces us to operatives in an economic machine – whether as producers, exchangers or consumers of goods, services and experiences – that is always waiting at the door like a 'roaring lion ... looking for someone to devour' (1 Peter 5.8).

When describing 'the Universal Right to Education', the Second Vatican Council described the purpose of 'true education' as 'the formation of the human person in the pursuit of their ultimate end and of the good of the societies of which, they, as a member, and in whose obligations, as an adult, they will share'.[47] It was the formation of the human person in the life of the kingdom of God that lay at the heart of Jesus' educational method of those closest to him as well as of those who more loosely associated with him. It was a method rooted deeply in the practices of Jewish faith, and in his own experiences of learning through Mary, Joseph and others in his family and village community, the synagogue included. The formation of the human person for the life of the kingdom of God is the inspiration behind the Church of England's vision for education for 'fullness of life'. Education is truly for *life*. It is, indeed, lifelong but the foundation on which the future is built is laid at that stage of life when the human person is growing in body and mind, spirit and soul, emotion and character, when values are being absorbed and virtues nurtured. Schools, according to this embracing vision, are 'signs of fullness of life for all, as they educate children for wisdom, knowledge and skills, for hope and aspiration, for community and living well together, and for dignity and respect'.[48]

As I visit church schools seeking to live out that vision, meet young people, spend time with headteachers, read the values and aspirations often inscribed on the walls, I see many such 'signs of fullness of life' in city, town and village. I hear of the highest ideals for education and I see a good deal of evidence of transformative learning experiences taking place. I also hear, though, of great frustration from headteachers and their staff from the relentless pressure to meet – and to demonstrate that they have met – some fairly limited educational standards. As vital as those standards are in themselves, they are not the sum total of education. I see good teachers and headteachers leave the profession because they feel they have been reduced from educators of the whole person to producers of products, albeit well educated for the next stage of life and equipped with some of the basic skills for employment. I also see educational leaders and their governing bodies constantly battling with budgets that do not allow them to fulfil their aspirations for their children and young people, and the communities they serve. I see similar anxieties about finances when I visit well-established and well-run independent schools – there is never enough money to do all the good that we would like do – but often my breath is taken away by the resources available to them. I leave impressed by the quality of the education they provide not only in terms of academic standards but also in terms of the opportunities for fullness of life and the flourishing of futures. When I compare the sums of investment in each child between that sort of school and the state-funded schools I visit more regularly, at least some of the reasons for the educational gap between them becomes clear.

'For where your treasure is, there your heart will be also' (Matt. 6.21), said Jesus. Children are not only society's future who require our present investment. They are society's treasure that command the priority of our hearts and they deserve the full benefits of our assets. Kevan Collins, who was appointed by the then prime minister to plot a course of educational recovery for the country's children after the Covid-19 pandemic, saw something of the imperative that the educational needs of children placed before society when he called for a determined and ambitious reinvestment in education in the region of £15 billion. The figure promised by the government fell far short and he resigned in the absence of the 'comprehensive and urgent response' for which he was calling.[49]

Government funding is always changing, and it is difficult to predict what the future will hold for the resourcing of education, but the scale of the task is clear. There are many competing demands for funding in the face of multiple challenges facing humanity, several of them at crisis point. Choices facing governments are complex and the resources at their disposal are limited. But just as an ethic of life confronts us with the moral demands of life that is not yet born (Chapter 2) and with the threats to the futures of life young and old from nuclear weapons (Chapter 4) and environmental damage (Chapter 5), so it places *in our midst* the responsibility that society as a whole has for the fullest development of children and young people, and calls each (adult) individual voter to make the child's fullness of life so much their own priority, that it becomes the priority of our elected representatives in government.

Notes

1 Gregory of Narek, 'Ode for the Theophany' in *The Festal Works of St. Gregory of Narek: Annotated Translation of the Odes, Litanies, and Encomia*, ed. and trans. Abraham Terian (Collegeville, MN: Liturgical Press, 2016), pp. 213–17.

2 Tina Beattie, *Rediscovering Mary: Insights from the Gospels* (Liguori, MO: Triumph Books, 1995), p. 28.

3 Cyril of Alexandria, 'Third Letter to Nestorius' in *Cyril of Alexandria: Select Letters*, ed. Lionel R. Wickham (Oxford: Oxford University Press, 1983), pp. 12–34.

4 Ronald F. Hock, *The Infancy Gospels of James and Thomas: With Introduction, Notes, and Original Text featuring the NEW Scholars Version Translation* (Santa Rosa, CA: Polebridge Press, 1995), pp. 51 and 127.

5 Gerard Manley Hopkins, 'The Blessed Virgin Compared to the Air we Breathe' in *The Poetical Works of Gerard Manley Hopkins*, ed. Norman H. MacKenzie (Oxford: Clarendon Press, 1990), p. 174.

6 'Life' is a strong ethical theme in Francis' thought and he speaks of 'an attack on life' in a variety of contexts from abortion to war as well as to attacks on nature and the environment.

7 For the different variations of the carol, see https://tinyurl.com/565ytyws, accessed 16.1.2023.

8 Joseph Cardinal Ratzinger, *Daughter Zion: Meditations on the Church's Marian Belief*, trans. John M. McDermott (San Francisco, CA: Ignatius Press, 1983), p. 12.

9 Ratzinger, *Daughter Zion*, p. 52.

10 Dietrich Bonhoeffer, *Ethics*, vol. 6 of Dietrich Bonhoeffer Works, ed. Clifford J. Green (Minneapolis, MN: Fortress Press, 2009), p. 84.

11 Bonhoeffer, *Ethics*, p. 84.

12 Natalie Carnes, *Motherhood: A Confession* (Stanford, CA: Stanford University Press, 2020), p. 12.

13 T. S. Eliot, 'The Journey of the Magi' in *Collected Poems 1909–1962* (London: Faber and Faber, 1927), p. 109.

14 See Tertullian, 'On the Flesh of Christ' in *The Ante-Nicene Fathers, Vol. III, Latin Christianity: Its Founder, Tertullian*, ed. Alexander Roberts and James Donaldson (Buffalo, NY: The Christian Literature Publishing Company, 1887), chapters I–IV, especially chapter IV, and *Protoevangelium*, chapters 19–20 in Hock, *The Infancy Gospels*. I am intrigued, though, by the apparent reappraisal of notions of Mary's virginity in birth by Beattie from her *Rediscovering Mary* (1995) to her *God's Mother, Eve's Advocate* (London: Continuum, 2002). See pp. 56–8 and 100–1 respectively.

15 See 'The 1001 Critical Days: The Importance of the Conception to Age Two Period' (2014), available at https://tinyurl.com/3maruc6f, accessed 16.1.2023.

16 For example, during bonding with their child, mothers produce the hormone oxytocin, making them more sensitive and empathetic. Oxytocin is produced by the mother and infant during lactation, which helps to lower stress levels in children from 0–3 years and promotes brain regulation, both of which are crucial to development. Fathers do not produce the same form of oxytocin. See Erica Komisar, 'Why Prioritising Motherhood in the First Three Years is Critical' (2017), available at https://tinyurl.com/3b9u2htd, accessed 16.1.2023.

17 I am especially conscious here of the complexities that I mentioned in the Preface. I am writing as a man about a bodily action of which I have no direct experience. Moreover, I am a western man of late modernity musing on the experience of a Palestinian woman from an ancient and remote culture. Breast feeding is a profoundly intimate and sensitive bodily reality, touching deeply the strongest emotions, bound up with joy, elation, disappointment, shattered dreams and broken hearts. It is freighted with the changing views of health science, commercial interest, family structure and social policy. Women disagree about its merits. My ignorance goes deeper. My birth was induced and, because of the medication, my mother had no milk to feed me. I have watched with awe as my own children have been breastfed and lived through something of the contrasting experiences of breast feeding among my daughters-in-law. Nevertheless, I hope the inaccessibility of the actual experience of breast feeding to me as mother or child has

not produced too many naiveties in the words I have written and, even more, that they have not caused hurt.

18 St Gregory, 'Encomium on the Holy Virgin' in *The Festal Works of St. Gregory of Narek: Annotated Translation of the Odes, Litanies, and Encomia*, ed. and trans. Abraham Terian (Collegeville, MN: Liturgical Press, 2016), p. 299.

19 For the image, see https://tinyurl.com/ea3d4fan, accessed 16.1.2023. I am grateful to Christina Maranci for directing me to several helpful sources, this among them.

20 Christina Rossetti, 'A Christmas Carol (In the bleak mid-winter)' in *The Poetical Works of Christina Georgina Rossetti*, ed. William Michael Rossetti (London: Macmillan and Co., 1914), p. 246.

21 I am grateful to Matthew Murphy for bringing this carving to my attention.

22 See Ashley Cocksworth and David F. Ford, *Glorification* (Grand Rapids, MI: Baker Academic, 2023).

23 The studies undertaken by McElwain and Volling in 2004 and Steele in 2002 provide evidence for the importance of the role of the mother in developing peer relationships. See Gabriela Misca and Jo Smith, 'Mothers, Fathers, Families and Child Development' in *Contemporary Issues in Family Studies: Global Perspectives on Partnerships, Parenting and Support in a Changing World*, ed. Angela Abela and Janet Walker (Oxford: Wiley-Blackwell, 2014), p. 158.

24 Gregory of Narek, 'Encomium on the Holy Virgin', p. 298.

25 Quoted in Andrew Louth, 'Mary in Orthodox Theology' in *The Oxford Handbook of Mary*, ed. Chris Maunder (Oxford: Oxford University Press, 2019), p. 241.

26 Beverly Roberts Gaventa, 'Nothing will be Impossible with God: Mary as the Mother of Believers', in *Mary Mother of God*, ed. Carl E. Braaten and Robert W. Jenson (Grand Rapids, MI: Eerdmans, 2004), pp. 33–4.

27 Oratio X, in Franz von Sales Schmitt, *S. Anselmi Cantuariensis Archiepiscopi Opera Omnia* (Stuttgart: Frommann, 1968), VIII, p. 41, translation by Christine Walker.

28 St Ephrem, 'Three Homilies: On Our Lord', in *Nicene and Post-Nicene Fathers, Series II, Volume 13: Gregory the Great – Part II; Ephraim Syrus*, ed. Philip Schaff (Oxford: James Parker and Co., 1893), p. 327. For a helpful analysis of offering in the Syrian tradition, see Rowan Williams, *Eucharistic Sacrifice: The Roots of a Metaphor* (Nottingham: Grove Books, 1982), pp. 21–3.

29 Church of England, *Common Worship: Daily Prayer* (London: Church House Publishing, 2005).

30 UNHCR, 'Forced Displacement in 2020', online at https://www.unhcr.org/globaltrends.html, accessed 19.3.2023.

31 The only way I know for accounting for the apparent discrepancy between Matthew, who says the family returned to Nazareth from Egypt, and Luke, who says that they did so from Bethlehem or Jerusalem, is that they represent different traditions about the early life of Jesus circulating in different early Christian communities.

32 Infancy Thomas, chapter 19, in Hock, *The Infancy Gospels*, pp. 141–3.

33 Quoted in Elizabeth A. Johnson, *Truly Our Sister: A Theology of Mary in the Communion of Saints* (London: Continuum, 2009), p. 202.

34 Johnson, *Truly Our Sister*, p. 202.

35 On John Wesley, see Michael Hurley (ed.), *John Wesley's Letter to a Roman Catholic* (London: G. Chapman, 1968).

36 Basil of Caesarea, *On the Holy Generation of Christ*, p. 5, quoted in Tina Beattie, 'Mary in Patristic Theology', in *Mary: The Complete Resource*, ed. Sarah Jane Boss (London: Continuum, 2009), p. 98.

37 Beattie, *God's Mother, Eve's Advocate*, p. 178.

38 Beattie, *God's Mother, Eve's Advocate*, p. 180.

39 Johnson, *Truly Our Sister*, p. 198.

40 See Geoffrey Curtis, *Paul Couturier and Unity in Christ* (London: SCM Press, 1964), pp. 282–4, where part of the Meditation is quoted at length.

41 For a sensitive and insightful study on this theme, see Dane C. Ortlund, *Gentle and Lowly: The Heart of Christ for Sinners and Sufferers* (Wheaton, IL: Crossway, 2020).

42 I use the KJV here because it seems to me closer to the Greek of *en meso auton*.

43 For a detailed analysis of the figures, including definitions of the different forms of measurement, see https://tinyurl.com/mtn5we74, accessed 16.1.2023.

44 See the Children's Society 'Good Childhood Report 2022', https://tinyurl.com/4vys2dhj, accessed 16.1.2023.

45 See the findings of *Independent Review of Social Care* published in 2022, https://tinyurl.com/mtamwsws, accessed 16.1.2023.

46 See the Church of England Child Poverty Review published in 2022, https://tinyurl.com/43v7rvha, accessed 16.1.2023.

47 Second Vatican Council, 'Declaration on Christian Education: Gravissimum Educationis', in *The Documents of Vatican II*, ed. Walter M. Abbott (New York: Herder and Herder, 1966), p. 639.

48 The Church of England Education Office, *Church of England Vision for Education: Deeply Christian Serving the Common Good* (London: Church House Publishing, 2016), p. 8.

49 Quoted on the Times Educational Supplement website, 2 June 2021, https://tinyurl.com/yc8m6j52, accessed 16.1.2023.

4

Redeemed

She alone is Your mother,
but she is Your sister, with everyone else.
She was Your Mother, she was Your sister,
she was Your bride too,
along with all chaste souls.
You, who are Your mother's beauty
Yourself adorned her with everything.
('Nativity', Ephrem the Syrian)[1]

'Where did this man get all this?': Ministering life

In the last chapter we explored some of the ways in which Mary formed the life of Jesus, his body, character and self-understanding. At some points we were on fairly sure historical ground, at others we were working with more speculative soil. The reality of Mary's influence on Jesus is indisputable. Its extent is more open to debate and interpretation. Mark tells us the people of Nazareth were astounded at the words and works of Jesus that they had heard about him from his travels to other places. 'What is this wisdom that has been given to him? What deeds of power are being done by his hands! Is not this the carpenter, the son of Mary?' (Mark 6.2–3). Jesus was a familiar figure – the local carpenter and builder with a mother and family like others in the community. They would have accepted that Jesus had received much from his mother and his brothers and sisters but they could not account for the wisdom and wonders that were being attributed to him.

On one level, of course, they were right. From his conception, Jesus was different. He was a new creation of God's

Spirit and the 'Son of the Most High'. There would 'be no end' to the kingdom that he would bring (Luke 1.32–33). But it would miss the subtlety of the incarnation to say that the usual features of earthly existence came to him from his mother, family and community, while the unusual characteristics of his heavenly identity were given by some other divine communication which bypassed the more ordinary elements of his human life. Just as we say in the creed that 'the only Son of God ... was incarnate from the Holy Spirit *and* the Virgin Mary', so we can say that Jesus was formed in life and for ministry from 'the Holy Spirit *and* the Virgin Mary' as by others around her.[2] As we saw in Chapter 2, the incarnation requires the new creative act of the Spirit and the willing consent of Mary. We also saw that this work of God in, through and *with* Mary was by God's grace – and through 'grace upon grace', as John puts it (John 1.16) – for God chose Mary by grace and enabled her by grace to respond to God's call with her own, 'Here am I, the servant of the Lord.' The Gospels leave us in little serious doubt that Mary's availability to form and shape Jesus' life continued through his childhood and into his adulthood, quite possibly into his public ministry itself. So, in that sense, as we have already proposed, the answer to the question of the people of Nazareth, 'Where did he get all this?' was *in part* to be found in their own words – from Mary, his mother.

However, none of this is to imply that Mary did not have a great deal to learn from Jesus' wisdom as a child and as an adult, or that she was not herself also astounded by his activity, especially the miracles that would happen around him. In the words of the Second Vatican Council that we have already quoted, Mary 'advanced in her pilgrimage of faith'.[3] There would be more 'grace upon grace' for her to discover from the 'Most High' and from the Spirit who would empower 'the Lord's Messiah', and more for her to receive from 'God [her] Saviour' through believing in her son and following his way (John 1.16; Luke 1.32, 2.26, 1.47). Like other mothers before and after her, Mary would need to learn the reality of Cecil Day-Lewis' poem about parenthood, that 'Love is proved in the letting go.'⁴ If her nephew's role was to prepare Israel to meet its Messiah, hers was to prepare the Messiah to meet Israel and the world. That would mean releasing him, when the time was right – when in John's terms, his 'hour had come'⁵ – for his messianic ministry that would exceed the imaginations even of her own heart. It would also mean that her belief and faithfulness would need to grow in proportion to the revelation of the height, width and depth of his work, and it would include her becoming fully part of the new family, the new messianic community that would grow around Jesus. Mark, together with Matthew and Luke, recounts an incident at the beginning of Jesus' ministry in which several of these themes – letting go, learning from, believing and following, joining the new community – are woven together. John tells us of another.

Devoid of a birth narrative, Mark's Gospel soon launches into a rapid-fire account of Jesus' ministry in the communities around the Sea of Galilee. 'The time is fulfilled, and the kingdom of God has come near,' Jesus announced (Mark 1.15). There was a dynamic authority about his teaching. It astounded those who heard it. People afflicted by evil spirits were set free, the long-term ill were healed, unlikely people were invited to become his disciples. People flocked to see, hear and touch Jesus. Celebration was in the air. Fasting was over. New wine was flowing. Peace was breaking out as people were put right with their minds, their bodies, their communities and with God. Now that God's life-giving kingdom was coming near in so many ways, Jesus appointed followers to be sent out to take their part in his messianic mission; and then, Mark tells us, he 'went home' (3.19).

The commotion that surrounded Jesus in Galilee reached Nazareth, and so did scribes from Jerusalem with serious complaints against him on their lips. Mark tells us that when Jesus' family heard about what was happening, 'they went out to restrain him, for people were saying, "He has gone out of his mind"' (Mark 3.21). Later, Mark tells us that Mary was among them (Mark 3.31–35). Perhaps this was one of those moments when Mary had to learn to let go. She may well have been fearful for Jesus' safety. There was a lot of talk in Nazareth and there was clearly growing concern in Jerusalem. She may have thought that Jesus was moving into his ministry too quickly, saying and doing too much too early, failing to bring people with him. All of this would have been entirely understandable and a predictable stage in Mary's 'pilgrimage of faith' as she learned to trust him. Perhaps, though, Mary joined the relatives as they went in search of Jesus in the hope of bringing some peace. She was in a unique position to mediate between the son whom she knew well and the family who were behind the curve. Was the Holy Spirit at work in Jesus, or was it some spirit? That was the question of the day that swirled around Jesus (Mark 3.22–30), and there was much that Mary would have had to say about it. The question would remain hanging over Jesus throughout his ministry and, ultimately, its answer would determine whether he would live or die.

Perhaps there was an element both of Mary letting Jesus go and of her helping others to take hold of his work more fully. Whatever the case, it was important for Mary to be reminded by Jesus' response to those who told him that his family were looking for him that the root of her motherhood was her readiness to do 'the will of God' (Mark 3.35) and, in that sense, her motherhood was shared with all those who would do the same. That decision had taken her on a journey of (in John's words) 'grace upon grace' through which she would be brought (in Paul's words) to the 'obedience of faith' to which God leads all 'who are called to belong to Jesus Christ' (Rom. 1.5–6).

John tells us another story where we see Jesus' relationship with his mother intersecting his ministry (John 2.1–12). It takes place 'on the third day' as Jesus begins to emerge as the Messiah. This is the first time we encounter Mary in John's Gospel and one of only two occasions in which we glimpse something of Jesus' relationship with her. The details of the story will be familiar. Jesus and his newly called disciples are invited to a wedding in Cana, fairly near Nazareth. The wine runs out and 'the mother of Jesus' tells him about the problem. Jesus' response – 'Woman, what concern is that to you and to me? My hour has not yet come' – is usually interpreted as a rebuke of some sort, made even more so by the remote and impersonal manner of address. Perhaps it was so and, as we have seen, there was much for Mary to learn about the scope of Jesus' ministry (that it would go far beyond the immediate needs of the people of Galilee) and the nature of the relationship between them (Jesus would follow the Father in deciding what he would do and when he would do it). The story may be John's way of showing us how 'the mother of Jesus' needed to let her son take on his true glory as 'the only Son, who is close to the Father's heart' (John 1.18). Tina Beattie has a different reading of the incident, though. She suggests that the wedding in Cana acts as an alternative birth narrative in John's Gospel.[6] Rather than reluctantly letting Jesus go into the ministry that *he* will define, Mary is releasing Jesus into the ministry that *she* knows to be his, even helping him to see that now is the time for it to begin. In other words, the running out of wine, as unlikely as it first appears to Jesus, is in fact of great concern both to him and to her because now, in this ordinary, domestic gathering of a small Galilean town, the glory of Jesus' abundant, transformative, life-changing ministry where the impossible becomes possible is to be revealed.

Again, whatever the case, the words that Mary spoke to the servants – the last words we hear her speak in John – were as important for her to hear as they were for her to say: 'Do whatever he tells you.' John brings the story to a conclusion by telling us that Jesus 'went down to Capernaum with his mother, his brothers, and his disciples'. Mary was part of the company that believed Jesus and followed him. The mother was taking her place as a disciple with a distinctive place among the other servants of the Messiah's kingdom where the good wine would flow and never cease.

'Meanwhile standing near the cross of Jesus were his mother and …': Dying for life

Jesus' ministry of *life-giving* increasingly met forces of *death-dealing*. It was like that at the creation of humanity. The life freely given to human life was tempted away by the beguiling forces of evil. Life gave way to anti-life and death came, with all its attendant suffering. As the pages of the Book of Genesis unfold it does not take long for the history of humanity to be overwhelmed by deception and deceit, injustice and depravity, famine and poverty. The peace of Eden gives way to the violence of the world. Humanity's helplessness in the face of its own destructive capacities soon becomes evident. Its reliance on God's promise to give life and to bless life, in ways that fast appear almost impossible, becomes the overriding hope of the story that follows through the Bible's many books.

Those forces of anti-life threatened to overwhelm Jesus before his birth, at his birth and after his birth. Roman systems, Herod's megalomania and even the conventions of his own Jewish culture and religion all conspired against him and his mother. Bound together in his earliest days, mother and son would also be together in his last hours. It is little wonder that the mysterious vision of John the Seer on Patmos Island of 'a woman clothed with the sun' has been applied to Mary in many phases of her life, including when she stood near to her dying son: 'Then the dragon stood before the woman … so that he might devour her child' (Rev. 12.1–6). The body she bore was being destroyed before her eyes. The life that she had given to her son was ebbing away. The Spirit that had overshadowed her in Nazareth, enveloping her with the life of God, seemed now eclipsed by the darkness that had descended on Jerusalem. The peace proclaimed by the angels to all the earth was being ridiculed by the 'ruler of this world' (John 14.30). Her son cried out, 'My God, my God, why have you forsaken me?' (Mark 15.34) in the words of the psalmist, which go on to say:

Yet it was you who took me from the womb;
you kept me safe on my mother's breast.
On you I was cast from my birth,
and since my mother bore me you have been my God.
Do not be far from me.
(Ps. 22.9–11)

The incalculable emotional trauma of seeing her son suffer in such extreme pain and public ignominy was given little attention by the theologians and leaders of the centuries following the writing of the New Testament. That was due to a number of reasons: part respect for scripture's own reticence, part desire to maintain Mary's dignity and part proper concern to keep the focus on Christ's saving action. At the same time there was also little concentrated interest in theology or piety on the sufferings of Jesus himself. The emphasis was more on his defeat of death and his victory over sin and evil. In the Eastern Church all this changed very dramatically around the end of the eleventh century. The shift may well have had something to do with Anselm's great work on the atonement with its focus on the sufferings of Christ.[7] Anselm's attention on Jesus' passion led him, as a consequence, to contemplate Mary's emotional agony:

My most merciful lady,
what shall I say of the streams of tears
which overflowed from your most pure eyes,
when you saw your blameless only son
bound, beaten and slaughtered before you?
What may I know of that flood
which flowed down your most holy face,
when you looked upon your son,
your Lord and your God,
stretched guiltless on the cross,
and the flesh of your flesh torn by wicked men?[8]

A more affective piety or devotion swept across western Europe, reflected in art, music, prayers, poetry, plays and other writings, with spiritual attention on the Servant Song's 'man of suffering ... acquainted with infirmity' (Isa. 53.3) and on his mother. Mary's grief at the suffering of her son became not just the example of how to respond to the passion of the Son of God but a point of connection or access to the suffering of Christ itself, and to the suffering of humanity which he carried. Mary's lament in the twelfth-century collection of spiritual folk songs, the Carmina Burana, captures the intensity of emotion and devotion that surrounded the recollection of Mary's experience at the cross:

> Alas, alas, the grief is mine today and forever,
> alas, how now I look upon
> the dearest child that ever
> in this world any woman brought forth.
> Alas, my lovely child's body!
> I will look upon it forever.
> Have pity, women and men.
> Let your eyes look there.[9]

The East developed this sort of attention to Mary's experiences at the cross of Christ centuries before it became common in the West, with the turn towards a more affective piety evident in Maximus the Confessor's seventh-century *Life of the Virgin*, the first complete biography of Mary, passed on to us today in the form of an Old Georgian translation. Maximus knew that Mary's emotional, mental and spiritual agony was beyond description but he also knew that he could not 'remain silent' for – as he said – 'the arrows of the pains of her suffering have stricken me'.[10]

While the West sings the Stabat Mater in Holy Week, Mary's vigil at the cross is embedded in the daily prayer of the East in short hymns chanted every Wednesday and Friday known as *Stavrotheotokia* that celebrate the victory of the cross and acknowledge the cost to the mother of the Saviour.

Beholding Thee, the Lamb and Shepherd,
the Saviour of the world, upon the Cross,
she that gaveth birth to Thee said, weeping:
The world rejoiceth, having received deliverance;
but my womb doth burn, beholding Thy crucifixion,
which Thou dost endure on behalf of all, O my Son
    and God![11]

All of these writers and sources would have seen Mary's
presence at the cross as the fulfilment of the soul-piercing
sword prophesied by Simeon in the temple years before with
their implication that Mary's travails have some part in the
purposes of God (Luke 2.33–35). Hence, they raise the particular question of the relationship between her suffering and
her son's, as well as the more general question of the relationship between the suffering of the Church through the ages
and of Christ on the cross. There are undoubtedly dangers in
dwelling too closely on Mary's suffering, and these came to
the fore in the West during the fourteenth century. St Bridget,
for example, claimed that Christ had said to her in one of her
revelations, 'Therefore I can well affirm that my mother and
I saved man, as it were, with a single heart – I by suffering in
my heart and flesh, and she with the suffering and love of the
heart.'[12] Centuries earlier in the East, Maximus even mused
that Mary may have suffered more than Christ because 'he
suffered voluntarily and knew everything that would come
upon him … but you [Mary] suffered unimaginably, and you
were still ignorant of the mystery of the Passion'.[13] This sort of
spiritual and emotional empathy is one of the drivers that led
to calls in the Roman Catholic Church for Mary to be formally
declared co-redemptrix with her son in the work of salvation.
Many people, especially those who are not Roman Catholics,
myself included, will be relieved that Pope John XXIII resisted
pressure for such a definition at the Second Vatican Council
and that the Council decided to integrate its main teaching on
Mary within its document on the Church rather than issue new
and problematic Marian Dogmas; and they will be heartened

by Pope Francis' affirmation that '[Mary] never wanted for herself something that was of her son ... never introduced herself as co-redemptrix. No. Disciple.'[14]

Maximus, in fact, would have been glad to align himself with Francis' words because his aim in giving attention to Mary's sufferings was to give greater attention to the saving suffering of her son. 'How could you bear to behold such a dreadful sight, unless the grace and power of your son and Lord strengthened you and confirmed the glory for you in his mercy,' he asks Mary.[15] Mary's suffering has the intensity of a mother witnessing her child's cruel and unjust death, and it belongs uniquely to her. Like mothers before and after her, Maximus imagines her crying out,

> O my son, would that I were tormented instead of you!
> O would that your wounds were upon me!
> O that I might take death upon me instead of you!
> But now it is more bitter to me than death
> that I cannot substitute myself for you.[16]

Mary cannot substitute herself for her son; but suffer she does. When she carried Jesus within her, Mary sang, 'my spirit rejoices in God my Saviour'. Now she sees her son carry the sins of the world and bearing its suffering as the 'Son of the Most High' (Luke 1.46, 32). The life that she gave to her son is now given by her son for the life of the world, so that everyone who, with Mary, 'believes in him may not perish but may have eternal life' (John 3.16). 'Only by God executing God's judgement on God can peace grow between God and the world, between human and human,' wrote Bonhoeffer.[17] Mary cannot take his place, for here 'in Christ God was reconciling the world to himself' (2 Cor. 5.19). The unique agony of Mary's sufferings at the cross is because the eternal Son of God who hangs on the cross for the salvation of the world is Jesus, her own child. Anselm captured something of the cosmic redemption gained solely by Christ's atoning work and the way in which his mother, among all the recipients of the salvation it wrought, was uniquely and intimately associated with it when he said, 'For there is no reconciliation except the reconciliation you conceived, O Chaste One. There is no salvation except the salvation you bore, O Virgin.'[18]

With Mary, other Christians and the Church as a whole become associated with Christ's sufferings as recipients of his redemption. We are baptized into Christ's death so that we can share in his resurrection. We have been 'crucified with Christ', so that 'the life [we] now live in the flesh [we] live by faith in the Son of God' (Gal. 2.19–20). We turn from our sins in 'the repentance that leads to life' (Acts 11.18) so that we can be at peace with God. By the Spirit we have put to death the sins of the body so that we may live (Rom. 8.13). In these ways the 'single heart' of which St Bridget speaks finds its proper place in Christ and in our dwelling and remaining in him.

Paul also talks about his own sufferings 'completing what is lacking in Christ's afflictions for the sake of his body, that is, the church' (Col. 1.24). A few verses earlier, though, he wrote majestically about God dwelling fully in Christ and decisively reconciling all things through him (Col. 1.15–20). So, there can be no question that his own ministry or the work of the whole Church supplements in some way the sufferings of Christ. That may be why he chose to speak here, uniquely in the New Testament, of Christ's 'afflictions'. Paul is acknowledging, though, that the Church is the body of Christ and that its commission to bring the life of Christ to the world will cause Christ's people to suffer. He also knew that because we are Christ's body, the suffering of the Church brings suffering to Christ – 'Saul, Saul, why do you persecute *me*?' (Acts 9.4). Perhaps we see something of that readiness to suffer with Christ, as well as the compassion of Christ for his followers who suffer for his sake, in the way that Mary in John's Gospel was not among those who were 'scattered, each one to his home' when Jesus' hour came, leaving him 'alone' (John 16.32). She was 'standing near the cross' of her son, perhaps hearing Jesus recite Psalm 22, praying that despite feeling the absence of God in his agony, Jesus would still find strength in

God's faithfulness to him 'since [the day] my mother bore me' (Ps. 22.10). As she made her home at the cross of Christ, so Jesus gave her to his beloved disciple to take to his home to form the community of solidarity in suffering and hope. We will return to these ideas about the character of the Church formed around the cross shortly, but first there are two other associations of Mary's suffering to explore.

The first we have already touched upon. Mary's suffering as a mother unites her with the suffering of mothers across the continents and centuries, especially those who suffer the effects of violence on their children. Anyone who has officiated at the funeral of a young person killed through the violence of others, whether the neglect of a road traffic accident, the feuding of gangs with knives and guns, or the strategies of war, will recall the harrowing sight and sound of a grieving mother, made even sharper if she had witnessed the death of a child. So, although I respect Ambrose's reticence when he said, 'I read that she was standing. I do not read she was weeping', and I agree that Pope Julius II was right in the early sixteenth century to resist calls for a Feast of the *Spasimo* to mark Mary swooning at the foot of the cross, I have a good deal of sympathy for those like the Armenian theologian Elishe, writing around the fifth century, who allowed themselves to imagine 'the crushed heart, choking soul, the grieving mind, and the emotions of Mary' as she watched the 'extreme torment' of her son's 'great sufferings'.[19]

It is important for Elishe that Mary stands at the cross with other women. This directly connects her – and, with her, each of us – not only to the visceral suffering of other women whose children are wrenched from them through violence but also with the 'maternal thinking' that Sara Ruddick argues is necessary to peace-building in our world. In a chapter on 'Mothers and Men's Wars', Ruddick quotes a number of women across the world who have protested against the wars and conflicts of the world, among them a group of women she describes as Patriotic East Germans who wrote to their Government in the GDR in this way:

We women do not regard military service for women as an expression of our equality, but as standing in contradiction to our existence as women. We regard our equality as consisting *not* in standing together with *those* men who take up arms, but in solidarity with *those* men who have like us recognized that the abstract term 'enemy' in practice means destroying human beings ... We feel that as women we have a particular mission to preserve life and to give our support to the old, the infirm and the weak.[20]

Decades later and some months into the war in Ukraine with its scenes of appalling suffering, Kaja Kallas, the Prime Minister of Estonia and mother of a child, said, 'When I see the pictures from Ukraine, I'm constantly thinking how sad it is that all the military equipment destroyed is not going to profit any economy or the well-being of any people ... Maybe it's sexist, but I'm going to say it: if you have given birth to human life, taking away the life of another mother's child is just so cruel.'[21]

Soon after Germany was reunited, Kathe Kollwitz's statue, *Mother with Dead Child*, was placed in the Neue Wache (New Guard) on Berlin's famous Unter den Linden street as the Federal Republic's 'Central Memorial to the Victims of War and Tyranny'. Originating from a 1903 etching, the image had a long history in Kollwitz's art bound up with the effect of war on ordinary German people, especially its poorest, and on her own experience of bereavement, notably the loss of her son Peter in World War One. It became for her a symbol of universal maternal grief in the face of violence. It belongs also to the longer history of the *Pietà* in European art – depictions of the *Mater Dolorosa* – the Mother of Sorrows – where Mary holds the body of her dead son.

Pope Benedict writes about the significance of the traditional *Pietà* scene, drawing on the emphasis of Bernard of Clairvaux in the eleventh century and Origen in the third, on the *compassion* of God, the suffering of God *with* (*mit-leiden* as Benedict puts it in German) the creation that God has loved into being.[22] Benedict roots Christian convictions about the suffering of God through compassion with the creatures God has made in the Hebrew notion of *rah'mim*. The literal meaning of *rah'mim* is womb and, with Hebrew preference for the concrete over the abstract, it is the bodily image of compassion – 'being with another', as Benedict calls it – just as 'heart' symbolizes feeling and 'loins' desire. Benedict describes the image of the *Pietà*, with 'the Mother grieving' (*leidend*), as the 'vivid translation' of *rah'mim*. 'In her,' he says, 'God's maternal affliction [*Leiden*] is open to view. In her we can behold it and touch it. She is the *compassio* of God, displayed in a human being who has let herself be drawn wholly into God's mystery.' That mystery, Benedict goes on to suggest, is that God transforms suffering through 'the redemptive being-with of love', healing its pain and restoring the life that humanity has lost through its sin.

Simeon's prophecy to Mary was fulfilled. Her son was, indeed, opposed all the way to death on a cross and there, as Bonhoeffer says, 'The world exhausts its rage on the body of Jesus Christ.'[23] The rejection of God's presence that lies at the root of sin was repeated in the rejection of Jesus. But God refused to be rejected. Through the cross Jesus redeemed the disobedience and opposition of humanity into the obedience of humanity and its acceptance of the judgement of God upon it. The weapons of human violence are turned by the God who took the form of humanity in the womb of Mary into the means of peace and the way to life. God remains with us in love, 'even [to] death on a cross' (Phil. 2.8), to defeat death by death so that every eye can not only see the salvation that has been 'prepared in the presence of all peoples' (Luke 2.31) but also, with Simeon, take hold of the gift of new life and give God praise.

We will move on to the life that comes through the death of Christ in the next section. Before doing so, though, there is more to say about John's scene of Mary 'standing near the cross' (John 19.25–27). Although John is clear that Mary is accompanied by other women, his narrative eye focuses on her and 'the disciple whom he loved standing beside her'. With

Jesus they form a triangle of attention familiar from art and iconography over the centuries. John tells us that when Jesus saw his mother and his beloved disciple standing near, 'he said to his mother, "Woman, here is your son." Then he said to the disciple, "Here is your mother."' It is a scene both tragic and tender, taut with tension as the dying Jesus takes what control he can of the situation to reconstitute the relationships of those who have proved to be closest to him, those who have not scattered, each one to their home (John 16.32). As at Cana, so now at the cross, Jesus addresses Mary as 'Woman'. His way of speaking to her is both respectful and intimate; 'Dear Woman' may be a better translation, and yet there is still a measure of formality to the exchange. Something more than the outworking of familial relationships seems to be at work.

John's Gospel gives us many lenses through which we may view the scene. One is Jesus' teaching on himself as 'the true vine, and [his] Father as the vine-grower' (John 15–16.4). Those who bear no fruit have been removed from the scene and only those who remain with Jesus, those who abide in him, can be seen. They are to love one another as Jesus has loved them and as Jesus has been loved by the Father. 'No one has greater love than this, to lay down one's life for one's friends,' said Jesus before his death and now proves by his death. 'You are my friends,' he told them, 'if you do what I command you.' Now he says to his mother, 'Behold thy son' – 'Here is your son'. Then to the disciple, 'Behold thy mother' – 'Here is your mother' (KJV). John's literary conventions make their full effect. Jesus does not say, 'Here is John, he will look after you from now on for I can no longer be with you and care for you.' He says, 'Here is *your* son' – here, in the disciple whom I love, is your son. This believer will be as I to you. I will come to you in this disciple whom I love. I do not name him because there are – and will be – many others whom I love, and who obey my commands. Behold them. My beloved is your beloved. My relationships are your relationships. He does not say to the disciple, 'Here is my mother for you to look after, for I cannot be with her and care for her.' He says, 'Here is *your* mother' –

here in my mother is your mother. My beloved is your beloved. My relationships are your relationships. Remember my words, 'I am giving you these commands so that you may love one another.' John concludes the scene at the cross by telling us that 'from that hour the disciple took her into his own home' (19.27). They abide together.

There are several layers to the relationships that John's Gospel unfolds here in this moment and at other points in Jesus' ministry. Because Jesus is life itself, his death will not mean his absence. Yes, death must do its work and there will be a time before his resurrection when the disciples and his mother no longer see him. They will mourn his parting, but Jesus promises that their pain will turn to joy as he comes to them again. 'When a woman is in labour, she has pain, because her hour has come. But when her child is born, she no longer remembers the anguish because of the joy of having brought a human being into the world,' Jesus had told his disciples (John 16.21). Mary knew the truth of his words more deeply than they. In giving his mother to his disciple and in giving his disciple to his mother, Jesus is not giving them away, he is giving himself to them through each of them. As they love one another they will abide in him. As they receive the gift he sends them, they will receive him and the one who sent him (John 13.20). They will be bound together with him in a community of friendship, constituted as a communion of love within the community of God who is love. They will abide together in one home, the home where the Son will come to them with the Father in the Spirit who abides with those who love him (John 14.17), to make their home with them (John 14.23). They will be one with Jesus 'where I am' (John 17.24), 'close to the Father's heart' (John 1.18), infinitely loved by God and 'completely one' (John 17.23) with each other.

Much has been written and said over the years on when Jesus formed the Church, and some have doubted whether he founded the Church at all.[24] The New Testament gives us many ways of answering the question. John seems to give us one here. The Church is formed at the foot of the cross. It is made

up of those whom Jesus loves and who keep his commandments, Jesus' disciples with Mary his mother. It is a community
of the relationships of Jesus, divine and human. It is a community of mutuality: a community of *solidarity in suffering*
where the grief of one is shared by the other and a community
of *solidarity in joy* where each rejoices in the joy of the other.
It is a community at peace with itself in the peace that Christ
gives, serving the God of peace. It is the community of the
cross that knows the reality of the persecution of the Church
and the pains of the world's suffering. It is a community that
knows the life-giving power of the water and the blood that
flow from the stricken side of Jesus, and that his wounds are
for the healing of the nations. It is a community that believes
his words, 'It is finished' (John 19.30) and receives his Spirit
that he sends in God's name. It is a community that testifies to
Christ and bears fruit. It is a people who pray in Jesus' name as
friends of Jesus who belong in one house together. It is, John
seems to be telling us, a church of love, a church of 'the disciple
whom Jesus loved' and the 'mother of Jesus'.[25] That is why
Origen, who wrote one of the earliest commentaries on John's
Gospel, told his readers, 'Nobody can really understand this
gospel until they too have reclined on the heart of Jesus and
received Mary as mother as the beloved disciple did.'[26]

'Including Mary, the mother of Jesus': Rising to new life

The resurrection of Jesus Christ is a new creative act of God.
It is, in the words of the New Testament scholar and bishop,
N. T. Wright, 'creation not merely out of nothing but out of
anti-creation, out of death itself'.[27] The resurrection is the
fulfilment of the ancient promise of life to Abraham. It marks
the beginning of the new history of humanity and the age fore-
told by the prophets. The new heavens and the new earth are
coming into being. The God of life raises Jesus to life by the
Spirit of life, the Spirit promised for the end of time as we know

it and the start of a new time when God's Spirit of life would be poured out on all flesh. The God of peace is establishing 'the kingdom ... [of] righteousness and peace and joy' (Rom. 14.17). The Book of Acts describes the fulfilment of prophecy of the coming of the Spirit on the Feast of Pentecost – the Day of the First Fruits – in suitably dramatic terms (Acts 2.1–42). Sounds like a rushing wind are heard. Tongues like fire are seen descending. Jewish pilgrims from across the Roman Empire are amazed and perplexed to hear their local languages. 'What does this mean?' they say to each other. Peter, filled with the life of God's life, tells them: the Spirit has come, God has raised Jesus of Nazareth from the dead, we are witnesses 'that God has made him both Lord and Messiah'. 'What should we do?' they respond. 'Repent,' says Peter, 'be baptized ... in the name of Jesus Christ so that your sins may be forgiven; and you will receive the gift of the Holy Spirit.'

'Put on the Lord Jesus Christ,' wrote Paul some time later (Rom. 13.14). Take on the life of Jesus Christ risen from the dead and live from the reality of that new life in which death and the forces that lead to death are overcome. Turn to Christ's life: be transformed by a renewal of your whole mindset. Be baptized: be immersed into Christ, go down into this death, rise into his life. Be justified by faith: believe that Christ has done this for you so that you can live in him and with him, and he can live through you, and be at peace with God (Rom. 5.1). Be filled with the Spirit: taste the first fruits of the coming age. Christian existence for Paul is the gift of being 'brought from death to life' (Rom. 6.13). Commenting on Paul's invitation to the Christians in Rome to 'walk in newness of life' (Rom. 6.4), John Barclay writes,

Paul imagines not just an imitation of Christ, but a form of participation, such that believers' new life is no ordinary existence, but the product of an impossibility, the resurrection of Christ.[28]

Barclay notes how for Paul, and in Jewish thought, resurrection necessarily concerns bodies and, therefore, that the fullness of this new life lies in one very real sense in the future when our bodies – like Jesus' body – are themselves reconstituted. Nevertheless, because 'the Spirit of the One who raised Jesus from the dead' is given to us, we can be assured that our 'new and humanly impossible mode of existence' is already present and active in our mortal bodies. Jesus Christ, risen from the dead, truly lives within us.[29] Paul is able to speak in personal terms about each individual: every believer is a recipient of the Spirit, Christ lives in each person baptized into his life. At the same time, he always sets the believer in the context of the community: Christ lives in the community, the body of which he is the head. The new life of Christ which we bear as the first fruit of the fullness that is to come, is lived out in our 'mortal bodies' (Rom. 6.12, 8.11) and through the actions and interactions of our bodily existence. It is, therefore, inherently social. 'The highest goal of existence "in Christ",' writes Barclay, now commenting on Paul's letter to the Galatians, 'is not self-knowledge or self-mastery for the sake of individual perfection, but a pattern of pro-social behaviour issuing in love, joy, peace, patience, kindness, goodness, faithfulness, gentleness, and self-control.'[30] 'Social practice is, for Paul,' Barclay contends, 'the necessary expression of the Christ-gift.'[31] This is most certainly the pattern that we see in the Book of Acts. The Spirit came. The word was preached. Baptism was given and received. The common meal is shared with joy. A small community of 120 believers in the resurrected Christ grew into a community of 3,000. 'All who believed were together and had all things in common' (Acts 2.44).

We have no record of whether Mary was among those who personally witnessed the risen Christ but we are told that after the disciples returned to Jerusalem to be 'clothed with power from on high' (Luke 24.49), they were 'together with certain women' in the upper room, 'including Mary the mother of Jesus, as well as his brothers' (Acts 1.14). Others at some point joined them as well, and we are given every indication that it was this group of 120 people – Mary among them – who 'were all together in one place' and all 'filled with the Holy Spirit' (Acts 2.1–4). Luke has already told us about Mary's earlier experience of the Spirit: 'The Holy Spirit will come upon you, and the power of the Most High will overshadow you; therefore the child to be born will be holy; he will be called Son of God' (Luke 1.35). John's Gospel works with different timelines from Luke's as well as from the Gospels of Matthew and Mark. For Luke, as he continues the story of Jesus in the story of his people, the birth of the Church takes place on the Feast of Pentecost, when all the believers, including 'Mary the mother of Jesus', were filled with the Holy Spirit, God's power from on high. We hear no more of Mary as the story of the Church continues. In one sense, though, for Luke, Mary's work is done. She has given birth through the Spirit to the Son of God and played her part in preparing him for his ministry. She has seen her son give birth through the Spirit to the Church, and she has taken her distinctive place within it, not as an apostle but named among them as one of the first and founding members of the community of Jesus Christ.

Although we do not hear of Mary witnessing publicly to the resurrection of Christ after the Day of Pentecost, John's account of Jesus and his beloved disciple around the cross leaves us with intriguing questions about whether Mary's unique testimony to Christ helped shape distinctive theological and spiritual traditions that developed in the Johannine community that gave rise to the Gospel of John. The theological character of the Johannine writings, with their reflective style, ruminating on the life of Christ to distil their deepest meaning, is very much in the pattern of Mary, who pondered the angel's words and treasured memories of Jesus' life in her heart (Luke 1.29; 2.51). Those questions suggest another set of questions of how Luke and Matthew came to draw on Mary's testimony of Jesus' birth and childhood while John showed no interest in them. Unfortunately, they will have to remain questions. There is simply not the evidence to answer them. What is clear is that Mary's experience of Jesus' conception, birth and childhood, and the angle from which, as his mother, she would have viewed his ministry, death and gift of the Spirit, would have given her a unique perspective on the work Jesus did among the generation who knew her, just as it does, through that first generation, to people of whom she sang from 'generation to generation' (Luke 1.50). She would have been able to speak not only about the life of Jesus and the life that, overshadowed by the Holy Spirit, she gave to him, but also of the life that she saw in him and that he shared with her as son and Saviour, child and Messiah. The remarkable events in the early life of the Church we read about in the early chapters of Acts would not have been entirely new to Mary. The outpouring of the Spirit without measure, the transformation of fearful disciples into fearless preachers, the appearance of angels and other wonders, the newfound praise of God, the opposition and danger mirror the events around Jesus' birth in the beginning of Luke's and Matthew's Gospels. Perhaps Mary was able to interpret the work of God's Spirit to them in the life of the nascent Church in the light of God's work three decades prior.

Among the many lines of convergence between the early life of Jesus and the early life of the Church is the accessibility of the Jewish-born Messiah to the Gentiles. Luke recounts a quintessentially Jewish scene. Mary and Joseph are devoutly fulfilling their religious obligations. They come to the centre of their life, culture and religion, and in the temple they meet a priest. Events, as we have seen, then take several surprising turns, none more so than Simeon declaring that he saw in their child God's salvation for *all peoples* – the 'light for revelation to the Gentiles' as well as the 'glory to [God's] people Israel' (Luke 2.32). Perhaps that is why Luke tells us that Mary and Joseph, despite everything else they had seen and heard over the last months, 'were amazed' (Luke 2.33) at Simeon's words. Matthew places Gentiles at the heart of his birth and childhood narratives. Magi from the east see a new light in the sky and make their journey to Jerusalem so that they can pay homage to 'the child who has been born king of the Jews', kneel before him, open 'their treasure-chests' before him and offer their gifts to him (Matt. 2.2, 11) – gifts representing the universality of human life: the gold of commerce and industry, the frankincense of religion and aesthetics, the myrrh of medicine and mourning. Soon after the departure of the mysterious visitors from distant lands, Jesus departs to another Gentile land and remains among them until it is safe to return.

We do not know how long Mary lived. By the time of Jesus' death she was already approaching the life expectancy of a first-century Palestinian woman from a poorer background. It is likely, though, that she would have still been alive as the Church took its decisive and momentous step not only to welcome Gentiles into its life but deliberately to expand its mission to reach the Gentile world. If she had heard the once-fanatical Pharisee of Tarsus tell of how he had been sent by the risen Christ 'to bring [his] name before Gentiles and kings' as well as before 'the people of Israel' (Acts 9.15), surely she would have agreed with his preaching that Jesus 'came and proclaimed peace to you who were far off and peace to those who were near' (Eph. 2.17). And if she had picked up word from Peter about his journey to visit a Gentile household following visions – Gentile and Jewish – from God, and how, when he spoke to them about the peace that Jesus preached and named him 'Lord of all' (Acts 10.36), the Holy Spirit fell upon them, she would have rejoiced with Peter that 'God has given even to the Gentiles the repentance that leads to life' (Acts 11.18). Here the Church was being born into the Gentile world and Peter was right to conclude that there was nothing to stop them being baptized into the life of her son. The sign of the Magi and the prophecy of Simeon were coming to pass. Now she could sing her song in the Spirit with all the strength of the resurrection. God's promise to Abraham, and through Abraham to her, was being fulfilled:

By your offspring shall all the nations of earth gain blessing for themselves, because you have obeyed my voice.
(Gen. 22.18)

Life for peace – Case study 3: Nuclear weapons

'If you, even you, had only recognized on this day the things that make for peace! But now they are hidden from your eyes' (Luke 19.42), said Jesus as he wept over the city where a few days later he would be violently put to death. On the way to that execution later in the week there was more weeping, this time from some women. 'Daughters of Jerusalem, do not weep for me, but weep for yourselves and for your children' (Luke 23.28). There was a mother in Jerusalem who surely wept for her child. In Chapter 3, we suggested that Jesus' beatitudes – the attitudes of the kingdom of God – may have been in some way inspired by that woman, his mother, through her own example and through her reflection – her 'pondering' – on the character of the kingdom that her son would bring, a kingdom that would have no end. We have seen how Mary, full of God's Spirit, sang of that kingdom: conceiving in her own spirit the ways of life-giving human community that the child conceived in her body would bring to the world. It was to be the kingdom prophesied of old, a world in which the conditions for the flourishing of all, especially the weak and the hungry, are reset and the forces of anti-life are overcome by the rule of God's life-giving mercy. It was to be a kingdom where the nations of the earth would learn the ways of God and where justice for all would lead to peace for all. In tune with her song, Jesus proclaimed, 'Blessed are the peacemakers' (Matt. 5.9). It was a kingdom that appeared impossible. But it is the kingdom of God, with whom, as Mary had come to know within her body, the body of her cousin and, later, the body of her risen son, nothing is impossible (Luke 1.37).

Nuclear weaponry is a force of anti-life that has cast its shadow over the world since the 1940s. The destructive capacity of nuclear weapons is barely imaginable. A 2021 study of their impact on the life of the world projected the following potential scenarios.

50 15-Kiliton airbursts targeted at urban zones in different countries would produce up to 17.6 million immediate deaths from blast and fires in the case of airbursts, up to 9.3 million similar deaths with groundbursts, and up to 2.6 million short term radiation deaths in the case of groundbursts. The highest number of deaths among the 13 countries evaluated occurred in China, followed by India. The total casualties for China in the case of 50 15-kt airbursts was estimated at 32.2 million; 20.6 million in the case of groundbursts.[32]

According to this study the 'weapons involved would constitute less than 0.04% of the total explosive yield and less than 0.3% of the number of weapons in the global nuclear arsenal'. The intense heat, radiation and radioactive fallout of such death-dealing intensity would cause lasting effects on a transnational scale: long-term harm to human health and well-being, large-scale displacement of populations, extensive damage to the environment, leading to food shortages and risk of global famine, enduring injury to infrastructure, socio-economic development and social order. No state or international body is equipped to deal with the long-term consequences of this scale of humanitarian disaster.

It is not just the use of nuclear weapons that poses a threat to humanity. Their production and testing come at a cost. Describing his experience of the 2014 Vienna Conference on the Humanitarian Impact of Nuclear Weapons, Tyler Wigg-Stevenson recounts that the 'most compelling moment' was of three testimonies on the lasting effects of testing nuclear weapons on the Marshall Islands in the Pacific, Australian Aboriginal communities and Utah 'downwinders' in the US.

… the greatest suffering from nuclear testing was borne by women and children, particularly around childbearing. Anjain-Maddison told of her cousin, who had never seen snow, playing with friends in the fallout ashes from a nuclear test, 300 miles distant, which no-one had warned them about. This caused acute radiation sickness. Marshallese women immediately began to suffer pregnancy complications, including 'jellyfish and monster-like babies'.[33]

Hopeful international efforts in the late 1960s led to the Non-Proliferation Treaty (NPT) signed by those states that had by then tested nuclear weapons – US, UK, France, Russia and China. It sought, on the one hand, to create a measure of stability between the Cold War superpowers by containing their nuclear weapon ambitions and, on the other, to prevent other states acquiring nuclear weaponry. States party to the Treaty committed themselves to the mutual reduction of their nuclear arsenal and to the eventual eradication of all nuclear weapons. Serious strides have been made in the reduction of arms, and the global number of nuclear armaments is lower now than it was then. But, with existing arms control frameworks faltering and geopolitical instability increasing, the US and Russia are beginning a renewed arms race, upgrading their nuclear weaponry together with non-nuclear offensive and defensive capability, 'limited' nuclear capability and other technological advancements. The UK Government is committed to renewing the UK's nuclear capacity and judges that, in order to maintain 'a minimal, credible, independent nuclear deterrent', its arsenal must increase. Although the UK Government's 2021 Integrated Review of Security, Defence, Development and Foreign Policy maintained pledges to use nuclear weapons only in defence of the UK and its NATO allies, it also stated that it will remain 'deliberately ambiguous about precisely when, how and at what scale we would contemplate the use of nuclear weapons'.[34]

The world has changed since the relative stability of the Cold War era. The nuclear deterrent had a simple logic on its side when two forces which stood against each other were held in balance by the mutual threat of destruction. There was a Christian realism of the twentieth century which, however reluctantly, accepted that maintaining a capacity for nuclear attack was necessary to hold the peace until each power moved in close step to disarm. I held that view myself.

But the inherently more complex geopolitical realities of the twenty-first century and the failure of the NPT to deliver on its promises, together with the experience of living with the effects of World War Two bombing of Coventry, Dresden and other British and German cities, combined with ongoing reflection on the application of the deep truths of Christian faith for every dimension of life, including international politics, have changed my mind.

Vertical proliferation of weapons (increasing the quantity of nuclear weapons held by possessor states) has returned, made all the more threatening to the life of the earth by the failure of the NPT to prevent some horizontal proliferations (more states acquiring them). North Korea, India, Pakistan and Israel have joined the company of nations possessing nuclear weapons, but have not signed the Treaty that was designed to bind together possessor states in a common journey towards disarmament. Further proliferation is likely to follow, with Iran and Saudi Arabia not far from the technical potential for nuclear weapons, and other states such as Egypt and Turkey which have been suspected of harbouring ambitions to join this powerful club of nations. They will have been further motivated by the war in Ukraine, determined to insure themselves against an invasion from a stronger power; and other states will join them as they reconsider their defence strategies. The greater the proliferation of states with nuclear weapons, the greater the risk of non-state actors finding it easier to obtain them, and the threat of terrorism to the peace of the world increasing exponentially. The more nuclear proliferation, the more chance of accidents taking place with disastrous consequences. Even the risk of states developing nuclear attack capability is politically destabilizing as we know from Israel's response to Iran's nuclear potential and, again, in Ukraine where Russian fear of Ukraine restoring its nuclear weapons played some part in feeding President Putin's narrative. The risks, dangers and threats look as if they are spinning out of control.

Nuclear weapons do not simply represent a threat to the

security of nation states. They present a catastrophic peril to every human being on earth, other life forms on which we are dependent and the fabric of the natural order of which we are part. These weapons of destructive immensity are a force of *anti-creation* that stand in proud contradiction to God's work in bringing all life into being and restoring the conditions for that life to be lived in abundance. We are better in the twenty-first century at recognizing the global nature of certain threats. The Covid-19 pandemic and the ecological crisis have instilled into us a stronger sense of our connectivity as human beings and of our embeddedness in the natural order of all life. That gives rise to a different perspective on nuclear weapons from the one that has dominated the defence policies of nuclear weapon possessor states, and those other countries that have chosen to live under their supposed protection. Rather than beginning and ending with rationales based on national security and protection of a country's citizens, there is a growing movement to think primarily in humanitarian terms that begin and end with the preservation of life. Security analysis has a propensity to abstraction which insulates its discourse from the full effects not only of the use of nuclear weapons but of their possession, testing and threat-making on human life and community. It risks, as the philosopher Luce Irigaray puts it, 'forgetting life' in its attempt to promote defence based on mass death and universal damage.[35] Its justification is that nuclear strategy works as a political power tool – it preserves peace. A humanitarian perspective, on the other hand, attends closely to the concrete, lived realities of all people and assesses that the protection of life of a country's citizens purportedly offered by nuclear weapons comes at too great a cost to the preservation of life of all the peoples and of the well-being of the planet itself. It challenges the rationale of nuclear strategists by questioning whether it does, indeed, deliver on its aims of safeguarding the security of their own people, quite apart from the security of all peoples. It responds to a shift in the angle of geopolitical vision which recognizes that we are no longer only vulnerable to a threatening 'other' who is our 'enemy' but that we are vulnerable to the intolerable threat that hangs over us all from multiple, increasingly unpredictable actors.

This growing humanitarian perspective on the menace of nuclear weapons led to the ratification of a new United Nations Treaty on the Prohibition of Nuclear Weapons (TPNW) in 2021. Eighty-six states have signed it. They are the nuclear 'have nots' who have grown tired of the unkept disarmament promises of the five nuclear 'haves' of the NPT and the refusal of the other four 'haves' even to sign up to it. Among them are some of the poorest nations on earth – the 'lowly' of whom Mary sang, raised up to confound the powerful, many without the resources to develop nuclear weaponry or the status to live under the shadow of its supposed protection. The UK abstained from the treaty's development, denounced its entry into force and, so far, has refused to engage with its underlying concerns or harness its energy in the shared pursuit of peace and the eradication of nuclear weapons, not even sending an observer to the 2022 Review Conference in Vienna.

As Bearer of Life, Mary received the gift of the life of the 'Son of the Most High' (Luke 1.32). She gave birth to the life of her child who was the life of the world. She nurtured this new life, determined to preserve the gift that she had been given for the world, to protect her child from the dangers the world posed and to promote the life that he would bring to all the peoples of the world. She lived by the sort of 'maternal thinking' described by Sara Ruddick that takes on the responsibility of 'preservative love, nurturance and training' demanded by the life of another human being to which one is bound.[36] It is a way of living that works for 'the things that make for peace' (Luke 19.42) because conflict and war threaten life with its antithesis – death. It is a way of thinking and acting grounded in the realization of the vulnerability of life that is demonstrated in the singular and lonely helplessness of a new life that cries out for care.

This way of thinking, acting and living questions the rationality of the security argumentation of nuclear deterrence and the methods by which it seeks to protect its citizens from the vulnerabilities of determined nuclear disarmament. The thought of disarming when others remain armed or when others, especially the most unreliable others, may retain the potential to arm or rearm nuclear weapons triggers deep fears – dark dreads that have been reactivated by events in Ukraine – among those who have sought to make themselves invincible by the possession of nuclear weapons and the threat of their use. But invincibility is an illusion. Life is always vulnerable. It has been made more vulnerable by the production, possession and proliferation of nuclear weapons. They force upon us the existential fear of elimination of vast swathes of human life, catastrophic suffering for those who survive and permanent damage to the fabric of the natural order.

Mary was no stranger to vulnerability. She faced her own vulnerability at the annunciation, the vulnerability of her child at his birth, the vulnerability of God's kingdom in the trials of her son's ministry, the vulnerability of his own life as the cross on which he would die loomed larger over them both. She encountered in her body, soul and spirit God's own embrace of vulnerability: God's redefinition of power in weakness in the incarnation, God's glory displayed in the suffering of the cross, 'the powers of the age to come' (Heb. 6.5) when 'the wolf and the lamb shall feed together' (Isa. 65.25) in God's resurrection of her son from the dead, and the 'first fruits' (Rom. 8.23) of the new creation in the gift of the 'Spirit of life' (Rom. 8.2) to God's people. Vulnerability is not safely met by violence. Indeed, 'Violence begins with a denial of vulnerability,' says Marisa Egerstrom. 'It is in the avoidance of our vulnerability that we become capable of evil and violence; the effort to defend our weakness from perception and exploitation is already on the way to enacting violence upon another.'[37] Vulnerability is better protected and life more securely preserved by building relationships that secure peace, by determined efforts of reconciliation and by policies that work at ways of promoting the interests of others as well as ourselves.

What does the global nuclear threat demand of the UK, one of the early acquirers of nuclear weapons? The UK has aimed to be an example to other nuclear weapon states. It played a leading part in the negotiation of the NPT including its disarmament commitments. It has sought to reduce its nuclear arsenal to a minimum needed to maintain its posture of deterrence. Now is the time (this time when threats and counter-threats have been made to use nuclear weaponry) to take a bold and decisive step in the same direction. A time to become a courageous and convincing example to every state of a people who refuse to live with the deceits and bluffs on which nuclear deterrence is based; a people who choose to give up the false security of invincible vulnerability; a people who decide to dedicate their resources to building the long-range weapons of peace-building through the patient growing of strong international relationships and by humanitarian interventions; a people who determine that, rather than adding to the threat of environmental disaster, they will lead the world in the healing of the planet.

Notes

1 St Ephrem, *Nativity* 11.2, quoted in Sebastian P. Brock, *The Luminous Eye: The Spiritual World Vision of Saint Ephrem the Syrian*, rev. edn (Collegeville, MN: Liturgical Press, 1992), p. 127.

2 See The Nicene-Constantinople Creed.

3 Second Vatican Council, 'Lumen Gentium: Dogmatic Constitution on the Church', chapter VIII, para. 58 in *The Documents of Vatican II*, ed. Walter M. Abbott (New York: Herder and Herder, 1966), p. 89.

4 Cecil Day Lewis, 'Walking Away' in *The Gate and Other Poems* (London: Jonathan Cape, 1962), p. 21.

5 See multiple references to the 'hour' in John's Gospel, among them 2.4, 4.21, 5.25, 7.30, 12.23, 12.27, 13.1, 16.32, 17.1.

6 Tina Beattie, *Rediscovering Mary: Insights from the Gospels* (Liguori, MO: Triumph Books, 1995), pp. 97–104.

7 For a contemporary translation, see St Anselm, 'Cur Deus Homo (Why God became Man)', in *Anselm of Canterbury: The Major Works*, ed. Brian Davies (Oxford: Oxford University Press, 1998), pp. 260–356.

8 *Oratio II: Oratio ad Christum* in Franz von Sales Schmitt, *S. Anselmi Cantuariensis Archiepiscopi Opera Omnia* (Stuttgart: Frommann, 1968), VIII, p. 8, translation by Christine Walker.

9 Miri Rubin, *Mother of God: A History of the Virgin Mary* (London: Penguin, 2010), p. 246.

10 Stephen J. Shoemaker, 'Mary at the Cross, East and West: Maternal Compassion and Affective Piety in the Earliest "Life of the Virgin" and the High Middle Ages', *The Journal of Theological Studies* 62 (2011), p. 580. Shoemaker argues, convincingly to my mind, for eastern interest in Mary's sufferings influencing western piety through the presence of Greek monastic communities in Italy and in Rome in particular.

11 For an example of this chant embedded in a liturgy, see Ode III in this 'Commemoration of Martyrs', https://tinyurl.com/2p9a4c56, accessed 16.1.2023.

12 Robert Fastiggi, 'Mary in the Work of Redemption' in *The Oxford Handbook of Mary*, ed. Chris Maunder (Oxford: Oxford University Press, 2019), p. 308.

13 Maximus the Confessor, *Life of the Virgin*, p. 78, quoted in Shoemaker, 'Mary at the Cross', p. 580.

14 Pope Francis, 'Feast of our Lady of Guadalupe: Homily of His Holiness Pope Francis, Vatican Basilica, Thursday, 12th December 2019', available at https://tinyurl.com/mwnzh65h, accessed 16.1.2023. Benedict XVI, when writing as Joseph Ratzinger, also expressed clear reservations over defining Mary as co-redemptrix. See Joseph Cardinal Ratzinger, *God and the World: Believing and Living in Our Time*, trans. Henry Taylor (San Francisco, CA: Ignatius Press, 2002), p. 306.

15 Maximus, *Life of the Virgin*, pp. 67–8, quoted in Shoemaker, 'Mary at the Cross', p. 580.

16 Maximus, *Life of the Virgin*, pp. 69–70, quoted in Shoemaker, 'Mary at the Cross', p. 581.

17 Dietrich Bonhoeffer, *Ethics*, vol. 6 of Dietrich Bonhoeffer Works, ed. Clifford J. Green (Minneapolis, MN: Fortress Press, 2009), p. 88.

18 I use the concept of 'association' here, recognizing that it was used in a short document of the Second Vatican Council in which Mary was separately treated (compared with *Lumen Gentium*, the main statement about Mary, where she is considered within the doctrine of the Church). *Acta Synodalia Sacrosancti Concilii Oecumenici Vaticani*. See Fastiggi, 'Mary in the Work of Redemption', pp. 312, 306.

19 See Shoemaker, 'Mary at the Cross', p. 587.

20 Sara Ruddick, *Maternal Thinking: Towards a Politics of Peace* (London: The Women's Press, 1990), p. 147.

21 As reported by George Grylls in *The Times*, Saturday 16 April 2022, p. 13.

22 Joseph Cardinal Ratzinger, '"Hail, Full of Grace": Elements of Marian Piety', Hans Urs von Balthasar and Joseph Cardinal Ratzinger, *Mary: The Church at the Source*, trans. Adrian Walker (San Francisco, CA: Ignatius Press, 2005), pp. 75–9.

23 Bonhoeffer, *Ethics*, p. 83.

24 For a thorough contemporary study of the issues, see Paul Avis, *Jesus and the Church: The Foundation of the Church in the New Testament and Modern Theology* (London: T&T Clark, 2020).

25 See John D. Dadosky, 'The Official Church and the Church of Love in Balthasar's Reading of John: An Exploration in Post-Vatican II Ecclesiology', *Studia Canonica* 41 (2007), pp. 468–71.

26 Alan England Brooke, *The Commentary of Origen on St John's Gospel: The Text Revised with a Critical Introduction and Indices* (Cambridge: Cambridge University Press, 1896), p. 6 (wording updated).

27 John M. G. Barclay, *Paul and the Gift* (Grand Rapids, MI: Eerdmans, 2015), p. 496.

28 Barclay, *Paul and the Gift*, p. 500.

29 Barclay, *Paul and the Gift*, p. 501.

30 Barclay, *Paul and the Gift*, p. 430.

31 Barclay, *Paul and the Gift*, p. 425.

32 See Ray Acheson, 'Unspeakable suffering – the humanitarian impact of nuclear weapons', https://tinyurl.com/4fxebdb2, accessed 16.1.2023, p. 23.

33 Tyler Wigg-Stevenson, 'The Humanitarian Impact of Nuclear Weapons: A Problem for State Authority', *Christian Scholars' Review* 44 (2015), p. 370.

34 HM Government, 'Global Britain in a Competitive Age: The Integrated Review of Security, Defence, Development and Foreign Policy' (2021), p. 77, https://tinyurl.com/mv4ru2pv, accessed 16.1.2023.

35 Luce Irigaray, quoted in Tina Beattie, *God's Mother, Eve's Advocate: A Marian Narrative of Women's Salvation* (London: Continuum, 2002), p. 90.

36 Ruddick, *Maternal Thinking*, p. 17.

37 Marisa Egerstrom, 'The Advent of Occupy Wall Street' in *The Open Body: Essays in Anglican Ecclesiology*, ed. Zachary Guiliano and Charles M. Stang (Oxford: Peter Lang, 2012), p. 203.

5

Fulfilled

The King of Kings who sits enthroned in you,
Whom the heavens cannot contain, the
Word beyond measure,
Distributes his salutary, life-giving body
And sacred, immortalizing and incorruptible blood.
The heavenly hosts encircle you,
Those who cover their faces with awe mixed with fear;
They sing melodious praises
To the One who made all things by his Word,
Christ the Saviour who crowned you,
To whom befits honour and glory always.
('Ode for the Church', Gregory of Narek)[1]

'Do whatever he tells you': Life in the community of life

Shortly before his ascension, Jesus told his disciples that they would be baptized with the Holy Spirit 'not many days from now'. After they witnessed him being 'taken up ... into heaven', Luke tells us that the remaining eleven apostles returned to Jerusalem as instructed by Jesus and spent these few days largely in an upper room of the house where they were staying. We are then told that as the apostles devoted themselves to prayer, they were joined by 'certain women, including Mary the mother of Jesus, as well as his brothers' (Acts 1.4–14). There are several significant features of that compressed historical record. The early Christian community consists of more than the apostles.

It includes women. Right from the start men and women are together, doing as Jesus said. They are praying, waiting for the gift of the Holy Spirit to empower them as his witnesses. The nascent community of followers includes members of the family of Jesus. The relationships he inherited through family identity are woven into the relationships he chose through messianic ministry, with both sets of people united in a common sense of calling to follow him. Mary, his mother, is uniquely named among them. Luke, like John, places Mary in the heart of the Church from its earliest days. This chapter will consider ways in which Mary is not only rooted in the historical origins of the Church but has an ongoing role in the continuing reality of the Church in terms both of how we understand the Church and how the Church acts as the people Jesus appoints as his 'witnesses in Jerusalem, in all Judea and Samaria, and to the ends of the earth' (Acts 1.8).

Dietrich Bonhoeffer described the Church as 'nothing but that piece of humanity where Christ has really taken form. It is solely the form of Christ that matters, not any form besides Christ's own.'[2] Bonhoeffer does not make connections here between the Church and Mary but his definition of the Church provides a helpful guide to the road we will travel in the pages that follow. Jesus' humanity quite literally took form in Mary. The creator of humanity took the form of a human being from the humanity of Mary. As we have seen, poets through the ages – John Donne among them – have mused on the mystery of Mary's pregnancy, 'Whose womb was a strange heaven, for there God clothed himself and grew.'[3] We have also seen how the forming of Jesus did not end with his birth but continued into his childhood under Mary's intimate influence. Christ took the form of a growing child who entered adulthood with an understanding of his unique place in the love and purposes of God. Like any relationship, it was by no means a one-way relationship. Mary was changed through the conception of Jesus. We have seen it in her song. She was shaped through her mothering of Jesus. We can see it in the way she held close all that she discovered about him and about God and the life of

God's world through him. She was stretched and challenged by his ministry. We can see that in the way she responded to Jesus at Cana's wedding, Nazareth's commotions and Jerusalem's Golgotha.

Mary's womb and home became the tabernacle in which the real and concentrated presence of God dwelt among the people of God. She knew, though, that her calling was not to contain the uncontainable but to provide the bodily and social environment in which the incarnate presence of God – the temple that is Christ's body (John 2.21) – would be made ready to reconcile the world to God and to form a people who are themselves 'a holy temple in the Lord ... a dwelling-place for God' (Eph. 2.21–22). It is this interplay between the mother in whom the son was formed, Jesus in whom the form of God took the form of a human person, and the Church that is called to take the form of Christ, that has led to Mary being seen as an archetype, image, or figure of the Church.[4] That sort of linkage is present in Protestant theology, albeit tentatively, but it is made more confidently in contemporary Catholic and Orthodox traditions, often drawing on ancient Christian patterns of thought. The connection between Mary and the Church runs deep in the Armenian Orthodox tradition and is made by Gregory of Narek in his typically poetic and profound way. Mary, for Gregory, is the 'precious pearl discovered ... holy Bearer of God ... Daughter of Light ... the foundation of faith laid without hands ... after which heavenly model you were anointed and sealed',[5] while the Church is the 'Treasure of profound goodness, desired, discovered, and concealed, absolute fullness that gathers everyone, never wanting', whose calling is to 'reunite those who have severed themselves from [God], through the mediation of the One who sits enthroned in [her]'.[6] Gregory would have agreed with Bonhoeffer that when we are defining the Church and discerning the Church's activity, 'It is solely the form of Christ that matters, not any form besides Christ's own.' At the same time, as he contemplated the heights of the Church's stature and the breadth of the Church's work, he found great inspiration in Mary – literally 'that piece of humanity where Christ has really taken form'. Drawing on that same line of thought, we will look at three marks of Mary's life that the Church too is called to embody: Mary as faithful believer, Mary as bearer of Christ, Mary as Spirit-empowered woman.

Mary is a believer who steps into the call of God, rising to the challenge of faith. She accepts God's word. She trusts that God is her saviour. She gives herself over to the call of God. Mary is an embodiment of the gospel virtues that Paul commends to the Corinthian Church: faith, hope and love. Her faith is in the grace of the 'Most High' given in Jesus Christ. Her hope is in the coming of God's kingdom in Jesus Christ that will have no end (Luke 1.32–33). Her love is for Jesus Christ and the community of faith that gathers around him, beginning with Elizabeth and her child and continuing to the beloved disciples and other followers of Christ who take Mary to their home and hearts. 'For the riddle that torments the world is this: Shall Sorrow and Love be reconciled at last, when the present Kingdom comes?' asks Balthasar, one of the Magi, in Dorothy Sayers' play, *The Man Born to be King*.[7] Mary answers that, 'Wisdom and Power and Sorrow *can* live together with love.' Believing in the wisdom of God makes foolish the wisdom of the world. Putting one's hope in the promise of God defeats the despair of the world. Holding on to the goodness of the world in faith and hope in the face of the suffering of the world addresses the torments of the world. The riddle of the world's existence and its suffering that troubled the Magi is answered with the gentle word of God's favour spoken to Mary and the heavenly sound of God's goodwill heard by the shepherds. The unlimited, unexpected, undeserved grace of God to humanity – God's favour – was made known to Mary at that moment, and it was confirmed to her as her son grew and loved and gave himself in love. She was the first to believe that, as Bonhoeffer was to put it two millennia later, God has overruled 'every reproach of untruth, doubt, and uncertainty raised against God's love by entering as a human being into human life, by taking on and bearing bodily the nature, essence, guilt, and suffering of human beings'.[8] Mary embodied the *evangelical virtues* of the Church of God.

Mary is the bearer of Jesus Christ. She carried Jesus within her, visiting Elizabeth's home: the earliest Christian evangelist. She took Jesus in her arms in the stable offering her thanks to God for him and she carried him to the temple making her sacrifice of praise: the first Christian worshipper. She carried him in her heart, treasuring all that God had promised through him, and suffered the cost of loving him: the first Christian disciple. She shaped a family for him and joined a community of followers that he gathered around him. She knew that the work of the Most High and coming of the kingdom that would have no end needed the material of her body, the consent of her spirit and the forming of a new community of faith, hope and love. She learned that the scope of God's grace, rooted in Israel's life, extended to the Gentiles, and she felt the power of the new creation coming into life within her. Mary embodied the *catholic virtues* of the Church of God.

Mary is the Spirit-empowered woman. 'Twice-Spirit graced', as Ann Loades describes her, Mary received the Spirit through whom God's Son was conceived in her, the power of life that overshadowed her.[9] Elizabeth had prophesied over her in the Spirit. Mary, inspired by the Spirit, sang her scriptural song magnifying the Lord, envisioning the new form of life that her son would bring. Again, she received the Spirit in Luke's account of the birth of the Church when 'they were all together in one place' and the Spirit came upon them in the upper room (Acts 2.1–2). Propelled into the streets of Jerusalem, the Spirit-filled believers – Mary among them – were endowed with unimaginable courage and energy, and the Church took form in proclamation and baptism, teaching and fellowship, breaking of bread and prayers, common life, praise and healing. The Syriac Rubulla Gospels, one of the earliest illustrated versions of gospels dating from the sixth century, placed Mary in the centre of the apostles, the Spirit descending upon her first, setting the pattern of later eastern iconography of Pentecost: Mary at the heart of the Spirit-empowered

Church. Mary embodies the *pentecostal virtues* of the Church of God.[10]

These marks of Mary can be seen reflected in the characteristics of the Church. We are a community of faith, hope and love, made up of believers in the grace of God whose hope is audacious and love is visible. A people that bear Christ, each believer giving birth by the Spirit to Christ in the depths of their soul, and every believer together as a body, giving birth to Christ in the world. We are a Spirit-empowered people, freed by the liberating strength of God to respond to God's call and to be sent into every part of our local communities and every corner of the world to lift up the lowly. What Gregory of Narek says of Mary he says also of the Church, 'the personal chariot of the living will of the Giver of Life', and he exhorts us, as the angel did to Mary, to rejoice that we have found God's favour.

This high calling to serve the Giver of life works out in the life of the Church in a number of fundamental ways that relates to its reality and structure. The Church is the community of faith, hope and love. Our *faith* is in Christ who comes to bring fullness of life. Our *hope* is in God's purposes of life for all creation. Our *love* is given by the Spirit of life drawing us into the life of the new creation. In so being and doing, the Church is a community of the word, a community of the sacraments and a community of service to the world. Like Mary the Church is called by the word of God's grace: 'Do not be afraid, for you have found favour with God.' We are founded on the promise of God's word of grace: 'you will bear a son ... and he will be called the Son of the Most High.' We are animated by the Spirit who makes God's word of grace active in our midst: 'The Holy Spirit will come upon you, and the power of the Most High will overshadow you' (Luke 1.28–35). *Therefore* (Luke 1.30, 35), the angel goes on to say – the 'therefore' of the gospel! Because God's word is the word of grace, *therefore* you do not need to be overawed by the greatness of God. You do not need to be overwhelmed by the scale of the world's needs. You do not need to be overcome by your own smallness and helplessness. You simply need to take hold of the grace of God and let it take hold of you, 'For nothing will be impossible with God.' Like Mary the Church is the community that believes 'that there would be a fulfilment of what was spoken to her by the Lord' and says, 'Here am I, the servant of the Lord' (Luke 1.37, 45, 38).

Believing in the word of God's grace, the Church is the community that 'continue[s] in the grace of God' (Acts 13.43) through the sacraments of the gospel of grace. After entrusting his mother and beloved disciple to each other in John's Gospel, Jesus cried out, 'I am thirsty,' drank the wine given to him on a sponge and then, after declaring, 'It is finished,' 'gave up his spirit' (John 19.28–30). John goes on to describe how, as Jesus' body was pierced with a spear to check that he was indeed dead, blood and water flow from him. Artists of the Church East and West have imagined Mary still standing by Jesus with a vessel in her hands to collect these fluids that once sustained her son's life. After Peter preaches about God raising to life the one whom the world put to death by the lawlessness of the world, the crowds call out, 'what should we do?' and Peter replies, 'Repent, and be baptized every one of you' (Acts 2.37–38). At the beginning of the Church, at its very root, is the sign of life – water and birth. By taking on the mortality of human life and being obedient to death, even death on a cross under the judgement of God, God gives new life to human life. Mortality is not denied. It is faced head on. But it is overcome by the natality of the new birth of the resurrection. Christ is given life in the waters of Mary's womb. His followers are christened, conformed to his form, in the waters of baptism. Christ is born into the household of Mary and Joseph in the community of Nazareth. His followers are born into the household of faith in Jesus' community of the new creation.

'Those who welcomed the message were baptized' and 'devoted themselves to the apostles' teaching and fellowship, to the breaking of bread and the prayers' (Acts 2.42). The community of new life of the resurrection is sustained by apostolic teaching, the fellowship and the prayers that culminate in the breaking of bread. Mary spread a table for her son and her household with the bread that she had made, perhaps wine as well. Through long years she sustained him with the food he needed to keep him alive and strengthen him for his work. It was her work for him that began from his earliest moments of life and continued into his days of feeding from her breast. She gave of herself to him, sharing her body with his body. Like Mary, the Church makes bread for its Lord to share with his family and spreads a table for him to feast with his friends. It brings the staple food of human life to 'the Author of life' (Acts 3.15): bread for the Bread of life. Now though – with Mary – we find that the table we prepare becomes the banquet the Lord provides. The bread that we make becomes for us the bread that Christ gives – the bread of eternal life, the bread that Christ is. The cup that we fill becomes for us the cup of salvation – the new wine of the kingdom of God that Jesus longed to share with his disciples and that will have no end. We who gather as a body of people are grafted deeper into the body into which we have been baptized. Christ feeds us – his body – with his own body, his body given for our life, his blood shed that we may live. As the curtain of the sanctuary in Armenian churches is drawn open after the consecration of the elements, the priest stands before the people and announces: '*This is life.*' He invites them to commune with their Lord and be – if I may apply and adapt the words of an Anglican collect to an Armenian liturgy – transformed in the substance of their flesh by the one who came to us in substance of our flesh to raise us into life with him.[11]

Ephrem the Syrian knew that there is more than water, bread and wine in the Church's rites, just as there was more than water and natural nourishment in Mary's womb. There is the Holy Spirit, ever overshadowing with 'the power of the Most High' (Luke 1.35).

See, Fire and Spirit in the womb that bore You,
see Fire and Spirit in the river in which you were baptized.
Fire and Spirit in our Baptism,
in the Bread and the Cup, Fire and the Holy Spirit.[12]

Baptism and Eucharist, water, bread and wine – the ordinary
things of life, used according to Jesus' word of grace – are animated and activated by the fire of God's love, the Spirit who
is, in the words of the Nicene Creed, 'the Lord and Giver of
life'. The actions of the Church become, in Gregory of Narek's
image, the 'personal chariot' of the living Lord. The Church
is the *epicletic* community – the community that continually
invokes the Holy Spirit, conscious always that it depends
entirely on the same 'power of the Most High' that overshadowed Mary. The Church is the *agapeic* community – the
community that is bound in love together in its substance, its
being, its deep identity as the body of the Lord of love. Therefore, however hard it might try to divide itself, the Church is
one. It is one with Christ because its people have been baptized
into his life. It is one with Christ because it is fed by the one
Lord who communes with his people. It is one with Christ
because it drinks of the same Spirit. And being one with Christ,
united in his love, the Church is bound with God, united in
the love of the Son for the Father. The Church is the *chairistic*
community – the community of joy and gladness that rejoices
and sings praise. *Chaire!* announced the angel: Rejoice, Mary!
And she did: she sang. And as she sang, the prophecy came to
pass, 'Sing and rejoice, O daughter of Zion' (Zech. 2.10, KJV).
John leapt in the womb. Elizabeth was jubilant in her home.
The Magi 'rejoiced with exceeding great joy' (Matt. 2.10) in
Bethlehem.[13] Simeon and Anna praised in the temple. The
Church in its earliest days tasted the unbounded joy of the age
to come as bread was broken with 'glad and generous hearts'
(Acts 2.46). A thousand years later, Gregory had lost none
of the delight and wonder at the Church's stature in Christ
and calling in the Spirit: 'Be glad,' he exhorted the Church, 'O
Queen, glorious Bride, crowned, great wonder, rejoicing with
many children.'[14]

The God who *is* – God who is beyond all definition except
God's own self-definition of *I am* that itself cannot be truly
spoken in words – shared life with all creation as an act of
grace. When, in 'the fullness of time' (Gal. 4.4), God took on the

reality of human life in Jesus Christ, that divine life in human form was a life for others, a life lived and died so that we 'may not perish but may have eternal life' (John 3.16). God's life in Christ is life to be shared. When people are brought into the life of Christ though word and baptism, and sustained in life by teaching, fellowship, prayer and breaking of bread, it is *for* the work of God in the world: the coming of the kingdom of God and the fulfilment of God's purposes for the renewal of creation. God's act of grace is made known by the grace-filled life of the Church. Like Mary, we cannot contain the uncontainable or confine the unconfinable. In Mark's resurrection narrative, the women and men who discover the empty tomb are told by the angel that the risen Jesus 'is going ahead of you to Galilee' (Mark 16.7). Just as the disciples' eyes are opened in the breaking of the bread in Luke's Emmaus story, he disappears from their sight. It is when they return to Jerusalem that he appears to them again (Luke 24.31, 36). In John, Jesus says to Mary Magdalene, 'Do not hold on to me … But go to my brothers and say to them, "I am ascending to my Father and your Father, to my God and your God"' (John 20.17). In Matthew, the risen Christ sends the disciples into all nations to make disciples who live out their baptism in obedience to his word, promising them that 'I am with you always' (Matt. 28.20). Here we see the originating pattern of Christian existence. The presence of the risen Christ is received fully into the life of the Church, with each believer responsible for the fullest initiation of each member of the Church into the personal reality of Christ's risen life so that each person is brought fully to life by the life of Christ. The risen life of Christ received by individual people manifests itself in the life of the community of Christ's risen life. Those tasked with overseeing its ministry are given responsibility for ordering the life of the Church so that the social reality of Christ's risen life is embodied in its relationships and actions. The community of the risen life of Christ is compelled by the love of Christ 'to participate', as Bonhoeffer put it, 'in Christ's encounter with the world', sent by him to serve all peoples as his community of love for the world. The Church is the community of life that gives itself to God's purposes of life for the world. In the next section we will explore how the Church, like Mary, responds to its call and the Church truly says to God, 'Here am I, the servant of the Lord; let it be with me according your word' (Luke 1.38).[15]

'They have no wine': Serving the kingdom of God

There is a sequence of scenes in the middle of Luke's Gospel that show us how Jesus formed his followers to serve the kingdom of God in the world. Woven through the stories are the two contrasting ways in which the Church manifests and ministers the life of Christ: the *vita contemplativa* and the *vita activa*. Over the centuries the contemplative life and the active life have often conflicted with, rather than complemented, each other. The life of prayer and worship for the individual follower of Christ and the Church as a whole has sometimes made claims to being the fundamental calling of Christian existence, reducing the mission of the Church in its various forms of engagement with the world to a lower or secondary concern. At other times, the opposite has been in play, and life *in* God has been downplayed in favour of life *for* God and for God's purposes in the world. Both the contemplative and the active can be seen in Mary's life. We have seen how she was ready to take time to think and question, to reflect and ponder, and how she was faithful and devout in her religious life. We have suggested that, like other mothers, she would have spent many hours holding her child, looking at him, loving him. Mary was by no means passive, though. It was in speaking and doing that she gave personal shape and public presence to her faith in God's grace, relating to others through her questions and concerns, and acting with them to fulfil God's call on her. We have seen that the life of a mother taking her part in the sustenance and care of a household in first-century rural Galilee would have meant plenty of activity for her, much of it exhausting and exacting, and a lot of interaction with others, essential for survival.

In Luke's account of Jesus' ministry in these chapters, and his interactions with those who wanted to follow his way, he seems to be balancing the *vita contemplativa* and the *vita activa* together and suggesting how they can be integrated. Jesus sends out 70 people into the towns and villages of Galilee to 'cure the sick who are there, and say to them, "The kingdom of God has come near to you"' (Luke 10.9). They are to spend time with the people in each community, staying for as long as they are welcome, sharing with them the peace of God's rule. They return to Jesus and spend time with him, reflecting on what has happened and sharing his joy that God is at work through them. Luke immediately follows his account of the Mission of the Seventy with Jesus' dialogue with a lawyer who asked him what he needed to do 'to inherit eternal life' (Luke 10.25–37). Jesus, always good at answering a question with a question, asked him what he saw written in the law. The lawyer, who clearly knew the law well, came back quickly with the answer that it says to love God fully and to love your neighbour as yourself. Jesus replies, 'Do this, and you will live.' The lawyer, well versed in the rabbinic style, asks another question in return: 'And who is my neighbour?' Jesus then goes on to tell a story about a Samaritan whose heart is moved by a Jewish person in need and who goes out of his way to care for him. Jesus' listeners knew well the bitter enmity between Samaritans and Jews, giving the story its shock factor. The answer Jesus seems to be giving to the lawyer's question is that life is to be found in becoming a neighbour to whoever is in need, whatever their background and identity: the *vita activa*.

'Now as they went on their way,' Luke tells us, they rest at the home of Mary and Martha (Luke 10.38–42). Martha is preoccupied with the myriad of tasks that fell to women of her culture, especially when providing hospitality, and she is not a little annoyed by her sister Mary who 'sat at the Lord's feet and listened to what he was saying'. Jesus dismisses Martha's protestations, saying to her, 'There is need of only one thing. Mary has chosen the better part, which will not be taken away from her.' Here Jesus seems to be giving a different inflexion

to the lawyer's question on how we can take hold of the life
that God has for us and enter the 'eternal life' of God's kingdom. Mary is loving God not by serving others and not even
by serving Jesus in the sort of activity that consumed Martha.
She was simply resting and listening. She was taking delight
in Jesus, enjoying his presence, feasting on his words: the *vita
contemplativa*.

In the next scene, Luke shows how the *vita activa* and the
vita contemplativa belong together in an integrated life of faithful discipleship (Luke 11.1–4). Jesus is praying. The disciples
are drawn to the quality of his prayer and ask to share in it, so
that they could be more fully identified with him and share in
his work. Jesus' contemplation of God in prayer leads to action
towards others who want to know God better. The prayer that
Jesus teaches them is itself a combination of adoration of the
God whom Jesus makes better known – 'Father, hallowed be
your name' – and intercession for the fullest manifestation
of God's goodness that they can see breaking into the world
through Jesus' work – 'Your kingdom come.' It is a prayer that
makes those who pray it participants in the promises of God
to all creation. It is a prayer that commits those who pray for
the kingdom to take their part in its coming: in being forgiven,
we are to forgive. It is a prayer that calls the followers of Jesus
to follow his way of prayer and action: in doing so we follow
the pattern of God who not only *is* but chooses to *act* so that
we may live.

Hannah Arendt's mid-twentieth-century study, *The Human
Condition*, shows how the *vita activa* and the *vita contemplativa*
have vied with each other through the course of western civil-
ization, pre-dating the Christian era.[16] Her arguments for why,
in large part, the *vita activa* has eclipsed the *vita contemplativa*
in the modern era need not detain us, but her particular understanding of the *vita activa* is of real value when it comes to
considering the way the Church witnesses and works for the
kingdom of God in the world. For Arendt, the essence of the
vita activa is not the activity dedicated to the meeting of basic
human needs for life (water, food, shelter, etc.), the 'labour

of our body' as she calls it. Neither is it the activity dedicated
to the meeting of human wants (the making of things, simple
or sophisticated that improve the quality of life), the 'work of
our hands' as she calls it. Rather it is the activity that derives
from 'our plurality as distinct individuals' as we order the
common life together.[17] It is this *living and acting together* as
distinct individuals, each of us the fruit of the natality of the
world, that gives our lives its truly *human* character. Arendt's
analysis has many parallels with Christian thought which
defines human life as *life lived together*. Accordingly, it corre-
lates both with the deep *identity* of the Church as the people
of God, bound together in Christ's life, and with the *activity*
of the Church in the world, to serve God's purposes for the
reconciliation of humanity with God and with itself – the healing of its self-inflicted wounds, the restoration of its lost peace
and the renewal of the creation of which it is part.

Arendt's interest is specifically in the political life of human
beings which she understands to be the whole sweep of activity
through which people relate to each other and decide together
how they will live with each other in human community for
the good of all. The Church of the New Testament took its
name (*ekklesia*) not from the religious sphere but from the
political – the ordering of the life of the city state in Greek culture. In ancient Greek culture, the *ekklesia* was the assembly
of citizens summoned together to deliberate and decide about
its life together. The identity of the Church – its being – is a
community of people called together by God, bound together
by a common confession of one Lord and by one baptism into
him, empowered together by the same Spirit and nourished
together in one body by the one bread. The activity of the
Church – its doing – in its various forms, with each person in
some way involved, is directed towards the 'common good' so
that 'the whole body ... promotes the body's growth in building itself up in love' (Eph. 4.16). In its being and doing the
Church witnesses to the 'city that is to come', as it prays for
God's kingdom to come. The relationship between the holy
city 'coming down out of heaven from God' (Rev. 21.2) and

the cities of earth in which people live out their lives today has taken many forms in Christian thought over the centuries. But even in times when Christians have been tempted to withdraw from engagement in the wider political and social dimension of human life and neglect the call of Jesus to be light for the world and salt for the earth, they have continued to pray for God's will to be done on earth as it is in heaven. In every age the sweeping vision of Mary's Magnificat for a just and peaceful society stands as a touchstone, challenging God's people to step up to the call to believe in and work with the God who has promised to transform the earth as well as heaven.

Hannah Arendt identified two particular challenges for human beings as they seek to live well together in the *vita activa*: irreversibility and unpredictability. Human activity is often harmful and always difficult to undo. The damage our activity causes and the hurt we do to each other sets in motion a spiral of further events from which it seems impossible to escape. Human life is also unpredictable. We do not know what will happen in the future and the capacity of human beings to act badly, and to cause problems that we cannot presently conceive, means that it is very difficult to enter into any sort of cooperation with others. The risk is too great. Arendt identifies 'the faculty of forgiving' as the 'possible redemption from the predicament of irreversibility' – of being unable to undo what has been done. Similarly in her mind, the 'faculty to make and keep promises' is 'the remedy for unpredictability, for the chaotic uncertainty of the future'.[18] Here Arendt acknowledges the unique contribution Judeo-Christian thought and practice has played in commending to the world the virtues of forgiveness and promise-making and promise-keeping to human culture. She pays special tribute to Jesus' ethic of forgiveness and 'his insistence on the "power to forgive"' which he not only exercised himself but taught his followers also to do.[19]

The extent to which Jesus' understanding of forgiveness was shaped by his mother's attitudes and behaviours is impossible to say but her place within the life of the earliest Church suggests that she was a person who learned to forgive, and that she may have taught others what she learned from her son about the way forgiveness breaks the bonds of the past, as well as what she may have taught him. Peter had let Jesus down on several occasions and had denied that he knew him when he was on trial. He had proved to be a false witness to Christ by failing to stand by him and was complicit in his death. Now, shortly before Pentecost, they were in the upstairs room together along with others who had deserted her son at his hour of greatest need, and Peter was taking the lead in the community that he had formed. Crowds of people in the streets of Jerusalem had cried out for her son's execution. Later she was out on those same streets as thousands wanted to be baptized into his name and follow his way. We do not know whether there was any overlap between the two crowds, but it is likely that many of those who joined the Christian community 'in Jerusalem, in all Judea and Samaria' and other places Jesus visited were those who had once rejected her son or failed to support and protect him. There would have been much for a mother to forgive and it could not have been easy for Mary to accept all those 'the Lord added to their number' (Acts 2.47).

Scripture tells us more about Mary's experience of promise-making and promise-keeping. She hears God's promise that she will bear 'the Son of the Most High' in fulfilment of the ancient promise about a young woman conceiving a child who will be called *Immanuel* (Luke 1.31; Isa. 7.14). She exercises the faith of Abraham, believing God's word and entrusting herself to the promise. She makes her own promise to be the servant of the Lord and the bearer of life. She keeps her promise through the days of his life even at that moment when it looks as if God had reneged on the promise made to her. Mary hears and believes God's promise. She makes and fulfils her promise to God. She herself belongs to the promise made long ago to Abraham. It is through her and in her and with her that God blesses all the peoples of the earth with the life of God in Jesus Christ.

In 1954, Lesslie Newbigin, who became one of the twentieth century's leading missiologists, set a course for understanding the identity and activity of the Church that became enshrined in several ecumenical statements and agreements: 'The church lives in the midst of history as a sign, instrument and foretaste of the reign of God.'[20] It is not difficult to see these ecclesial realities concentrated in the life of Mary. Mary is a *sign* of God's covenant to redeem the world and dwell on earth – 'Therefore the Lord himself shall give you a sign; Behold, a virgin shall conceive, and bear a son, and shall call his name Immanuel' (Isa. 7.14, KJV).[21] She is a *foretaste* of God's promise to pour out the Spirit on all flesh – 'The Holy Spirit will come upon you' (Luke 1.35). She is a personal *instrument* or agent through whom God brings to new life the promised covenant in the 'new covenant in [Christ's] blood' (Luke 22.20).

This is the character and dignity of the Church. Believing God's promise, we commit ourselves to God's promise, we engage in God's work and we become the means by which God's promise of life to the world is fulfilled in the world. It is a staggeringly high calling and one that is all too easy to doubt or dilute. We reach for ways to relativize the Church as just one of God's agencies among many. We look for ways to deny that, although the Bible, human history and present experience all affirm that God is at work in the world in all sorts of ways through all sorts of people, the Church that God calls into existence plays a decisive part in making known 'the wisdom of God in its rich variety' (Eph. 3.8–10), and preparing the way for the coming of Christ and of his kingdom that will have no end (Luke 1.33). Nevertheless, given the scale of the work that God entrusts to the Church, Hannah Arendt's affirmation of the particular Christian contribution to the value of forgiveness and promise-keeping in political life is worth pursuing. Attention to them may help strengthen our confidence in the experience and wisdom the Church can bring to the political sphere. One way in which the Church participates in God's promise-making and keeping is through its ministry of intercession, and one way the Church participates in God's work of forgiveness is through its peace-making activities. As we shall see, both of those themes will move us on from Mary's part in

Jesus' earthly life and the Church's early ministry to consider the place of Mary in the ongoing work of Christ and the life of the Church. Before doing so, though, it is worth drawing on another of Arendt's insights.

We have seen that Arendt placed great hope on the natality of human life, the reality of the birth of new people into the world. She liked to talk of 'men not man', distinct and different people in all their plurality who choose to work together, rather than humanity as some sort of monolithic whole. Her thinking at this point does not perfectly map on to the life of the Church but it comes very close. To be sure, there is such a reality of the Church which is greater than the sum of its individual parts and takes the form of the body of Christ. That body, though, is constituted by Christ through the people he calls in the fullness of their own personhood and individuality. The Church is continually renewed by those Christ draws into his life and each person, whether newly baptized or well-established in the faith, is appointed by the Spirit to make a difference to the Church's life and empowered by the Spirit to witness to Christ and his kingdom in the world. The Church is new every morning.

Scripture is clear that salvation for human beings and renewal for the whole of creation has been *achieved* by the life, death, resurrection and ascension of Jesus Christ. At the same time, it is in no doubt that the redemption gained is still in the process of being *applied* to human life and the whole created order. We wait, expectantly, for the consummation of God's purposes in the *parousia* of Christ when God's saving sovereignty will be fully manifested and experienced in the coming of Christ and his kingdom, when 'the home of God is among mortals' (Rev. 21.3). This in-between time in which we find ourselves is the era of Christ's ascension and the Church's ministry, and it is defined by intercession. The Church's prayer for the coming of God's kingdom is always oriented to the future and lives with the disciplines of hope. It is always, though, simultaneously a prayer that looks to the present, calling on God's name to be hallowed and God's will to be done on earth as in heaven. It is the prayer of faith that God's saving love is active in the present as the blessings and benefits of Christ's saving work are made present and available to a world in need.

The work of the salvation of humankind and the renewal of creation remains always the work of God, an act of God's grace. We have seen, though, that the way God chooses to act is through the inside of humanity. God chooses a people. God comes in person in Christ. God extends those people to include the Gentiles and inhabits them by the Spirit. Mary stands at the pivotal point in the purposes of God and we see how deeply and participatively God works with those to whom God has promised to give life in its fullness. Tina Beattie puts it this way: 'The God of the Annunciation is a God who submits himself to the human will, made manifest in the will of one who has no power and authority.'[22] Mary's response, 'Here am I,' is the attitude of Christian prayer. We simply say that we are ready to take our part in the purposes of God in what we do and say, to become, as Gregory of Narek said, 'the personal chariot of the Giver of Life'. We saw in Chapter 2 that although Mary made her 'yes' for herself she did not make it by herself. God prepared her for her 'yes' and enabled her to take part in God's work. The Church's intercession is the prayer of the whole Church – the head and the body inhabited by the Spirit. Paul tells us that Christ is interceding for us and the Spirit is interceding within us (Rom. 8.34, 26). The incarnation is not a temporary event. It is a permanent reality for the life of God and the life of the world. The ascended Christ holds our humanity in heaven and, as 'the pioneer and perfecter of our faith' (Heb. 12.2), leads our prayer in the power of the Spirit he has shared with us. God's sovereignty remains God's own but – or, rather, we should say *and* – God has chosen to embrace a people into those sovereign purposes as *participants* and not only *recipients* in the giving of the gift to the whole world. The mystery of the incarnation involves the humility of mediation. The 'one God' chose to act through humanity by becoming in Jesus Christ the human being the 'one mediator' (1 Tim. 2.5); and Christ chose people to be sent in his name, 'entrusting the message of reconciliation to us' (2 Cor. 5.19).

Although it became more prevalent and influential around the ninth to the eleventh century, belief in Mary's intercession has ancient origins in the Church, and that is both in the sense of believing that Mary continues to pray in and for the Church and in the sense of believing that her prayers carry special weight. It is closely related to the mediatorial ministry of the Church as a whole and to the question of whether Mary has a particular role or ministry in the Church, even allowing her to be called Mediatrix, as many Roman Catholic and Orthodox Christians propose. Although silent on that contested question, Pope John II's *Redemptoris Mater* notes that any talk of Mary's mediation is 'in the nature of intercession'.[23]

Luther's attitude to the prayer of Mary is complex and ambivalent. On the one hand, he concludes his sermon on the Magnificat with a prayer that 'Christ will grant this through the intercession and for the sake of His dear Mother Mary' and commended the Hail Mary (the *Ave Maria*) in his *Little Prayer Book, 1552*.[24] On the other hand, only a year later, he complained of his time as a monk before his evangelical experience that:

> We believed Christ sat in heaven in judgement, not caring about us on earth, but that he would only give us life after death (even if we had done good deeds) if the mother had reconciled him with us ... Therefore I wish that the Ave Maria would be completely rooted out because of this abuse.[25]

These are clearly serious concerns that strike at the heart of the gospel. They give us some parameters within which any responsible talk of Mary's intercession needs to operate and remind us of how deeply misunderstandings of the place of Mary in the life of faith had become embedded in the life of the Church before the Reformation. The brunt of Luther's attack on the Marian practices of the Church lay in the prayer to Mary (in which he believed hid all manner of deformations of the gospel) rather than the prayer of Mary (for which he was thankful). We will return to these vexed questions shortly, but for now I would like to remain with Luther on the less contentious ground of Mary's prayer on earth and the way that reveals something of the character and dynamic of our intercession today.

In a very insightful essay, the Lutheran scholar Lois Malcolm draws attention to Luther's emphasis in his sermon on the Magnificat on Mary's experience of the Holy Spirit, the way she was 'saturated with the divine sweetness and Spirit'.[26] Before she could see the full evidence of God's goodness, she was given to 'taste' that 'the LORD is good' (Ps. 34.8) whose word is 'sweeter also than honey (Ps. 19.10). Like the psalmist, Mary trusted God; believing in God's promises she lived into the future. Malcolm argues that the Magnificat has the quality of the apocalyptic, that genre of biblical literature that lifts the veil on the future that God is bringing. In this way her song shifts the perception of its readers – and singers – so that we begin to share with her the new world that God is creating out of the conditions of sin and suffering in the present age. The wisdom of the proud is unmasked for what it is – the imagination of human minds. The strength of the mighty is brought down as the lowly are lifted up. The wealth of the rich is emptied as the hands of the hungry are filled. Mary's song sounds like a utopian dream full of the misplaced aspirations of other social revolutionaries reaching after the impossible. But Mary has been brought into the realm of God's promise by God's Spirit and she has 'believed that there would be a fulfilment of what was spoken to her by the Lord' (Luke 1.45). What demonstrates Mary's faith most persuasively for Luther is the way she trusts in the 'bare goodness' of God.[27] He contends that Mary believes in God's goodness even where the goodness of God seems to be thwarted and even when it looks as if God is absent. In this way, Mary's prayer of praise provides a template for our prayer of intercession. We pray according to the promise, not in relation to the evidence. Our sights are not limited by what seems realistic, they are set on the reality of God's coming kingdom. Our hope is not in the politically possible but in the God for whom nothing is impossible. Like Mary – and Paul – we believe that God can create out of the 'things that are not' (1 Cor. 1.28) and that the new creation has come to life in her.

There is undoubtedly much in Mary's past example to inspire our present practice of prayer, and Luther was right to commend the faith underlying her prayer and praise. But is there any sense in which her prayer is also a present reality and, if so, is it a ministry of prayer on which we should call? That set of questions relates to a prior question of whether those who have gone before us into death – those who scripture tells us have 'fallen asleep' in Christ (1 Thess. 4.15, NIV) – pray for us. They in turn raise questions of eschatology and the nature of existence for those in Christ between death and resurrection. We will touch tentatively on those in the next section but suffice it to say for now that the affirmation of the Communion of Saints in the Apostles' Creed summarizes well the witness of scripture. We remain in a continuing fellowship with the followers of Christ who have been gathered into his presence and, with us, await the fullness of the kingdom in the renewal of creation. The ARCIC Agreed Statement on Salvation and the Church captures something of the Christian experience of the presence and encouragement of the 'cloud of witnesses' described in the letter to the Hebrews (Heb. 12.1–3): 'The believers' pilgrimage of faith is lived out with the mutual support of all the people of God. In Christ all the faithful, both living and departed, are bound together in a communion of prayer.'[28] Without denying that those who have died in Christ continue to pray for us, Luther and other reformers had their misgivings about asking for their prayer; and the 39 Articles of the Church of England rejected 'the Romish doctrine of the invocation of the saints'. They were teaching against the backdrop of the sort of excesses of Marian devotion, to which we have already referred, that obscured the unique mediatorial place of the humanity of Christ.

Joining the monks praying in St Macarios Monastery in Egypt, and watching them drift into chapel for prayer in the half-light of the early morning, I saw the way they acknowledged each other with a bow as they entered the church and then made a point of placing a hand on the tomb of the three Macaria – the three Matthews – whom they revere as their spiritual fathers. It all felt entirely natural and normal. We were praying with those who were physically present *and* with those who were spiritually present with us through their communion with Christ, whether they were living in Egypt, elsewhere in the world or with Christ in the heavenly places. We were praying 'with all the saints' and any invocation to those whose life in Christ continued beyond this life was not so much prayer *to them* or *through them* as request for their prayer *for us*.

Gregory of Narek preserves and develops an ancient pattern of prayer deriving from the Syriac tradition. Its closest western form is the litany. The content of Narek's litanies, treasured by the Armenian Church, is often related to a particular feast or theological theme but they all conclude with an invocation that follows a well-established order: Mary, John the Baptist, Stephen, the apostles and prophets, Gregory the Illuminator (the founding father of the Armenian Church) and the martyrs and ascetics of the Church. Mary is clearly placed within the communion of saints and at the same time she is named as first among them. Often Gregory's litanies will include a petition that runs like a refrain through the prayer. We met one in Chapter 2, when Gregory prays, 'Life-giving Saviour, Give life to the lost.'[29] At other times Gregory invokes the prayers of the apostles as he pleads to Christ for mercy and sometimes calls on Mary 'to present [our prayers] to your Son our God'. Gregory is clear that God – Father, Son and Holy Spirit – is the Giver of life and that Christ is the mediator of God's life to us through the Spirit. He is also, though, entirely comfortable about seeking the prayers of all the people of God, including particular categories of believers on the basis of their distinctive discipleship, and Mary on the basis of her motherhood.

Although this is exactly what Luther cautioned against, the Lutheran theologian Robert Jenson, writing in a very different context, commends the practice of asking Mary to pray for us. He does so on two grounds.

First. Mary is Israel in one person, as Temple and arch-prophet and guardian of Torah. To ask her to pray for me is to invoke all of God's history with Israel at once, all of this place-taking in this people, and all the faithfulness of God to his people, as grounds for his faithfulness to me.

Second ... To ask Mary to pray for us is to ask 'the whole company of heaven' to pray for us, not this saint or that but all of them together. It is to ask the church triumphant to pray for us.[30]

Jenson is doing more than appealing to a symbolic role for Mary. It is not just that she is the figure or type of Israel and the Church, representing the faithful response of Jew and Christian to God. She is a person and, in the economy of God, we relate not just to ideas and concepts but to people. Moreover, as a person, she has become *Theotokos*, the Bearer and Mother of God. The response which God was looking for in Israel was found in her. 'Mary is Israel concentrated,' he says. God found a space in which to dwell in creation, and so 'there must be a mysterious sense in which Mary is heaven, not only the container of the uncontainable Son, but of all his sisters and brothers'.[31]

Jenson's emphasis on Mary's personhood and motherhood is important. Mary is not an object used in God's work, discarded when her purpose has been served in the conception and birth of God's Son. She is a subject who is caught up in the ongoing work of God through Jesus' childhood, ministry, death, resurrection, giving of the Spirit and the life of his Church. She remains his mother as he ascends to heaven bearing our humanity to the right hand of God. She is structured into his relationships. As Luther was fond of saying, 'We have communion with Christ and all the saints.'[32] That communion includes Mary in her 'unique vocation' as Mother of God and, thereby, as the mother of Christ whose kingdom has no end, our mother in him, the mother of the Church. Our prayer for the world is joined with her prayer for the world – 'They have no wine' (John 2.3) – and our work is shaped by her word – 'Do whatever he tells you' (John 2.5).[33]

It is said that Pope Francis is drawn to a relatively new Marian devotion inspired by a Baroque style painting by Johan Schmidtner. It pictures Mary, aglow with the light of the Spirit emanating from a dove hovering above her and surrounded by angels, untying knots in a long strip of cloth or string. 'But being from above ... you straightened what was tangled,' said Mary to Gabriel in Romanos the Melodite's sixth-century reimagination of the Annunciation.[34] Schmidtner's painting seems to be depicting Mary doing the same with the prayers of all those who pray. She is untangling the complex web of conflicting human prayer so that it can be brought into some sort of order and presented to her son. It is an evocative image of the Church's life in both its *vita contemplativa* and its *vita activa*. The world is tied up in thick knots of problems, each compounding and complexifying the other. As the Church prays in the Spirit, it seeks to bring the needs of the world to the throne of grace through petitions in the name of Jesus, clarifying the world's concerns through the lens of the kingdom of God. Just as Mary did not meet the needs of the family whose wine had run out, the Church does not answer the prayers of humanity. But with Mary, the Church discerns the underlying threads of human need amid the snarled and tangled suffering of the world and offers them to God in prayer. And, heeding Mary's words, as we pray, we wait for Christ to show us how we are called to work with him in responding to those needs.

I had a rare opportunity to visit a Yazidi temple in Georgia and to spend time with their clergy telling me more about their faith and the troubles of their community, especially the Yazidis around Sinjar in the Nineveh region of northern Iraq. When I visited Iraqi Kurdistan in the past, the security situation did not allow me to go to their homeland around Mount Sinjar but I was able to meet some of their leaders and speak to Kurdistani politicians about their situation. I thought I understood things reasonably well and had some sort of handle on how Yazidis could be protected from the sort of genocidal persecution they had experienced at the hands of ISIS during the wars in Syria and Iraq in the twenty-first century. Listening to Pir Dimitri Pirbari, the Yazidi Akhtar of Georgia, I realized that there were layers of complexity to their plight in Sinjar of which previously I had little inkling.[35] I valued greatly the opportunity to find out more about this ancient community with their gentle religion that had been almost unknown by the international community until violence was wreaked upon them. There is much the international church community could do to make their fears and hopes better known, and that work will be sustained by prayer. We also talked together about the Yazidi respect for Mary and the place she has in their prayers and scriptures. As we sat in their small and simple temple, I was intrigued to see pilgrims, some of them looking as if the troubles of their persecuted community weighed heavily upon them, tie knots in pieces of cloth. 'These are the needs they bring to God hoping that others will pray for them,' I was told. I was glad of the invitation to pray for one of those needs knotted into the cloth and to untie it as I did so.

Mary has often been seen as Protectoress, and many threatened communities have turned to her as a child turns to their mother when in danger. Not all of this tradition is by any means wholesome and there is no doubt that Mary has been manipulated by men to justify their claims to power and legitimize violent means to achieve their ends. Indeed, there has been chilling evidence of Mary being militarized by Russia in the Ukraine war as well as moving examples of Ukrainians turning to the tender care of Mary evident in the face of its famous twelfth-century Virgin of Kyiv icon. As we have seen, the Magnificat shows that there is a deep connection between Mary and those who live in fear of violence and war. Mary stands on the side of those oppressed by human violence – economic, political, cultural and every sort – and she knows first-hand the terror of physical violence and the further degradation when caused by the manoeuvrings of law and religion. The Church that honours Mary as mother of the Son of God whose body still bears the scars of violence, will stand for peace in the face of the powers that slaughter the innocent. The Church that looks to her as mother of believers will do as Jesus tells us and be peacemakers in the power of his gift of peace (Matt. 5.9; John 14.27). That is one reason why Pope Francis on Marian Feast Days called for the intercession of Mary for the peace of Russia, Ukraine and the whole world.[36]

The causes of conflict are usually complex, creating a maze of problems that seem impossible to untangle. Violence in any form leaves long legacies, and the violence of war weaves threads of hatred and distrust through the generations that sow in them the seed of further violence. The damage inflicted on human relationships by war and conflict is an example writ large of the 'irreversibility' of human action that Hannah Arendt identified. Undoing the dense knots by which whole communities are bound into patterns of behaviour that are themselves the cause of further problems requires a patient exercise of virtues that are rarely trusted. Forgiveness, as Arendt saw, is prime among them and has the capacity to release the tension that allows the loosening of the knot. My experience of Coventry's story of war and peace is that reconciliation between war-time enemies is built not first on forgiveness of the other or even on apology of one to the other but on mutual humility before God. The prayer inscribed on to the bombed-out ruins of Coventry Cathedral after its destruction by German bombs in 1940 was simply, 'Father, forgive'. It was not well received in bombed-out Coventry at the time. Even 'Father, forgive *them*' would have felt like several steps too far, especially with retaliation in the minds of many, government, military and citizen alike. It is, indeed, a radical and demanding prayer. It is a prayer that demands the sort of 'poverty of spirit' that resists justifying one's attitudes and actions against those who have caused hurt or damage, even when they have rained down terror on those who could not defend themselves. It is an acknowledgement of the way the affairs of human beings are knotted together in such a way that responsibility for events is denied by every side and blame assigned in different ways. It accepts that it is better to speak first to God than to each other. It is a costly confession of complicity that recognizes the permeation of sin through the common life of humanity and asks for mercy. It is a lament for the virus of evil passed from person to person, society to society, nation to nation. Standing together in the solidarity of sin and suffering, enemies find a new freedom to acknowledge the damage they and their peoples have done to each other. The long road to lasting reconciliation begins. Although it is marked at different points by new tolls of forgiveness, the irreversible changes direction and the lasting hurt of what has been done in the past is undone.

Christians believe that human beings are made in the image and likeness of God. It is because God forgives and opens for us a new future that we have the capacity to forgive and unlock new possibilities for peace between peoples. It is because God is the promise maker who covenants to keep and fulfil promises, that we have the capacity to make promises and enter into covenants and agreements to keep them. Forgiving and promising are rooted in truth telling and are sustained by all manner of virtues that structure relationships and bring stability to society at every level: family, community, nation, global. Providing a distinctive Christian witness to the transformative effect of forgiveness and promise-making and keeping is one of the ways in which Christians bring near the kingdom of God.

'To Our Lady Undoer of Knots' by Charlie Annis, Anglican priest and monk, brings together the themes we have been discussing in much of this section: God's promise-keeping and our prayer, God's gift of peace and our work of reconciliation, the image of the Church in Mary whose 'yes' to God's grace is also a 'no' to the violence of the world.

> They say that you can plot
> on the short end of a bell curve
> how long it takes a great man with a knot
>
> to reach for the scissors or his sword.
> Thus the king of kings
> and scourge of Asia Minor
>
> hacked apart the coil of Gordias
> with his generals standing by
> like a kingpin rounding on a traitor

and for this was hailed
a genius and a god, and from there
rode roughshod over half the world.

Likewise, the wisest man
that ever lived lost no time
when he found himself

umpire in the field
of fraught maternal politics
to recommend the acumen of steel.

Not so with you though, is it?
Our nimble-fingered mother
our lady of perpetual patch-it-up

queen of the trouser tuck
and the button jar
your hands were made for defter work

the supple motion of the wrists
the patient finger tips
like the eyeless creatures on the seabed.

And you blind also
or might as well be
as the cherubs go on feeding you

the endless rosary of human mishap
and default, that one by one
is dispatched and straightened

and the whole thing loops back
wrinkled to the earth again.
O Sancta Maria

Mère de Dieu
whose heart's immaculate 'no'
the one sword passed through.[37]

'The Spirit and the bride say, "Come"': Looking to the life of the life to come

Mary's conception of Jesus brought her into the sphere of the new creation. God's gift of Christ to the world through her was a new and defining event in the history not only of humanity but of the whole of creation. God who brought life out of nothing now renews life in a newly creative moment of grace that will transform humanity and the whole of creation. The life of God in human form – God in creaturely existence – manifests the life that will overcome death. The Spirit of life overshadows Mary with the liberating favour of God, empowering her to step into the promise of God's future where 'the home of God is among mortals' (Rev. 21.3). Some of the early theologians of the Church described Mary as 'rational paradise'. In the freedom and dignity of her humanity she becomes the virgin soil of redemption. She is the body of the earth in which the body of God – God in human form and likeness (Phil. 2.7) – grows with the fecundity that will 'renew the face of the ground' (Ps. 104.30).[38] The creation God has brought into being through the word of God's love and life will be renewed by the same word, now becoming flesh in her through the energy of the Spirit and the powers of her flesh: 'For us and for our salvation, he came down from heaven, was incarnate from the Holy Spirit and the Virgin Mary, and was made [hu-]man,' as the Nicene Creed says. The vision of the new creation with which the Christian Bible concludes in the final chapters of the book of Revelation layers multiple images of life, one on top of the other: 'the spring of the water of life', 'the Lamb's book of life', 'the river of life', 'the tree of life', culminating in the invitation to every person to 'take the water of life as a gift'. Mary responded to the invitation at the Annunciation and the one who was seated on the throne said, 'See, I am making all things new' (Rev. 21.5).

Mary's participation in the work of God's new creation where 'Death will be no more' (Rev. 21.4) is one of the reasons why there has been such theological and spiritual attention to her bodily relationship to the risen Christ. At a relatively early point, though still distanced from the New Testament period by some centuries, traditions began to emerge of God acting uniquely at her departure from earthly life in a way that mirrored God's distinctive work at her conception. Stephen Shoemaker's detailed studies suggest that these traditions were circulating by at least the fourth century, especially prevalent in heterodox circles.[39] They gathered pace, gaining more recognition in mainline streams of the faith and by the sixth century they were clearly well established, given voice and credence in writers and preachers such as John of Damascus and Germanus of Constantinople. The Eastern Church in its different forms commemorates *The Dormition of Mary*. As we can see from the Icons of the Dormition, Mary dies surrounded by the apostles and Jesus comes to carry her soul to Paradise. Touchingly, her soul – white and pure – takes the form of an infant held in the arms of Jesus. A few days after her death her body also is taken into the presence of the ascended Christ. The traditions developed with a different emphasis in the Western Church. Rather than the more intimate scenes of Mary's death, she is usually pictured – as in Titian's medieval classic, painted on the eve of the Reformation – rising triumphantly into heaven, body and soul, earth no longer able to hold on to her, the blue of her dress dazzling with regal splendour. Although celebrated and confirmed by Popes from the eighth century, it was not until the twentieth century that the Assumption of Mary, as it came to be called, was proclaimed 'a divinely revealed dogma'. In 1950 Pope Pius XII declared in his Apostolic Constitution, *Munificentissimus Deus*, that 'the immaculate Mother of God, the ever Virgin Mary, having completed the course of her earthly life, was assumed body and soul into heavenly glory'.[40] Whether the completion of her earthly life included her death or whether her freedom from the effects of original sin preserved her from death is left open by the Papal definition; and so, Roman Catholics are free to believe the latter, though most affirm the former.

Although the Roman Catholic Church and the Orthodox

Churches maintain that the belief in Mary's bodily presence with Christ has a basis in scripture, they would be less confident about claiming that it can be proved through scripture. Rather these traditions are seen as mysteries that have been made known to the Church through its ongoing life of prayer and learning in the Spirit, revealing what is present in scripture, albeit in a somewhat hidden form. As with other distinctive Marian doctrines, I feel no obligation as an Anglican to accept the Assumption of Mary as a divinely given truth that Christians are bound to believe. At the same time, out of respect for the two largest communions of the Christian Church and the millions of Christians among them, I do feel obliged to explore what lies behind these ancient and devoutly held beliefs about Mary's life with Christ beyond this present life, and to learn what belongs to the gospel from them.

Giving thought to what happens to Mary beyond her life on earth leads us into questions of immense theological and ecclesiological importance that have consequences not only for our spiritual status in Christ but also for our political engagement in the world, including, as we shall explore later, our responsibility to the earth, its environment and ecology. Paul sets out Christian identity and destiny in his letter to the Romans, especially chapter 8. 'Those who are in Christ', whom God raised from the dead, live in 'the Spirit of life'. We are adopted as God's children as 'joint heirs with Christ'. What belongs to him is shared with us through our share in his life. The effect and evidence of this work of God in us through Christ is that we now, together, call out to God as 'Abba! Father!' by the Spirit. The dynamic of Christian existence is seen most clearly in prayer. We are caught up into the intercession of Christ through the Spirit who 'intercedes with sighs too deep for words'. God's work for us and in us has a deep origin and a glorious fulfilment. Paul writes of how we have been 'predestined to be conformed to the image of his Son, in order that he might be the first-born within a large family'. Being 'predestined', we have been 'called', and being 'called', we have been 'justified', and being 'justified', we have been 'glorified'.

Paul is working with complex patterns of perspective that stretch our concept of time. We have been predestined according to God's purpose beyond the origins of time. We have been called within history, within our time. Likewise, we have been justified now by God's grace. Already, though, Paul is slipping into a future perspective. He is seeing things eschatologically, from the point of the end of this age and the beginning of the new. We are truly justified by the grace of God which we receive by faith and baptism and, thereby, adopted into the life and love of God's trinitarian life. This undeserved gift of salvation takes place now while we remain sinful and before we are fully sanctified in grace-given anticipation of the transformation that will come to us as God's gift in 'the resurrection of the dead' (1 Cor. 15.42). Paul's eschatological focus sharpens further when he speaks of our glorification. That too for Paul is a present reality. What else could adoption into the trinitarian relationships of God as 'those who are in Christ' and 'in the Spirit' mean? We are given a real and present participation in glory. And yet we remain in a world immersed in 'hardship, or distress, or persecution, or famine, or nakedness, or peril, or sword'. The suffering they bring is a reality for the body of Christ and, of course, death comes to everyone. We have been glorified. That is a theological and spiritual reality. But our glory is still to be manifested physically in the material conditions of human life within the life of the whole creation. That is why 'creation waits with eager longing for the revealing of the children of God'. We have been saved 'in hope'; it is a hope that binds us to the whole of creation as we wait for it to be 'set free from its bondage to decay'.

We can see a similar pattern in the letter to the Ephesians. We hear of how we have been chosen in Christ 'before the foundation of the world', and of how we have been 'blessed ... in Christ with every spiritual blessing in the heavenly places' in such a way that God has not only 'made us alive together with Christ' but also 'raised us up with him and seated us with him [enthroned us, as it might be translated] in the heavenly places in Christ Jesus'. All of this is *for* the present *because* of the future.[41] Our identity and destiny are clear. Their reality is truly but proleptically experienced in the present. We are 'marked with the seal of the promised Holy Spirit' which is 'the pledge of our inheritance towards redemption as God's own people'. Our life today in Christ is an inheritance of the life that we will know tomorrow, the life that we wait for in expectant hope when 'fullness of time' will come (Ephesians 1.3–4, 2.5–6, 1.13–14).

The Doctrine of the Assumption affirms the theological and spiritual identity of Christian existence that we are raised up with Christ and 'seated [enthroned] with him in the heavenly places'. Additionally, it proposes that Mary's destiny in Christ which we share with all other believers is no longer in the realm of promise and hope but has become a personal actuality for her in differentiation from other believers. Whereas the living and the dead in Christ, together with all creation, are waiting for the *parousia* – the coming – of Christ in glory, the resurrection of the dead, the redemption of the body and the renewal of creation and the dwelling of God among mortals, Mary experiences it now.

It could be argued that what the doctrine says about Mary applies equally to us despite the pattern of salvation that I am suggesting is laid out in the New Testament with its tension between gift given now and promise for the future for which we wait and work in hope. Indeed, a good deal of Christian piety, pastoral care and funeral ministry equate life in Christ beyond death with resurrection from the dead and fullness of salvation. We die in the Lord and we rise in the Lord in an individualized, sequential resurrection. I think that the schema of death followed by immediate personal resurrection into the life of heaven – on, as it were, a 'one-by-one' basis – is incorrect. It may not be exactly the same as the views of 'Hymenaeus and Philetus, who have swerved from the truth by claiming that the resurrection has already taken place' (2 Tim. 2.17–18), but it still fails to hold the proper tensions of Christian faith and risks undermining the full gift of salvation as a corporate and bodily reality in a renewed creation.

Working with the sort of linear pattern of eschatology that N. T. Wright describes as death followed by 'life after-life death' followed by resurrection 'as newly embodied life', could also be challenged on the ground that our historically bound concept of time makes it very difficult if not impossible for us to conceive of things eternal.[42] We have just seen how Paul struggled to express the different dispensations of God's work in Christ with their different dimensions of time as well as space. In our own age, Einstein has shown us that time, and our perception of it, is a very much more complex matter than it appears to be, and certainly more complex than it appeared to be to the biblical writers.[43] We should abandon any attempt to constrain the eternal realm of life with God by our time-bound existence. I am more sympathetic to that sort of critique of the limitations of our conceptuality, but I am also cautious about departing from the historical, time-oriented patterns of the scriptural mind that protect the corporate and material character of salvation. I do not want to isolate my salvation from the salvation of others or abstract it from the renewal of creation. I am bound to both in the family of humanity and the community of creation.[44]

It is this pattern that the Roman Catholic and Orthodox traditions maintain. Jesus Christ risen from the dead goes before us into the new creation to be joined at some point by his mother in 'a singular participation in her Son's Resurrection and an anticipation of the resurrection of other Christians', as the *Catechism of the Catholic Church* says.[45] The reasons – in the absence of clear biblical data or early credal basis – for dis-connecting Mary from the eschatological experience of other Christians, in order to reconnect her bodily with her risen Son, are worth examining. The first is to be found in Mary's par-ticular relationship with Jesus and her unique vocation to be the mother of the Lord. Mary's intensive participation in the new creation through the conception and birth of Christ, and God's preparation of her for her part in these transformative stages of redemption, together with the continuing relationship she has with him through his life as his mother who was found at his side when he died, has led, in the words of the ARCIC Agreed Statement on Mary, to her being given a 'distinctive place in the common destiny of the Church'.[46] We have seen how there is some evidence for the singling out of Mary in the life of the earliest Church. Luke tells us at the beginning of Acts that the apostles gathered in the upper room after the ascension 'together with certain women, including Mary the mother of Jesus, as well as his brothers' (Acts 1.14). Scholars have wrestled with an especially mysterious section in the book of Revelation which appears to suggest that Mary has a particular place and role among the people of God in the heavenly ministry of Christ. Whereas the 'servants, the prophets and saints ... both small and great' have been waiting for the time of 'judging the dead' and 'destroying those who destroy the earth' (11.18), a woman 'clothed with the sun ... and on her head a crown of twelve stars' is caught up in a great battle with 'a great red dragon' (12.1–17). As she gives birth 'to a son, a male child, who is to rule all the nations', the dragon tries to devour the child. The child is whisked from his mother's arms and 'taken to God' while the woman flees to the wilderness, 'where she has a place prepared by God'. War breaks out in heaven with 'Michael and his angels' pitched against the 'dragon and his angels'. Satan is thrown out of heaven and a loud voice proclaims that 'Now have come the salvation and the power and the kingdom of our God and the authority of his Messiah'. The fight continues on earth as the dragon pursues the woman but the earth comes to help, swallowing 'the river that the dragon had poured from his mouth'. The dragon, 'angry with the woman', turns his attention to 'the rest of her children'. The imagery here is complex and multi-layered. It is little wonder that there is no consensus on its meaning. Generally, scholars, often mindful of the persecution the church in Rome was enduring at the time of the book's writing, have concluded that the woman in the passage refers to the church rather than to Mary herself. While I agree that there are good reasons for holding that the passage's primary attention is on the church, and that there is little to be gained here to prove a point about Mary's ongoing relationship with Christ and her place in heaven, it feels very odd today – and was perhaps even more so for the early hearers and readers of Revelation's prophecy – to ignore the passage's resonance with the actual woman who gave birth to a child destined to rule the nations.

The second reason why many Christians believe that Mary was lifted into the presence of Christ, body as well as soul, in advance of the rest of the Church, is less about her bio-logically given relationship with her Son and more to do with her faithful discipleship, though the two are closely connected. According to the ARCIC Statement, Mary is 'a disciple with a special place in the economy of salvation'.[47] She both received the Christ who came to redeem humanity in her body and received the redemption that he brought by the act of her faith. She believed God's word and accepted God's Spirit. That pro-cess of receiving the gift of salvation through her son began before his conception into human life and continued not only to his death on the cross but beyond into the coming of the Spirit of God that he promised to his disciples. Elizabeth called her 'Blessed … among women' because she has been chosen to be the 'mother of [her] Lord' and because she believed God's word and accepted God's gift of life for her and all the world.

There are some fine but definite lines to draw here. Human-ity is redeemed by Jesus Christ through his own faithful and obedient humanity. It is the humanity which Christ redeems in his own person that we share through faith and baptism, Eucharist and ongoing discipleship. But Mary shows us what redeemed humanity looks like in someone who has received it *from* Jesus and grown into it through her life of faith. Edward Yarnold, Roman Catholic priest, monk and theologian, help-fully works within these lines when he describes Mary as 'the archetypal redeemed human being'.

I say 'redeemed' because in our devotion to Mary we must never forget that the archetypal human being *tout court* is Jesus, 'the last Adam'. It is through participation in his human life in its total dedication to his Father, in drawing life from him who is our Head, that we, the cells of his body, are redeemed. His humanity is the *source* of redemption. Mary's humanity is the *model* of redeemed humanity, the sign that the redemption brought by her Son is effective.[48]

I can see Christian logic in both of these claims for the Assumption of Mary. Mary's relationship with Christ is intrinsic to his identity, and her part in his saving purposes is unique. It is fitting that she should remain with him distinguished from the 'servants, the prophets and saints ... both small and great' (Rev. 11.18) as the 'mother of the Lord', made mother of the faithful disciples by the gift of her son. Mary's redemption through Christ is both distinctive and emblematic. Her acceptance of the grace of the gospel is shaped by her reception of the gift of Christ as his mother. In that sense, it differs from ours and has its own unique aspect. In another sense, though, she receives the gift of Christ as we do – by faith – and she allows the form of this gift to take full shape in her through her faithful discipleship throughout her life. As 'a *model* of redeemed humanity', it is fitting that Mary's redemption should be seen to encompass her body as well as her soul, and for her to be the 'image and beginning of the Church as it is to be perfected in the world to come ... a sign of sure hope and comfort to the pilgrim People of God', in what *Lumen Gentium* describes as the 'interim' – that is, in the time and space between the resurrection of Christ and the resurrection of those found in him.[49]

It is from this eschatological perspective that Anglican theologians agreed with their Roman Catholic dialogue partners in the ARCIC Statement on Mary that the 'teaching about Mary' found in the Doctrine of the Assumption 'can be said to be consonant with the teaching of the Scriptures and the ancient common traditions', providing it conforms at all times with Christological norms.[50] This does not commit Anglicans to accepting the doctrine as an article of faith, but it does not charge those church communities and individual Christians, members of Anglican churches among them, who do affirm it with departing from scripture. For my own part I prefer the greater reticence of John Keble's poem 'Mother Out of Sight' on the exact form of Mary's heavenly existence:

> What glory thou above hast won,
> By special grace of thy dear Son,
> We see not yet, nor dare espy
> Thy crowned form with open eye.
> Rather beside the manger meek
> Thee bending with veiled brow we seek,
> Or where the angel in the thrice-great Name
> Hail'd thee, and Jesus to thy bosom came.[51]

I detect something of my own concerns about the need to preserve the tension between the full redemption of the individual and the coming of the new creation in Pope Benedict's writings as Cardinal Ratzinger, a staunch advocate of the traditional eschatological schema I have outlined. In affirming that Mary 'has entered into full community with Christ' – and, therefore, compared with other saints, 'lacks nothing' – he explains that 'part of this community is *another corporeal identity, which we cannot imagine*'.[52] In the face of the absence of greater scriptural guidance and of the dangers, doctrinal and spiritual, of imagining that which we cannot imagine, I think there is wisdom in Basil of Caesarea's advice from the fourth century that the 'dignity of the mysteries is best preserved in silence' rather than defined in doctrine.[53] Nevertheless, with all generations I believe that what Jesus said is true, and that it applies most especially to his mother:

> 'Blessed are you when people revile you and persecute you and utter all kinds of evil against you falsely on my account. Rejoice and be glad, for your reward is great in heaven.'
> (Matt. 5.11–12)

And with all generations I call her Blessed.

Life for the earth – Case study 4: Environment

'I mean people are scared because it's existential. It's about life itself.'[54] That was the assessment of John Kerry, US Climate Change Envoy, in mid-2022, pressing world leaders to keep to the commitments made at the 26th United Nations Climate Change Conference of the Parties that took place in Glasgow in 2021 (COP26). Alongside biodiversity loss and pollution, climate change is one of three main ecological crises facing the world today. These crises for the whole planet are part of what António Guterres, Secretary-General of the UN, has called a 'confluence of crises' that include the ongoing effects of Covid-19, with which the world will be living for years to come, and the highest number of conflicts the world has known since the UN was first established in 1945. These conflicts – the war in Ukraine only the most extreme example among them – are exacerbating the multiple crises of food, energy and refugees, 'that threaten the very survival of humanity'. Climate change operates as a 'crisis multiplier' among these manifold crises, intensifying their effects and causing further crises as their consequences.[55]

The statistics of environmental degradation are overwhelming in every sense of the word.[56] Patterns of consumption are causing 10 million hectares of forest – the lungs of the earth – to be destroyed, 90 per cent because of agricultural expansion. Over the coming decades 40,000 species of life are at risk. Over 17 million metric tons of plastic are dumped in the oceans annually and increasing acidification of the seas threaten marine life and limit the oceans' capacity to absorb CO_2 emissions. More than 85 per cent of the world's wetlands have been lost over the last 300 years, with at least 733 million people living in countries with high and critical levels of water stress. With energy-related increases in CO_2 rising to their highest recorded levels, the Intergovernmental Panel on Climate Change (IPCC) warned in 2022 that it was 'code red for humanity'; 'It's now or never, if we want to limit global warming to 1.5%C.'[57] Meanwhile there were 50,000 new fossil fuel developments planned across the world.

All of this pertains deeply and urgently to the Christian ethic of life, and the gift of life itself given to Mary in the vulnerability of a child, threatened from the first by the dangers of political powers, the self-interest of religious authorities, poverty, violence, displacement and more. How can Christian faith speak a word of hope into a threatened humanity, a word of life into a dying world? As with the unborn child in the womb (vulnerable to the decisions of adults and the culture they create), the child in the classroom (vulnerable to the policy-making of adults and their priorities), and all the peoples of the earth (vulnerable to the exigencies of geopolitics and the flawed political leaders and complex military-industrial machinery of the nations who possess nuclear weapons), life itself on our planet is vulnerable to the powers of humanity, especially its strongest contenders who lay waste the earth.

The environmental threat that faces all life forms including human life maps clearly on to the Christian analysis of the life of the universe and human history. At the genesis of life itself, so the biblical book that bears that name tells us, God gave to humanity the gift of 'everything that has the breath of life' (Gen. 1.30). Created in the image and likeness of God (according to one of its stories of our origin) humanity was called to be like God, to be God's agent of God's purposes of life, God's viceroy even, acting on behalf of God, exercising God's dominion of liberating love, and (according to the other story) 'to till it and keep it' (Gen. 2.15) nurturing creation into fullness of life. God is the creator, and God's creation was made good, 'indeed, it was very good' (Gen. 1.31). God places human life at the heart of creation, as a critical organ within an interconnected ecology of life. We are to receive this good gift of God's creation, to live within it well and to rise to the responsibilities God has given to humanity to care for it, tending and nurturing it into its full potential for mutually flourishing life.

As the story goes on, it becomes all too familiar. Rather than rising to its responsibilities as creation's pastor, humanity is consumed by its sense of its own rights, its desire for autonomy, and all creation suffers as a consequence. The ecological crisis of the twenty-first century leaves us in no doubt that humanity is the problem. That is a cause of despair, so deep is the human predilection for destruction, even of itself. But the Christian story – inherited from the Jewish story and inhabited in its own distinctive way – is a history of redemption that culminates in the coming of the Creator into the fabric of creation to reshape human life according to the intended pattern – the image and likeness of God. *Christ the Heart of Creation* – the title of a book by Rowan Williams on the meaning of Jesus Christ for our understanding of both the Creator and the creation – captures the Christian vision succinctly.[58] Humanity may have been creation's problem but humanity has become *in Christ* – through God's presence and act in Jesus Christ – creation's solution. This is the ground of Christian hope for creation even amid 'the clear and present danger' to its survival: creation, renewed through God's redeeming love, has a future.[59] Christian ethics is an ethic of future life as much as it is an ethic of present life. Indeed, it draws its strength *eschatologically* – from the promise of fulfilment of God's promises in the *shalom* of the redeemed creation.

Nevertheless, the condition of creation in the present time remains a momentous challenge to humanity in general and to those who confess Christ in particular. Mary, often called 'Mother of all the living' in the theological tradition, embodies the response to the seriousness – its existential quality – of the challenge before us. She said *yes to life*, to life itself, and yes to her part within it.[60] We have also noted how the theological tradition has compared Mary's yes to Eve's no. It is a theme that needs to be handled very carefully lest it both undermine Christ's unique redemptive role and reinforce degradations of women as, in some way, the root of human sin. But perhaps the ancient tag, 'by a woman death, by a woman life', has something to say here.[61] Eve's no to God prepared the way for Adam's sin. Mary's yes to God prepared the way for Christ's redemption. The challenge to humanity is to receive the new life of the renewed creation that God has wrought in Jesus Christ so that the pattern of the new creation can begin to take form in creation's present conditions. That is why Paul says that 'the creation waits with eager longing for the revealing of the children of God; for ... the creation itself will be set free from its bondage to decay and will obtain the freedom of the glory of the children of God' (Rom. 8.19–21).

Human beings are increasingly capable of extraordinary feats of technological ingenuity. Many offer us some optimism that despite the scale of the problems facing us – the problems we have caused – we have it within ourselves to find the technological solutions to sort them out and to return the earth to the equilibrium it needs to sustain itself, and us with it. The capacity for technology is itself a gift from God and, used rightly, it will be part of the solution to the planet's woes and the threat to humanity. When Adam stepped out from the garden of paradise into a now inhospitable world, the Lord provided 'garments of skins' (Gen. 3.21) to protect them from its hard conditions. From thereon in, humanity was forced to develop increasingly sophisticated forms of technology in order to cope with life in a damaged and disrupted world. But, of itself, technology is not sufficient and, as the story of Cain suggests, its capacity for good is easily turned to harm, such is the depth of the human problem. Earlier in this chapter we saw how Hannah Arendt argued that 'the work of our hands' will not address the needs of the world unless rooted in a deep-seated awareness and fundamental attitude of responsibility for each other that derives from our common experience of natality (that we are all born into the world through its life-giving capacities) and plurality (that we are bound together in a common life of mutual interdependence). We might call this a framework of rights for all and responsibilities of all that seeks life for all. At the heart of this reorientation is – in Christian terms – a *metanoia*, a turning towards God's ways for the world and the needs of everyone, especially the most vulnerable, that is essentially spiritual and moral.

Again, Mary can be a source of inspiration for this sort of ethic of life that imagines how the world might be if humanity were truly to receive and nurture the life that God gives. Her

Magnificat speaks of what the 'Mighty One' has done and sets the perspective that defines Christian ethics: the work of God. Ecological care is not primarily a response to the crises of the moment. It is stepping into the movement of God that desires justice for the world and has taken decisive action in Christ to establish the radical kind of social and political justice that Mary envisages. Her vision goes to the root causes of ecological damage – greed, wealth, consumerism – in the sort of reversal of roles which Ephrem imagines when he celebrates the upending of the world's structures that Mary's child brings (see pp. 10, 75). She envisages the dismantling of the pride and the unseating of powers that drive those forces that exploit creation, and the raising up of the lowly, hungry and poor who presently suffer their gravest consequences.

What does all this mean in terms of social and political policy? What would this sort of world look like in practice and how do we work towards it? The 17 UN Sustainable Development Goals (SGS) and 169 Targets for 2030 agreed at a world summit in 2015 have a Magnificat-like quality to them. They are the outworking of the '2030 Agenda for Sustainable Development', 'a plan of action for people, planet and prosperity ... [and] to strengthen universal peace in larger freedom'. The states party to the Agenda also declared:

> We recognise that eradicating poverty in all its forms and dimensions, including extreme poverty, is the greatest global challenge and an indispensable requirement for sustainable development. All countries and all stakeholders, acting in collaborative partnership, will implement this plan. We are resolved to free the human race from the tyranny of poverty and want and to heal and secure our planet.[62]

The goals address the dangers of climate change, damage to the oceans, degradation of ecosystems, plant, water and animal. They do so, however, within a web of other interconnected needs of people and planet that seek to establish a world 'where all life can thrive': freedom from poverty, access to health care, opportunities for education, equality for women and men, availability of water, affordable energy, inclusive economic growth, resilient infrastructure, reduced inequality, safe cities, sustainable consumption and production, peaceful societies and, *critically*, strengthening the global partnerships that are needed to implement the goals and achieve sustainable development for all that leaves no one behind.

The 2022 Strategic Development Goals (SDGs) progress report analysed the data available and concluded that the multiple crises the world is facing today are putting the goals in serious jeopardy, including the ambition to reduce world greenhouse gas emissions to zero in 2030.[63] Hence, the declaration by the bishops who gathered in 2022 from across the Anglican Communion that the SDGs 'are a vital vision for the mutual flourishing of people and planet' was well-timed. The bishops called on their churches to 'launch and support a campaign to reimagine our world and so encourage and equip the Communion to make a significant contribution to achieving the ambitions of the Sustainable Development Goals'.[64]

There are a number of ways in which the Church as a global community, and the Anglican Communion within it, can play a part in addressing the triple environmental crises of climate change, biodiversity loss and pollution and their several causes which the SDGs does well to identify and address. They are forms of the *via activa*: the active life of the Church in and for the world, and they have a Mary-like character to them. There is the fundamental readiness to *cooperate* with God's work, to lend our will to the will of God and to say our yes to active participation in God's redeeming purposes. There is *communion* within and across the churches of the world, the coming together of people in every land, some from contexts that have done more to cause the crisis and others from places that are bearing more of its effects. The encounter of people with people, made far easier by the internet, makes the statistics visible in human lives and communities and creates global connections that can lead to local differences. There is responsible *campaigning*. The Lambeth 2022 bishops were right to call on world leaders to 'commit to finance and action to enable all nations of the world to be able to fulfil the 2030 Sustainable Development Goals, including its vision to "leave no one behind"'.[65] Hannah Arendt's acknowledgement of promise-making and promise-keeping in the Judeo-Christian tradition takes on a real relevance in the environmental sphere as well as the other areas of the SDGs. The UN climate conferences rely on states making credible commitments to reduce their negative impact on the climate and then keeping those commitments judiciously. Here the Church, joining with other religions of the world, has an important role in holding governments to account. There is *caring* for the planet through the use of Church's own resources and actions. 'For the time has come for judgement to begin with the household of God' (1 Peter 4.17), and without putting our own house in order, it is difficult to address governments and other institutions with any sort of credibility. So, it is right that the Church of England has committed itself in its multiple forms to being carbon neutral by 2030, despite the many difficult and costly decisions it will involve.[66]

We saw earlier in the chapter how Luke pictured the *via activa* and the *via contemplativa* working together to serve God's purposes. That principle of Christian practice applies here too. The root problem of our multiple crises, environmental among them, is the disordering of the human heart and the misdirection of our desires. It begins from a refusal to receive the life of creation as God's gift for our blessing and a determination to turn it into a possession to serve the ends of those whose powers can most control it. Contemplating creation's true value – its extrinsic worth – as God's own gift, created as good and given for the good of all, resets our relationship with the earth, opening our eyes and hearts to see its own beauty and vitality as a witness to the abundant creativity of God and not merely as a resource for our use or, worse, exploitation. Creation as God's gift has its own intrinsic value and invites us to give voice to its splendour in praise of God: 'Let the heavens be glad, and let the earth rejoice; let the sea roar, and all that fills it; let the field exult, and everything in it. Then shall all the trees of the forest sing for joy before the LORD' (Ps. 96.11–12).

Through the contemplation of God in prayer, using everything that God has given to aid our prayer, especially the gift of scripture and, perhaps, most especially the psalms, we properly position ourselves within creation as stewards and guardians. The result is both a humility before God ('what are human beings that you are mindful of them, mortals that you care for them') and a renewed sense of dignity ('you have made them a little lower than God') as those who are to care for creation, sharing in God's own dominion of love over 'the works of your [his] hands' (Ps. 8.4–6). Contemplation of creation, and of God's purposes of life for it, resets our perspective. It liberates us from the denial or inertia that can set in when we are overwhelmed by the scale of the world's ecological woes. Contemplation calls us into times of sabbath and strengthens us with God's resolve for the whole of creation to be 'hallowed' by sabbath rest (Gen. 2.1–3).

Hannah Arendt's acknowledgement of the Judeo-Christian virtue of forgiveness may provide a route out of apparently irreversible situations where we seem entrapped in spirals of damage from which it is impossible to escape. Forgiveness relies on the mercy of God, which is not to be doubted. But it also requires repentance, a demanding process of changed mindsets and new ways of behaving that leads to the putting right of what has been done wrong. It is an orientation away from self-interest towards 'the interests of others' that draws us into 'the same mind ... that was in Christ Jesus' (Phil. 2.4–5) and inspires us to receive the life of creation as a gift for a life lived together where, as the United Nations vision for sustainable development puts it, 'no one is left behind'. The recognition of our need for forgiveness begins, as we say in Chapter 4, with a posture of humility before God and each other and towards the earth we share as God's gift, admitting and accepting our part in its damage. None of this will make policy decisions straightforward – they are immensely complex because the world's life is itself immensely complex – but it will set some ethical boundaries and policy priorities for the *vita activa* as the peoples of the earth seek to preserve its future in an ethic of life that looks not to its own interests but to the needs of generations to come.

Notes

1 St Gregory of Narek, 'Ode for the Church' in *The Festal Works of St. Gregory of Narek: Annotated Translation of the Odes, Litanies, and Encomia*, ed. and trans. Abraham Terian (Collegeville, MN: Liturgical Press, 2016), p. 129 (English anglicized).

2 Dietrich Bonhoeffer, *Ethics*, vol. 6 of Dietrich Bonhoeffer Works, ed. Clifford J. Green (Minneapolis, MN: Fortress Press, 2009), p. 97.

3 John Donne, 'A Litany: The Virgin Mary' in *The Complete English Poems*, ed. A. J. Smith (London: Penguin, 1986), pp. 317–25.

4 For the most worked-out example, see Max Thurian, *Mary: Mother of the Lord, Figure of the Church*, trans. Neville B. Cryer (London: The Faith Press, 1963).

5 St Gregory of Narek, 'Litany for the Church' in *The Festal Works of St. Gregory of Narek*, p. 99.

6 St Gregory of Narek, 'Litany for the Church', p. 99.

7 Dorothy L. Sayers, *The Man Born to Be King: A Play-Cycle on the Life of Our Lord and Saviour Jesus Christ* (San Francisco, CA: Ignatius Press, 1990), p. 49.

8 Bonhoeffer, *Ethics*, p. 84.

9 Ann Loades, *Grace is not Faceless: Reflections on Mary* (London: DLT, 2021), p. 128.

10 Ann Loades very helpfully draws attention to the Rabbula Gospels in her writings. See, for example, *Grace is not Faceless*, pp. 57, 71.

11 Church of England, 'Collect for The Presentation of Christ in the Temple' in *Common Worship: Daily Prayer* (London: Church House Publishing, 2005), p. 420.

12 St Ephrem, 'Faith', 10.17, quoted in Sebastian P. Brock, *The Luminous Eye: The Spiritual World Vision of Saint Ephrem the Syrian*, rev. edn (Collegeville, MN: Liturgical Press, 1992), p. 94.

13 I use the KJV because it stays so close to the Greek.

14 Gregory of Narek, 'Litany for the Church', p. 96.

15 Bonhoeffer, *Ethics*, p. 50.

16 Hannah Arendt, *The Human Condition*, 2nd edn (Chicago, IL: The University of Chicago Press, 1998).

17 Margaret Canovan, 'Introduction' in Arendt, *The Human Condition*, p. xxi.

18 Arendt, *The Human Condition*, p. 237.

19 Arendt, *The Human Condition*, p. 239 n. 76, n. 77.

20 Lesslie Newbigin, *The Open Secret: An Introduction to the Theology of Mission* (Grand Rapids, MI: Eerdmans, 1978), p. 110.

21 The KJV translation better reflects the LXX (Septuagint) translation of Isaiah 7.14 than the Hebrew version. I have used it because of the influence of the Septuagint on the New Testament and later Christian writers.

22 Tina Beattie, *Rediscovering Mary: Insights from the Gospels* (Liguori, MO: Triumph Books, 1995), p. 28.

23 Pope John Paul II, '*Redemptoris Mater*', para. 21, in *The Encyclicals of John Paul II*, ed. J. Michael Miller (Huntington, IN: Our Sunday Visitor, 1996), p. 376.

24 See Mary Jane Haemig and Eric Lund, eds, *Little Prayer Book, 1522, and a Simple Way to Pray, 1535: The Annotated Luther Study Edition* (Minneapolis, MN: Fortress Press, 2017), pp. 192–4.

25 Lyndal Roper, *Martin Luther: Renegade and Prophet* (London: The Bodley Head, 2016), pp. 58–9.

26 Quoted in Lois Malcolm, 'What Mary Has to Say about God's Bare Goodness' in *Blessed One: Protestant Perspectives on Mary*, ed. Beverly Roberts Gaventa and Cynthia L. Rigby (Louisville, KY: Westminster John Knox Press, 2002), p. 132.

27 Martin Luther, 'The Magnificat, 1520–1' in *Works of Martin Luther: with introductions and notes*, Vol. 3, ed. Henry E. Jacobs, trans. Albert T. W. Steinhaeuser (Philadelphia, PA: A. J. Holman, 1930), pp. 119.

28 *Salvation and the Church*, para. 22, quoted in The Anglican–Roman Catholic International Commission, *Mary: Grace and Hope in Christ* (London: Morehouse, 2005), p. 69.

29 Gregory of Narek, 'Ode for the Theophany' in *The Festal Works of St. Gregory of Narek*, pp. 212–17.

30 Robert W. Jenson, 'A Space for God' in *Mary Mother of God*, ed. Carl E. Braaten and Robert W. Jenson (Grand Rapids, MI: Eerdmans, 2004), p. 56.

31 Jenson, 'A Space for God', p. 56.

32 This phrase is used numerous times in Martin Luther, 'The Blessed Sacrament of the Holy and True Body of Christ, and the Brotherhoods' in *Luther's Works, Vol. 35: Word and Sacrament I*, ed. E. Theodore Bachmann (Minneapolis, MN: Fortress Press, 1960), pp. 50–1.

33 ARCIC, *Mary*, and Malcolm, 'What Mary Has to Say About God's Bare Goodness', p. 140.

34 Loades, *Grace is not Faceless*, p. 107.

35 The nearest equivalent to a Yazidi Akhtar in the Christian tradition is a bishop or archbishop. As with other encounters in Georgia, I am grateful to Archbishop Malkhaz Songulashvili of the Evangelical Baptist Church of Georgia for the opportunity to engage with the Yazidi community in Georgia.

36 On The Feast of the Annunciation, 25 March 2022; see Hannah Brockhaus, 'Pope Francis consecrates Russia and Ukraine to the Immaculate Heart of Mary', *Catholic News Agency*, https://tinyurl.com/4m498u9a, accessed 16.1.2023. On The Feast of the Assumption, 15 August 2022: Deborah C. Lubov, 'Pope invites faithful to visit Our Lady in a Marian shrine and to remember Ukraine', *Vatican News*, https://tinyurl.com/mrwynvun, accessed 16.1.2023.

37 Used here with the kind permission of Charlie Annis.

38 I use the *Common Worship Psalter* translation (where the verse is 32).

39 Stephen J. Shoemaker, *Mary in Early Christian Faith and Devotion* (New Haven, CT: Yale University Press, 2016).

40 Pope Pius XII, *Munificentissimus Deus: Defining the Dogma of the Assumption* (Boston, MA: St Paul Books and Media, 1980), para. 44, p. 20.

41 Joseph Cardinal Ratzinger, *God and the World: Believing and Living in Our Time*, trans. Henry Taylor (San Francisco: Ignatius Press, 2002), p. 305.

42 N. T. Wright, *For All the Saints? Remembering the Christian Departed* (London: SPCK, 2003). For the scholarly underpinning of his arguments, see N. T. Wright, *The Resurrection of the Son of God* (Minneapolis, MN: Fortress Press, 2003).

43 Albert Einstein's theories of special and general relativity explore the relationship between time and space, with Einstein's theory of special relativity arguing that time and space are woven together to form one continuum in which events that occur at one time for an observer can happen at another time for a second observer. This relationship between space and time can be distorted by large objects. For more, see Leo Sartori, *Understanding Relativity: A Simplified Approach to Einstein's Theories* (Berkeley, CA: University of California Press, 1996).

44 For a fuller rationale, see my *Prayer and the Departed* (Cambridge: Grove Books, 1997).

45 *Catechism of the Catholic Church*, rev. edn (London: Burns and Oates, 1999), para. 966.

46 ARCIC, *Mary*, para. 54.

47 *Catechism of the Catholic Church*, para. 57.

48 Edward Yarnold, *The Assumption: The 1980 Assumption Day Lecture* (Burnley: F. H. Brown, 1980), p. 48.

49 *Lumen Gentium*, para. 68, cited in *Catechism of the Catholic Church*, para. 972.

50 ARCIC, *Mary*, para. 78 (see also para. 79).

51 John Keble, 'Mother Out of Sight' in J. T. Coleridge, *A Memoir of the Rev. John Keble, Vol. II*, 2nd edn (Oxford: James Parker & Co., 1869), pp. 314–18.

52 Ratzinger, *God and the World*, p. 305. See Joseph Ratzinger, *Dogmatic Theology: Eschatology, Death and Eternal life*, trans. Michael Waldstein (Washington, DC: Catholic University of America Press, 1988), especially the Appendix.

53 Basil of Caesarea, *De Spiritu Sancto*, in *Nicene and Post-Nicene Christian Fathers, Series II, Volume 8: St. Basil: Letters and Select Works*, ed. Philip Schaff (Grand Rapids, MI: Eerdmans, 1988), p. 233.

54 John Kerry, President Biden's Climate Change Envoy, speaking on BBC Radio 4, 'The World this Weekend', 24 July 2022.

55 'The UN Sustainable Development Goals Report' (2022), p. 2, https://tinyurl.com/2u2ruesc, accessed 16.1.2023.

56 The statistics that follow are taken from 'The UN Sustainable Development Goals Report' (2022), p. 2.

57 See https://tinyurl.com/2dvcjb55, accessed 16.1.2023.

58 Rowan Williams, *Christ the Heart of Creation* (London: Bloomsbury Continuum, 2018).

59 Joe Biden, quoted in Kevin Liptak, 'Biden calls climate change a "clear and present danger" as he tries to find ways to take action', *CNN*, 20 July 2022, https://tinyurl.com/2xth7kze, accessed 16.1.2023.

60 Ruth Valerio's book, *Saying Yes to Life* (London: SPCK, 2020), is an impassioned call for Christians to rise to their ecological responsibilities.

61 As cited by Gloria J. Thurmond, 'Ecology and Mary: An Ecological Theology of Mary as the New Eve in Response to the Church's Challenge for a Faith Based Education in Ecological Responsibility', *Journal of Catholic Education* 11 (2007), p. 32.

62 Preamble to UN Department of Economic and Social Affairs, 'Transforming the world: The 2030 Agenda for Sustainable Development', https://sdgs.un.org/2030agenda, accessed 17.8.2022.

63 For example, even if nations adhere to their voluntary emissions reduction, they are (at least from 2022) set to rise by 14 per cent by 2030. 'UN Sustainable Development Goals Report' (2022), p. 3.

64 'The Lambeth Call: Sustainable Development' (2022), para. 4.1, p. 22, https://tinyurl.com/4hs4a2z2, accessed 16.1.2023.

65 'Lambeth Call', para. 43, p. 23.

66 See https://tinyurl.com/27zmyth3, accessed 16.1.2023.

6

Loved

O Precious Pearl discovered
through the inscrutable search in the sea of this world,
holy Bearer of God ...
– the foundation of faith laid without hands, the
true image –
after which (heavenly) model you were anointed and sealed,
bridal chamber for God,
the One who took a body from you:
Please be an intercessor for our reconciliation,
us who are transgressors.
O Forerunner, progeny of the saints called to eternal life,
wreath of the martyrs, along with the apostles and prophets.
And now, may the Lord God have mercy on us according to
his great mercy.
('Litany for the Church', Gregory of Narek)[1]

'Where is she?' – that was the question with which this book
began. Where is Mary to be found in Dresden's rebuilt Frauenkirche, in Wittenberg's Marienkirche, in evangelical theology
and spirituality, in all the churches, in my life and devotion? I
hope that the pages that followed the preface have shown that
Mary's part and place in the conception, birth, ministry, death
and even resurrection of Jesus require the Church of today in
all its forms, and contemporary Christians in all their diver-
sity, to find a place for the one woman named among 'certain
women' who joined the apostles in the upper room after the
ascension, 'constantly devoting themselves to prayer' (Acts
1.14) and waiting to be 'clothed with power from on high'

(Luke 24.49). As this book comes to its end, I would like to reflect on three spaces in the life of the Church and the devotion of the Christian that Mary fills in her own unique way as the one so close to Jesus – 'the Giver of life' as Ephrem liked to call him – that she is to be called blessed by all generations (Luke 1.48). Mary is a companion in the journey through life. Mary is a sister in faith as we live out the gospel of life in the life of the Church. Mary is the mother of the Church exhorting us to do as Jesus tells us (John 2.5): to be one in him and one in his work of drawing others into the life of God.

'The Lord is with you': Companion on the journey

Mary is counted as one of the saints of the Church, one – together with all the baptized who confess Christ's name – who is made holy by the broken body and poured out blood of Christ, and one who becomes holy by following faithfully in the way of Christ, walking in his truth, living his life. Like all the saints, Mary accompanies us as we journey with Christ, surrounding us amid the 'cloud of witnesses' who urge us on, helping us to look with them 'to Jesus the pioneer and perfecter of our faith' (Heb. 12.1–2). For those of us who have been especially shaped by the New Testament epistles, she is as real and present as Paul, taking us ever deeper into the depths of Christian truth. For those of us inspired by the martyrs of the Church and exemplars of Christian discipleship through the ages, she is as living a witness as Clare of Assisi, Catherine of Siena, Cuthbert of Lindisfarne, calling us to do as her son says and to stay with him wherever he goes.

Mary is shared by all those who seek to walk his way, for she was with him from the beginning – even before the foundation of the world (Eph. 1.4) – and remained with him even when others fled. She is also shared with those of other religions. As a faithful Jewish woman, well versed in her scriptures and observant in the practices and rituals of her community, Mary binds the Church of Christ to the Israel of God. Like Jacob she receives God's blessing and, even in the face of her own perplexity, prevails with God. Wrestling as Jacob had done before with God's messenger, she holds on to God, believes God's word, hopes in God, loves God and, as she gives herself over to the will and work of God, all the nations of earth are blessed (Gen. 32.22–32, 35.9–11).

As the one chosen by God 'above all the women of creation', who entrusts herself completely to God and is the first to name God as compassionate, Mary embodies – literally – the mercy of God, and so is none other than 'a sign for humanity and a Mercy from Us' says the Qur'an, rendering the voice of God.[2] Hence, the only woman mentioned by name in the Qur'an whose name appears more often than even Muhammad, Mary connects all Christians with the followers of Islam. Such is their respect for Mary that the Shias of Georgia give flowers to Christian and Jewish women on the day the Georgian Church celebrates the Dormition of Our Most Holy Lady, the *Theotokos*, and gladly call her 'our mother'.

As the one who carried Christ in her womb, Yazidis always speak of Jesus as 'son of Mary'. Their scriptures, unwritten but carefully preserved and passed on in an ancient oral tradition, tell stories about Jesus and his mother. Their liturgies – also carefully held in the memory of the clergy and other leaders – call on God's favour 'for the sake of Jesus, for the sake of Mary', and 'for the sake of the pencil and tablets [the Ten Commandments] and for the sake of Adam and Eve'.[3] Mary reminds us that her influence through her son goes deep into the memories of a religion whose riches have been hidden for centuries and a people whose vulnerability to unspeakable persecution has come only recently to the world's attention; and they remind Christians that Jesus is never without his mother.

As well as being the companion through life to all those who confess her son as their Lord, and a companion to those of other traditions of faith who seek the just and peaceful rule of God's righteousness in the world, Mary is also a companion of all humanity, especially women, among whom, according to Jewish Elizabeth, she is most blessed (Luke 1.42), and to all those who yearn for a better world in the future, chiefly those who suffer the worst of the world's failings in the present. She is a companion to the poor and powerless, to the hungry and thirsty, to the weeping and the worrying, to the women who fear the reproach of society or the loss of their children, to those perplexed at the workings of the divine and those who ponder the presence of God in the complexities of their lives.

To each of us, in whatever our circumstances and whatever belief systems, she points, like the icons of the Eastern Church, to her son Jesus, beckoning us to see in him God's word made flesh, inviting us to open our hearts to the goodness of God's word that transforms the world, calling us to receive grace upon grace by giving God space to dwell in us and among us. For those who yield with her their 'yes' to God, Mary becomes a companion in the origin and destiny of Christian identity for, like her, we too are foreknown by God and so 'predestined to be conformed to the image of his Son, in order that he might be the firstborn within a large family'. Her place in the purposes of God is a paradigm of ours: 'called … justified … glorified' (Rom. 8.29–30). This is the life 'that really is life' (1 Tim. 6.19), the life that Mary took hold of as she believed God's word and received the gift of life itself. It is the life that she prophesied would win the world: the life of the kingdom of God and its reign of peace which lies at heart of human hope.

'Blessed is she who believed': Sister in faith

As we noted in Chapter 1, there was some expectation that the bishops of the Roman Catholic Church gathered for the Second Vatican Council in the 1960s would produce a major statement on the role of Mary even, perhaps, requesting the Pope to promulgate a new dogma about Mary focusing on her unique participation in God's redemptive work in Christ, including a distinctive and, in some way, necessary mediatorial role. We have seen that although the bishops produced a short document solely on Mary, they reserved their main Marian attention for a concluding chapter to *Lumen Gentium*, a highly influential document on the Church as a whole.[4] It was an important decision, not only, in the words of the bishops, to dissuade 'theologians and preachers ... from all gross exaggerations as well as from petty narrow-mindedness in considering the singular dignity of the Mother of God' (para. 67), but also to set some safe and solid common ground on which all Christians could agree about the mother of Jesus.

While affirming Mary 'as a pre-eminent and singular member of the Church and as its type', the Second Vatican Council reset Roman Catholic teaching on Mary as 'excellent exemplar in faith and charity' (para. 53). It placed Mary firmly in the midst of the people of God, recovering a proper sense of Mary being *with* the rest of the Church – all those who seek to live in the faith and charity of Christ – and the rest of the Church being *with* Mary *in* Christ. Whatever we may say – as we have in Chapter 5 and will say again shortly – about the role of Mary's motherhood in the life of the Church, both personal and symbolic, we must first say that she is our sister in faith and discipleship. The Council's emphasis on Mary as believer among believers who 'advanced in her pilgrimage of faith' led to a renewal of reflection on Mary, often by women and many from a consciously feminist perspective, such as Elizabeth Johnson's seminal study *Truly our Sister*.[5] Johnson, like other similar writers, concentrates on Mary's concrete historical and cultural conditions, connecting Mary with the experience of women across the world's multiple contexts and centuries, from peasant farmers in subsistence economies, to women fleeing the violence of conflict, domestic, tribal or national, to women facing the opprobrium of society at their 'irregular pregnancies' (as Johnson puts it), to women of every age with all the demands of ordinary life, and the responsibilities they feel for others, crowding in on them.[6]

Mary belongs among the followers of Jesus in the community of the Church. That is where she is found in the New Testament – with Elizabeth, Zechariah, Joseph, Simeon and Anna at the beginning of Jesus' life; with the wider family of Jesus as they came searching for him in the early days of his ministry when 'people were saying, "He has gone out of his mind"' (Mark 3.21) and the Jerusalem authorities were on the look-out for him; with Jesus and the disciples as they head on to Capernaum after the wedding in Cana; in the 'company of sisters' at the cross with the beloved disciple, witnessing the death of Christ; in the upper room with the apostles, waiting for Jesus' promise of the Spirit's coming to be fulfilled.

As we said in Chapter 1, there are two things that Mary does for us that not even Jesus can do for us, and one of those is to show us what it means to be a disciple of Jesus. She does so as the first disciple. Mary has much to tell us about the agency that we have in our discipleship to respond and con-sent, believe and follow, but perhaps the most important truth we learn from her is that we become disciples through the 'favour' of God (Luke 1.28, 30, 48), the unbounded mercy of God that chooses to raise us up into fullness of life, that speaks of God's word of life to us, that surrounds us with God's Spirit of life and transforms us into bearers of God's life in the world. As with Mary, God reaches out to us not only in one moment of time but even before time – 'before the foundation of the world' (Eph. 1.4) – to prepare us for an encounter with the God of grace and to enable us through grace upon grace (John 1.16) to respond, 'For nothing will be impossible with God' (Luke 1.37). Uniquely in the New Testament's many scenes of people being called to follow the way of God, Mary's own response is made audible to us, challenging us to voice our own, 'Here am I' (Luke 1.38). She dares us to rise to the God-given dignity of human identity and breathe the air of personal decision and to find that the true exercise of that freedom, unlike Eve's and Adam's choices, need not turn the air stale. She inspires us simply to believe God's word of grace, and in believing to give ourselves fully as participants in God's life-giving purposes of redemptive love in a decaying world.

Mary also shows us that as important as deciding is, Christian discipleship is more than decision-making. It is leaning into the logic of the decision to follow the ways of Christ even when it seems contrary to the wisdom of the world. It is, as Paul says, to 'work out your own salvation with fear and trembling' (Phil. 2.12), learning what it means to be a sign of the kingdom of God. It is questioning when perplexed, pressing God and those who speak for God for answers that expand our understanding of God's will and word. It is taking time to ponder – to think deeply – when God's activity, or apparent inactivity in the world is overwhelming, not in some sort of detached, armchair amateur philosopher way, but in the wrestling of the mind and heart that will not let God go until we can take hold of the blessing that, faith tells us, God has promised. It is living into and living out of the life that Jesus has promised, rejoicing when the joy of heaven touches the things of earth (Luke 1.46–55), interceding when the pots of human possibilities run dry (John 2.3–5) and remaining steadfast when all our hopes for the redemption of Israel and the world seem to be falling apart (Luke 24.21; John 19.25–27). It is being fully part of the life of the Church, taking our place with those who have offended us or even betrayed our loved ones. It is waiting with them in continual dependence on the gift of the Holy Spirit, ready to be filled with 'power from on high' (Luke 24.49) to speak in all the tongues of humanity to all the peoples of the earth about the 'Author of life, whom God raised from the dead' (Acts 2.4, 3.15). It is being there for those ready to welcome the message and be baptized (Acts 2.41). It is abiding with the community that abides in Christ through the apostles' 'teaching, and fellowship ... the breaking of bread and the prayers' (Acts 2.42) and in the other ways through which their common life is lived out (Acts 2.43–47).

As well as showing us the essential character of personal discipleship (hearing, believing and keeping to God's words of grace in Christ as individuals), and as well as demonstrating the ecclesial dimension of discipleship (living out our friendship and following of Christ among all those he calls his friends), Mary opens our eyes wide to the expansive missional character of discipleship as we do as Jesus instructed us: to pray for God's will to be done on earth as in heaven, for God's kingdom to come in all the contexts and conditions of human culture overcoming the injustice, violence and degradation that inflicts societies and even threatens the life of the earth itself. Through the Church's prayers and liturgies, Mary invites us to join the song Bonhoeffer commended as 'the oldest Advent hymn' in a sermon for the Third Sunday in Advent in 1933 to which we referred in Chapter 2: 'a hard, strong, inexorable song about collapsing thrones and humbled lords of this world, about the power of God and the powerlessness of humankind'.[7] No wonder the Nazis killed him. No wonder the oppressive Guatemalan Government banned Mary's Magnificat in the 1980s and the British-owned and -run East India Company did the same more than a hundred years before, both fearful of the seeds of subversion it would plant in those who sang with Mary about the God who 'has brought down the powerful from their thrones, and lifted up the lowly' (Luke 1.52).

The Church throughout the ages needs this sister in the faith – this, in Bonhoeffer's words, 'passionate, surrendered, proud, enthusiastic Mary who speaks out here' – to encourage us to sing, to speak and even to shout out loud and clear to all the powers and principalities of the world that God has come to the world in Christ and will come in Christ to judge all the nations of the earth.

'Here is your mother': Mother of the Church

As we have just observed, the theological tradition has often seen Mary as an image or archetype of the Church – the pattern of her motherhood, a pattern of the Church in her ministry and mission. As we saw in Chapter 5, although this way of thinking both about Mary and the Church is more common in the Orthodox and Catholic traditions, it can be found in many expressions of Christian thought. We can see it in the popular Lutheran hymn, '*Es kommt ein Schiff geladen*', which pictures a ship coming laden with treasure, heavy with grace. On one level, the ship is Mary as she comes near to Bethlehem. On another level the ship is the Church carrying God's own Son who comes continually to the lost of the world.

Luther, Bonhoeffer and many others in the Lutheran tradition, as well as in the wider Protestant and Anglican families, have been glad to call the Church our mother, and to draw inspiration from the mothering of Mary. Like her, the Church, animated by the Spirit, embodies Jesus, not simply in the more functional sense of representing him but rather in allowing his body to be formed within us and then bearing that body into the world.

Like Mary, the Church learns from Jesus, from God's work in Jesus Christ. 'May your church see you as well as your mother,' writes Ephrem in his Hymn of the Nativity as he exhorts the Church to perceive Christ in its midst and to receive everything that he gives.[8] Such seeing – seeing deeply and truly – will involve the sort of pondering and reflecting to which Mary gave herself. The gift of Christ is both strikingly simple – God has come to us (Matt. 1.23) – and endlessly deep, always reliant on God's Spirit of truth to unfold to us 'the mystery that has been hidden throughout the ages and generations but has now been revealed to his saints' (Col. 1.26). As the Church, we need to acquire the receptivity and openness of Mary, and her courageous persistence, that allows the seed of God's word planted within us to grow through faith and faith's outworking in the life of discipleship: believing in Christ in daily life, speaking with Christ in prayer, listening to Christ through scripture, being where Christ is – with God in worship, with others who follow him, with those he is reaching out to in the world.

Like Mary, the Church witnesses to Jesus, enabled and empowered by the Spirit that overshadowed Mary at the conception of Christ and then, with all who 'were together in one place' on the Jewish Feast following his death, rested on her and filled her afresh with the life of Christ, risen from the dead (Acts 2.1–4). The Qur'an tells a story that clearly has great meaning for Muslims but has an even deeper meaning for Christians. Mary is derided as she rejoins her village community after giving birth to Jesus. But she has been well prepared for this first encounter by Gabriel. The angel told her not to try to defend herself, for that would keep the attention on herself, but rather simply to point to Jesus. She withholds her words, so that God's word – Jesus – may speak. And speak Jesus does, according to the Qur'an, from the arms of Mary his mother.[9] The Church does a lot of speaking in its ministry and mission, using a lot of words. The test of those words is how truly they speak of Christ and how fully they allow the words of Jesus to be heard.

Similarly, the Church does a lot of doing in its ministry and mission, with many practices and actions. On a warm Sunday in August, I attended the Eucharist in a Georgian village. It was a hauntingly beautiful liturgy with melodic chants sung by a small group of women, a gentle and godly priest clad in glorious vestments, prostrate at one point in devotion, people praying and bowing, incense wafting, bells ringing, icons shining. Then everything went quiet. The doors of the simple iconostasis were wide open. The priest had moved out of the way and all eyes were fixed on bread and wine standing on a table, transfixed by the searing shaft of light bursting from the heavens exactly on to this small space on earth. The test of the Church's activity is how truly it is the action of Christ himself and how fully it allows the world to encounter him. The closer the words and actions are to the words and actions of Christ, the closer the Church will be to the heavenly Jerusalem of which Paul speaks – 'the Jerusalem above', for 'she is our mother' (Gal. 4.26).

We can see here, as we have before, that there is a lot to be gained from seeing Mary as an icon of the Church – as an image or type of what the Church is called to be: our mother. Is there a case, though, for seeing Mary in her motherhood not only as a symbol of the Church but also personally, in her present reality, as mother of the Church, as our mother in Christ?

When the Second Vatican Council described Mary as 'our mother in the order of grace', it meant not only that Mary was the first to believe the good news of God in Christ and the first to model what the fundamental characteristics of discipleship look like but also that Mary is herself *our mother*.[10] Many centuries earlier, Luther agreed. As we explored previously in earlier chapters, the theological root of this belief is that confessing and following Jesus draws us into his own network of relationships, divine and human. 'God has sent the Spirit of his Son into our hearts, crying "Abba! Father!"' wrote Paul in one of his early letters (Gal. 4.6). When Jesus, dying on the cross, 'saw his mother and the disciple whom he loved standing beside her, he said to his mother, "Woman, here is your son"' and to the beloved disciple, 'Here is your mother' (John 19.26). John's Gospel introduces Jesus' Farewell Discourses by telling us that, 'Having loved his own who were in the world, he loved them to the end' (John 13.1). Here are two people who are most certainly his own who had not each scattered to their homes (John 16.32) but were with him *where he is* (John 17.24), standing at the cross, seeing him 'lifted up from the earth', living witnesses that by this means – by his death for the life of the world – he 'will draw all people to [himself]' (John 12.32). Jesus had already promised that 'whoever receives one whom I send receives me' (John 13.20). In giving his mother to his beloved disciple *as his mother* and his beloved disciple to his mother *as her son*, and in the disciple taking (or receiving – the Greek verb is the same) the mother to his own home, Jesus will come in his risen reality to dwell with both of them in one community of believers.[11] His mother is our mother because we are in him and he in us and his disciples are her children.

Mothers, good mothers – and we know that Mary's mothering is good – long for unity in their families and between families. As we acknowledged in Chapter 1, Mary has been for too long used as a figure of disunity in the Church. The same could be said between the Church and some other religions. In a profound study of Mary by Muna Tatari, an Islamic scholar, and Klaus von Stosch, a Christian scholar, they come to the view together that Mary is a meeting point between religions and, especially (as suggested earlier), a 'linking figure' between

Judaism, Christianity and Islam.[12] Tatari explains how she has come to appreciate better the central tenets of her own faith in the mercy and compassion of God through her encounter with Mary. She also reveals how she wrestled very hard with Christian understandings of the radical reach of God's grace and how Mary 'did not have to earn it'.[13] Although she critiques the Christian concept of grace from an Islamic perspective, she goes on to say, with real humility and honesty, 'Notwithstanding this, I am still fascinated by the idea of an unconditional consolation from God that has nothing to do with how I think or act.'[14]

So perhaps, therefore, we can see that Mary stands ready to help people from different religious traditions to appreciate the depths of their own faith, appropriating what is good from another faith and consistent with theirs; and, at the same time, that she is there to help the religions identify critical points of difference between them, and to do so respectfully, even holding out the possibility of further mutual learning.

The crucial point of differentiation between Christianity and other religions will always be over the question Jesus himself poses: 'But who do *you* say that I am?' The confession of Jesus Christ as 'the Messiah, the Son of the living God' (Matt. 16.15–16) and, in its fuller form, as 'My Lord and my God' (John 20.28), binds Christians together as one community over time and space despite everything we do to divide ourselves. Differing attitudes to and assessments of Mary have undoubtedly been one cause of division over the centuries and they remain sources of deep suspicion between Christians today. Of all that divides us, surely the arguments over his own mother are ones that bring Jesus especial grief. One of the reasons for writing this book has been to show that although theological, devotional and liturgical differences in relation to Mary will remain between Churches, a deeper encounter with her through scripture, the theological tradition and the practice of Christians in their different settings brings us closer to her son and thereby to each other. As we follow the example of the beloved disciple and take Mary to our home, we may find ourselves like Elizabeth – another person who invited Mary into her home – filled with the joy and love of the Holy Spirit, declaring, 'Blessed are you among women, and blessed is the fruit of your womb. And why has this happened to me, that the mother of my Lord comes to me?' (Luke 1.41–43). Perhaps her answer to our question will simply be, 'Do whatever he tells you.'

So, as I conclude these reflections on Mary on the eve of the Feast of the Dormition of Mary soon to be celebrated in the Georgian village where I am staying, join me if you would in making the traditional toasts of this land – a land that first heard about Jesus Christ from St Nino, a young woman sent, so the tradition goes, by Mary to tell of her son. The meal begins with a toast for God. Like the series of toasts that follow, it is a toast *for* God, in thanksgiving for who God is and what God has done for us. The meal is then punctuated with other toasts, some of them chosen by the host for the occasion; others, such as the toast for mothers, prescribed by custom ('Without my mother, my house was empty,' said one of the guests with whom I once ate); and then the meal ends with a toast for the Blessed Virgin Mary, giving God thanks for her gentle, grace-filled life of courageous faith, asking that we may be made ready to receive the gift of Christ more fully and, in so doing, welcome his mother and, with her, the whole Church into our own homes. And Mary's own prophecy is fulfilled not in this case through the Church's public liturgy or an individual's personal prayer but through an assembled community of ordinary people, young and old, meeting around a simple table, remembering the past, enjoying the present and looking ahead to the future: 'Surely, from now on all generations will call me blessed; for the Mighty One has done great things for me, and holy is his name' (Luke 1.48–49).

And blessed is she who believed
that there would be a fulfilment
of what was spoken to her by the Lord.
(Luke 1.45)

Notes

1 Gregory Narek, 'Litany for the Assumption of the Blessed Holy Bearer of God' in *The Festal Works of St. Gregory of Narek: Annotated Translation of the Odes, Litanies, and Encomia*, ed. and trans. Abraham Terian (Collegeville, MN: Liturgical Press, 2016), pp. 99–100. Gregory is referring to Mary at this point in his Litany.

2 The Qur'an 3:42; 19:21.

3 I am grateful to Pir Dimitri Pirbari, the Yazidi Akhtar of Georgia, and to Archbishop Malkhaz Songulashvili of the Evangelical Baptist Church of Georgia for the opportunity to meet with him and other Yazidi leaders.

4 Second Vatican Council, 'Lumen Gentium: Dogmatic Constitution on the Church', chapter VIII, in *The Documents of Vatican II*, ed. Walter M. Abbott (New York: Herder and Herder, 1966), pp. 85–96.

5 Elizabeth A. Johnson, *Truly Our Sister: A Theology of Mary in the Communion of Saints* (London: Continuum, 2009), p. 202.

6 Johnson, *Truly Our Sister*, p. 226.

7 Dietrich Bonhoeffer, 'My Spirit Rejoices: London, Third Sunday in Advent, December 17, 1933' in *The Collected Sermons of Dietrich Bonhoeffer*, ed. Isabel Best (Minneapolis, MN: Fortress Press, 2012), p. 116.

8 St Ephrem, 'Hymns on the Nativity: Hymn 11', in *Nicene and Post-Nicene Fathers, Series II, Volume 13: Gregory the Great – Part II; Ephraim Syrus*, ed. Philip Schaff (Oxford: James Parker and Co., 1893), p. 245.

9 Qur'an 19:27–33.

10 *Lumen Gentium*, para. 62.

11 I am grateful to David F. Ford, *The Gospel of John: A Theological Commentary* (Grand Rapids, MI: Baker Academic, 2021), from which I draw some connections.

12 Muna Tatari and Klaus von Stosch, *Mary in the Qur'an: Friend of God, Virgin, Mother*, trans. Peter Lewis (London: Gingko, 2021), p. 158. For another helpful study, see Hosn Abboud, *Mary in the Qur'an: A Literary Reading* (London: Routledge, 2014).

13 Tatari and von Stosch, *Mary in the Qur'an*, p. 305.

14 Tatari and von Stosch, *Mary in the Qur'an*, p. 306.

Acknowledgements

The *Luminous Eye* © 1992 by Cistercian Publications, Inc. © 2008 by Order of Saint Benedict, Collegeville, Minnesota. Used with permission.

The Festal Works of St. Gregory of Narek © 2016 by Order of Saint Benedict, Collegeville, Minnesota. Used with permission.

Accompanied by Angels: Poems of the Incarnation © 2006 by Luci Shaw, Wm. B. Eerdmans Publishing Co., Grand Rapids, Michigan. Used with permission.

Collected Poems 1909–1962 © 1963 by The estate of T. S. Eliot, Faber and Faber Ltd., London. Used with permission.

Index of Biblical References

Old Testament

New Testament

Index of Names and Subjects

Jesus in the temple 84
on Joseph 67
marks of a disciple 45
Mary as blessed 44–5
Mary's influence on Jesus 82
Mary's role in 119, 120
Mary's status and 30
ministry in Galilee 143
on Roman empire 60–1
on Simeon the Priest 74–5
women and God's promises
  63–4
Luther, Martin
Church as mother 191
Germany churches and ix–xi
invocation of saints 153, 155
Little Prayer Book 151
Mary and xi–xii, 4, 151–2
Mary's faith 37–8, 43
Mary's ordinariness 30
Mary's virginity and 81
nails 95 Thesis x

St Macarios Monastery, Egypt
  praying 153–4
makarioi 45, 83
Malcolm, Lois
on Luther and the
  Magnificat 152
The Man Born to Be King
  (Sayers) 135
Marienkirche, Wittenberg x,
  183
Mark, Gospel of
the empty tomb 141
family restrains Jesus 88
on Nazareth and Jesus 100
Marshall Islands nuclear
  testing 123–4
Martha of Bethany 143–4

Mary
the angel and 12–14, 31–3,
  36
Blessed 170
body's integrity 33–4
bread and 138–9
children and 93
chosen in grace 24–31
in the Church 11
as companion 184–6
at the cross xiv, 105–11, 193
death and Assumption
  of 161–70
different Christian traditions
  and 3–4
as a disciple 44–5, 89, 168,
  187–90
Elizabeth calls blessed 28–9,
  42–7
evangelical virtues 136
Eve and 70, 173
family and 29, 60, 79–80
follows to Capernaum 104
forgiveness 146–7
formation of the Church
  134–42, 167
German churches and ix–xii
God's purposes 5
the immaculate conception
  39–41
Joseph's children and 80
Judaism of 103, 184, 185
later life of 121
life-bearing 4, 9–10, 22–31,
  59–60, 73–6, 174–5
as a link 193–5
love and 5–6
Luther on xi–xii, 37–8
makaria 89
ministry of Jesus and 100–4